Why I Have Written *Ring of Tr*

Dear Reader,

This my first book, has been written especially for you.

It tells of my struggle and determination to overcome obstacles and to succeed in a world where no woman had before.

It is a story of burning ambition but also one of constant self questioning. It is a story of greed and selfishness but it is also a story of wanting to make a contribution, wanting to make a difference.

The story also reflects a growing awareness of an ultimate cosmic power that comes to the aid of all whenever they devote themselves to the greatest cause on earth, that of Liberty, Equality, and Fraternity. From this I drew my strength as earthly powers contrived to keep me in my place!

Ironically, I was not aware of this at the time of writing. I simply told it as it was. It was only later when I had read the book that I realised the many co-incidents. Then I recognised a series of events that although supernatural must have helped me to see things more clearly. I believe that we all have these moments and sometimes we are more susceptible to them when we are under extreme stress. I'm sure we could learn much more from them if we put our minds to it.

Ring of Truth is not just my story its our story and I hope you enjoy it.

Geraldine

Please note *Ring of Truth* is a true story, but the names of colleagues and companies have been changed to protect their identities.

Ring of Truth

Geraldine Bridgewater

Published by New Generation Publishing in 2015

Copyright © Geraldine Bridgewater 2015

The author asserts the moral right under the Copyright, Designs and Patents Act 1988 to be identified as the author of this work.

All Rights reserved. No part of this publication may be reproduced, stored in a retrieval system or transmitted, in any form or by any means without the prior consent of the author, nor be otherwise circulated in any form of binding or cover other than that which it is published and without a similar condition being imposed on the subsequent purchaser.

www.newgeneration-publishing.com

ISBN 978-1-78507-489-9

Printed and bound in the UK

A catalogue record of this book is available from the British Library

Cover design by Jacqueline Abromeit

Geraldine Bridgewater worked in the City of London for nearly twenty years starting as a telex operator before becoming authorised to trade in the ring as the first Woman Dealer on the London Metal Exchange.

Her struggle to achieve equality and become a trader during the 70's and 80's was recorded in the press and Radio. Newspaper and magazine articles followed her steps from lowly beginnings to the peak of success in an openly hostile environment that was proud to call itself *'A male dominated bastion'*.

In 1983 Geraldine was granted the Freedom of the City of London in recognition of her achievements and went on to become Head of Public Affairs and Training for the newly formed Association of Futures Brokers and Dealers.

By 1987 greener pastures beckoned and Geraldine moved to Exmoor where she developed her interests in Archaeology, Painting and Organic Farming.

After a short break Geraldine resumed her career in Public Relations for the Health Service before taking up a post as Sustainable Development Co-ordinator for West Somerset District Council.

In 2000 Geraldine moved to Sussex and completed a Master of Arts at Sussex University on Environment Development and Policy before joining local government in Sussex.

During her second chosen career, working for Local Government Geraldine has produced many Strategies and Policies including Waste and Recycling Plans, Environmental Policies, Local Agenda 21, A Strategy for Sustainable Development, Bio-diversity Action Plans, Community Plans and 'Bridging the Divide', Our Social Inclusion Strategy.

In 2007 Geraldine held her first painting exhibition in Brighton and is currently working on her next book.

Acknowledgements

Very special thanks to my Mother for her unwavering support and advise. Where would I be without you?!

Also to my sister Pamela for giving up so many hours over the dinner table to listen.

To my very close friend Vivien for her constant encouragement and 'When will it be finished, I can't wait to read it' quotes!

To my brother Robert for saying the story needed to be told and for reading the first proof. Thank you.

To my brother James who worked with me and became a successful trader too.

To my father who has been a source of great inspiration to me all my life.

To Pen Press the only publisher an author really needs today.

Thanks a million.

Contents

Chapter One	Rites of Passage	1
Chapter Two	Tournament	29
Chapter Three	Whittington Avenue	68
Chapter Four	The London Metal Exchange	97
Chapter Five	Chinese Whispers	143
Chapter Six	Win Some, Lose Some!	186
Chapter Seven	Daughters Wine	221

Chapter One

Rites of Passage

Close your eyes and breathe in deeply. Ah yes, nirvana. Now you have arrived! You're in a wonderful state of relaxation, not a care in the world. You can feel the angelic energy flowing in and around you. Your fingers and toes are tingling as you are caressed by a soft, warm yet very powerful energy. It tells you what you have been waiting to hear for a very long time and in an instant you know that what you did was right. What a relief! Now you feel that memory, so unsettling in the past, leaving you as, reborn, you enter your present consciousness. Here right now, you are much stronger, much more certain of yourself.

The sound of a sitar continues to play gently in the background as I replace the mundane with the spiritual. Kaftans, scents and soft music replace Ferraris, Rolexes and the colour red. Now I feel more like the person I used to be. Gone are the numbers in my head and I am feeling human once again, just like I felt when I was twenty-three.

Back then, the City of London was quite different. I'm not just talking about the place – I'm talking about the people too. Of course at my young age I found it awe-inspiring, a frightening and magical place full of ritual, wealth and power. Discipline ruled with an iron rod and there was no room for stepping out of line or being a maverick, not if you wanted to get on in the world. What a peculiar phrase! 'Getting on in the world' meant making it big, making lots of money, becoming rich and respected. It's what everyone wanted, what everyone expected. It's even what I expected from myself.

A blast of cold wind hits my cheek and I remember it's always windy here. I take some deep breaths and make the most of the fresh air. As I walk through the streets there's plenty to interest a West-End girl who has a liking for classical architecture. Large buildings with impressive entrances, some with wrought-iron railings painted black and gold, others with the name of the firm embossed in gold on the white stonework. I am particularly drawn towards the pillars and porticos. So elegant, and how important these embellished entrances look with their highly polished marble staircases. These imposing structures of capitalism certainly make a good impression, standing as they do, proud, barely visible, behind the swirling clouds of mingled fog and rain.

Walking past each building I scrutinise them in turn. I am imagining the layout behind the façade, trying to guess what business is served, how long it has been established and how much money has been made. Walking down Fenchurch Street, through Plantation House and past The London Sugar Market, I read the company names: Tate and Lyle, British Sugar, and E.D. and F Mann. Quite why I do this I'm not sure; perhaps it is part of an important ritual that I've made up for myself. What better place to be than right here in the middle of all this history in the making?

Oh yes, you can feel the tension around you, and it changes at different times of the day. For example, there is the lunchtime hustle and bustle of traders as they hurry to join a queue for the private Gentlemen's Clubs. Clubs whose traditional rules and regulations bar the uninitiated from joining. Clubs whose membership has remained unchanged over generations, passed down the line of privilege, down from father to son. All sorts of deals have been struck inside these hallowed places. Public school entrants from Eton and Cambridge, Harrow and Oxford follow faithfully in their fathers' footsteps. This is the foundation for all that is good and solid in the City of London. It is their inheritance and it has ever been thus, even since the British Empire rose out of the middle ages and from the ruins of the

Roman Empire right here under the City of London. Now castles and churches have replaced the once crowded bathhouses and amphitheatres. The buildings of governance are still here, though they once had different outlines. The wealth that built up these magnificent edifices came from the wars fought abroad and at home, as the opportunity for trade and commerce increased so the city grew.

The City of London was also a wonderful place of opportunity where the less privileged could work their way towards freedom and honour. As a Freeman of the City of London, you could trade anywhere within the city walls and you didn't need a licence. Free markets expanded at a rapid rate, fuelled by the Industrial Revolution – Commodity Markets, Banks, Insurance Brokers and the Stock Market, all competing within the square mile. No wonder they say the streets are paved with gold!

A golden phoenix clock on the building above tells me I'll be late if I don't get a move on. Two men jostle past me. Oh yes, if you work hard the sky's the limit. Yes, there were always stories of people making their fortune overnight. Sometimes there were losses but you hardly ever heard of them. Let's face it, if you couldn't make it here you couldn't make it anywhere!

All around me people are now rushing to work. They wear black bowler hats set at precarious angles. Impeccably smart with short, greased-back hair and long sideburns. Their dark suits are black or navy blue. Black overcoats complete their attire. Some of them have heel protectors under their very shiny shoes, providing an accompaniment to their black umbrellas as they hit the pavement. *Clickety-click. Clickety-click. Clickety-click!* One can't help but be impressed as they pass. So this is the opening ceremony of the day, performed by all as they posture and claim rights to the territory. At regular intervals I observe an umbrella or walking stick raised high into the air, usually at a road crossing, as if the owner is hailing a taxi but has then changed their mind. I am reminded not to stand too close because on some occasions I have been caught on the forehead, stabbed in the foot and once I was even poked in the eye.

Now I am not suggesting that because all these people dress the same they are the same. I think you know me better than that. But there is a sense of monotony, conformity, and a regimental atmosphere that feels quite depressing. I would have preferred more creativity and colour to start the day off. But there are some that appear less serious than the others – almost jolly even! Most prefer to start the day as they intend to finish it – wielding their power through moody indifference, portrayed by a constant sulking or frowning. I have learned to avoid them. I am happy to smile at the jolly ones with their bright red roses or pink carnations in their lapels. They are charming and polite. I feel almost at home with them!

At this hour in the morning there are very few women. It will be much later when they arrive, usually by bus from Liverpool or Cannon Street stations. Whenever I am late, I walk amongst the telephonists, secretaries, typists and telex operators, all arriving in a great hurry. Perfume fills the air, and the gentle rustle of clothes. Baskets and handbags replace briefcases while headscarves replace bowlers. You can hear the excited hum of time-limited conversation ending in a hurried 'See you for lunch later then?' So, if I am late, which is rare, this is a small part of heaven to see. Colour, creativity and warm smiles. Contrast this with the earlier entourage of bowlers and umbrellas, where if hell ruled the market yesterday, frowns still reflect the fortunes lost.

Later, about 10 am, the great and mighty arrive. These powerful and very rich men own and manage the great city institutions and multi-nationals. There is no great fanfare – on the contrary, barely a sound can be heard as their chauffeur-driven Rolls Royce whooshes up to their company headquarters. Doormen rush out to greet them with a smile, briefly touching their caps as the main man walks in. I am walking fast, sheltering along the inside of the pavement where I can feel the old buildings giving off a welcome heat. Sometimes the sound of marching feet behind becomes overbearing and I stand aside to let them pass.

New recruits to the city have traditionally come from England's wealthier classes and generally, employers demanded public school accents from their employees if they themselves were public school, which of course many of them were. Don't get me wrong: I love a public school accent, I just don't think it's that important a qualification. Anyway, for good or bad these rites of passage have been an integral part of the system. I knew that as soon as I heard a boss say, 'Ah yes, I knew your father', promotion would surely follow for the lucky blighter, even though he was as thick as two planks.

Thankfully, more diverse employers soon came to the city, often starting out as migrants themselves, so the employment market began to open up. This meant wonderful opportunities for some very talented people. Talented in more ways than one! I was hoping to be amongst them. Everything I planned to do today would take me that one step closer to making millions of pounds.

The damp darkness is now lifting to reveal a misty cold day with a hint of breakfast in the air. In front of me a grey view is thankfully broken by the reflection of a red bus on the wet road. I hurry along, my head, mostly bowed, tucking my chin into my scarf to avoid the damp drizzle now plaguing my walk to work. I am trying to calculate whether I will have enough money at the end of the week to go out. Like many of my age working in the city, I often go without a meal in order to supplement my weekend activities. I recall a particularly bad time left me eating tomato soup for countless meals before I could bear it no longer and succumbed to an unaffordable but succulent hot saveloy roll with French mustard. Only recently, I visited the pawnbroker in Shaftesbury Avenue. Out of work, I was like so many others, finding it difficult to get employed, though I was quite lucky because I had been working with a friend, designing and selling very colourful flower-power brooches. We used to sell them quite successfully to market stallholders and members of the public along Oxford Street. But there was a limit to this fashion accessory and both of us knew we were not going to become millionaires overnight. Time to get a proper job.

In the meantime, to keep us going, I decided to sell off a few personal items. Walking into a musty-smelling shop, I noticed an old man sitting in the corner warming his hands over a paraffin stove. 'Good afternoon,' I said as I closed the door quietly and a bell tingled lightly. 'I wonder what you can give me for these?' I stretched out an armful of records. He was deep in thought and I felt like an intruder. Eventually he peered up over his gold horn-rimmed glasses. I smiled, still waiting for an answer. He sported a pointed white beard that gave him a Father Christmas look. He raised his head. His hat, although worn, had retained its colour in parts. It was a deep red satin scull cap with gold embroidery around the edges from which his very white hair poked out. He repositioned it gently on his head before stroking his beard. He must be all of a hundred, I thought, maybe even older!

'Bring them over here into the light and let me see,' he said in a heavy foreign accent. 'Hmmm, there is so much of this stuff around these days I don't think I'll be able to offer you a lot... Look over there, see how much I have. The very best I can give you is... ten bob?'

'Ten bob!' I replied, shocked. 'They are worth much more than that – can't you pay a little more for them? Two pounds would help me. At least I can buy some food with that. Look, I've got the Beatles and Rolling Stones and even the Monkeys! And they are practically brand new!'

He sighed and looked away. He was sitting on an old wooden crate and his hands must have been cold as he moved closer to the small gas stove to warm them. I looked around his shop, slightly embarrassed but still waiting for his answer. Eventually he shook his head very slowly. 'I'm sorry... It's my best offer... take it or leave it!'

I was disappointed but he was poor too and what choice did I really have? Ten bob was better than nothing. I took a long look at my records, wishing I didn't have to part with them before agreeing his price. 'Thank you,' I said before taking the money from him. Just as I pulled the door to leave, he stood up and turned to a wooden desk in the corner, full of dusty old bric-a-brac.

'Wait, come here.'

I let the door go 'Yes?' I replied, walking towards him, all the while hoping he had changed his mind and would give me a little extra.

'Here, I can't give you any more for those records, they aren't worth it. But take this as well. It's very special and will help you.' I held my hand out as he pressed a small, round cold object into it. He looked up at me and smiled before holding my hand shut over it. Standing very still, I looked into his watery eyes as he spoke again. 'Now listen to me very carefully.' He breathed in heavily. 'If you keep this by your bed at all times, you will never be poor again. Keep it on your bedside table. Yes, that would be a good place, so that when you wake up you always see it. You understand me, girl?' He was shaking my hand with urgency and I found myself nodding without knowing what I was agreeing to. I was surprised by his gift. What on earth did he mean? I thought about it for a moment and knew he meant well. What harm could it do to follow his instructions?

I opened the door to leave. 'Yes thank you, I will do what you say.' Once outside, I smiled at him through the window and gave him a wave, not at all sure that he could see me. I was eager to see what he had put in my hand but I walked a respectable distance before stopping to look down at the glass object. It was a little glass ball, not a crystal ball to tell the future by, but a clear paperweight with pretty flowers in it. It was attractive but nothing special. Still, it was nice to believe in his gesture of goodwill. I smiled to myself; most people would think me mad. A crystal ball might have been magic but how could this paperweight stop me from being poor? I wondered.

I bought a bag of chips from the kiosk on the corner and made my way home. Of course as soon as I got in, I put it on my bedside table as the old man had instructed me to. I never thought about it again until a year later when I was passing the shop. By now I had got a job and had no need for the pawnbrokers. I peered through the dirty window and could just make out a few dustsheets. The place was empty of furniture and he was not there. I walked away disappointed, fearing he had passed away without me being able to tell him that he had been right. I said a little prayer, thanking him for the paperweight. I told him that the very next week after he'd given me the gift, I had been offered employment and hadn't been poor since.

Turning left into a doorway I arrive for a day's work at the office in Mark Lane. The warmth inside the building brings me back to the present. Untying my scarf, I walk through the lobby, saying good morning to the doorman, who is standing behind a large green plant. 'Good morning Gerry. How are you today?'

'Oh, I'm fine thank you, George.' He smiles and I smile back. It's the least I can do. I walk on through the swing doors, taking my coat off as I go.

Facing me is a large, and even at this time of the morning, smoke-filled room, full of noisy machines and telexes spewing out overnight reports from New York. I hang my coat and scarf up in the corner and shake my hair dry before using my hands to calm the sides down a bit. That'll do.

'Morning, Gerry.'

'Oh, morning, Henry, I didn't see you there. Would you like a coffee?'

He nods and turns away as he draws heavily on his pipe, snatching and reading reports taken from the telex overnight.

Henry is a small man. His clothes are expensive and his dark hair is thinning. He has small, grey-blue narrowing eyes that slope down at the end of his face and rest on puffy grey bags. His glasses lend him an intellectual aura, appropriate to the position of joint Managing Director. They are carefully positioned halfway along his nose above well-proportioned lips that imply a generous nature. His squirrel-like cheeks are most of the time blue, sometimes red, and often a combination of both. Wine at lunchtime helps his circulation. When he draws on his pipe quickly, as he often does to keep it a light, there is a gurgling noise rather like blocked drains being cleared.

Henry directs my workload because although I am a telex operator, I am also his general assistant. This is an important point because, by being his general assistant, I am not just a telex operator. I go beyond the call of duty to prove my worthiness. That is why I am usually in the office at 8 am and don't leave until 8 pm. Most of my lunch hours are spent looking after the office while I eat a toasted cheese and tomato sandwich.

I enjoy working with Henry and also for Mark. Mark is the big boss. Mark and Henry have worked together for many years and trust each other implicitly. Together they have been responsible for building up the company and are very proud of their achievements. 'Gerry,' Mark said to me one day, 'we are the tail that wags the dog – remember that!' I wasn't sure what he meant, but clearly he was very proud of being the tail and who was I to argue? In any case, although I took them both very seriously, I was quite amused by their appearances. When they stood together, which they often did, they reminded me of Laurel and Hardy. But I had the deepest respect for them. They were both Jewish immigrants who had made their way to England during the war years. Mark had been a merchant seaman and it was rumoured that he dreamt of trading sugar on a terminal market while he was washing down the decks! Some said he even ran a book on board. I never paid any attention to these stories because both Henry and Mark were wealthy beyond imagination. Over the years that they had been together, they had built up an enviable reputation. Not only did they have the confidence to oppose regulations that they considered hampered trading, they also worked towards modernising the image of the city by instigating market reform and supporting calls for a Clearing House System. They were multimillionaires and ran a highly successful business.

Much later in the day I sit on the telex machine with headphones on so that I can speak and listen to the traders on the Sugar Exchange. My job is to read the orders being given from an adjacent telex to the trader on the Sugar Market. All afternoon I watch a small screen to the left of me, showing the prices of the London Market, and type them over to our New York office. They would then respond with equivalent New York prices and orders to buy or sell sugar contracts.

Earlier, I circulated reports to the traders on the markets performance overnight in New York. They always welcome them and usually give me a smile. I hoped they value my hard work. It isn't easy remembering all my different duties and making sure that each is completed in the time allocated.

Twenty-three! I was young enough to be both idealistic and hard-working. I was on the constant look out for information and news, anything that would confirm that I was a valuable asset! Usually there was worthwhile information to gather ahead of the New York market opening. The Traders were only happy when they could have a punt. Misery reigned if the markets were quiet and there was no reason to trade. That was the worst ever so of course I did my best to supply them with the information. Information they could trade on and hopefully make money.

Morning progressed into the lunch hour and Henry asked me to cover the trading desk phones. 'No problem,' I beamed. I loved the opportunity to take a seat on the trading desk.

Now I could imagine what it was like to be a real trader. Ah, that was so good. I wished this was my desk and I was a trader. I didn't want to be a telex operator any more. Sitting on a stupid telex chair with my back turned to everyone. If I was a trader I would act like this and I would have two phones in my hand and one under my chin. I'd be drinking coffee and having a cigarette and I would be shouting to the new telex operator. 'Penny, tell him to buy another fifty tons at market!', and then I'd scream, '*Quiiiiick, quiiiick!*'

I felt someone looking at me and turned to see Karen. I smiled and she looked away, answering another telephone call. I picked up the phone as it rang.

'It's Tony for Mark.'

'OK, thanks Karen. Hello? Tony, Mark's in the boardroom, is it urgent? Do you need to speak to him or can I take a message?'

'Put me through quickly.' Tony was always horribly abrupt.

After I put the phone down, Karen was looking at me in that peculiar way of hers. 'What's the matter?' I asked.

'Nothing,' she replied, looking away in disgust.

Karen was the oldest employee we had. She had worked for sixteen years and was devoted to Mark. She delighted in telling everyone just how long it had been, but I'm afraid it didn't stop traders treating her and her friend Sacha as part of the office furniture! I felt sorry for them. They were taken for granted and I wondered why. Was it because they were older women? Whatever the reason, I resolved that no one would treat me that way, even if I was the only other woman in the room. When I heard traders making derisive remarks about the women, I would defend them and not let the men get away with their stupid comments.

Sacha would often stay late typing up contracts and I thought it unfair that they were rude about her behind her back. Karen already had my respect for being able to cope with answering all the telephones during a busy market session. But we did have our differences. Karen couldn't accept that my direct line telexes to New York were a more secure form of communication for trading. The line was open all the time, so there was no dial-up connection to lose, no scrambled line to decipher, just the clarity of the written word. What could be easier? But Karen wouldn't have it. She didn't believe that the company needed telexes at all and far less a young chit of a girl for a telex operator. She would say, 'It just doesn't make any sense having all these cumbersome ugly machines around the office. All we need is more lines on our switchboard and more telephonists.' I explained to her that it was important to have both, because our telexes had cables that went under the sea, which made them cheaper and safer and therefore the lines were very unlikely to go down in a storm.' I tried to convince her that the telex was not here to take over the telephones but to supplement them. She thought differently and our relationship suffered as a consequence.

Karen and Sacha's office was just to the side of the trading room floor. This gave them a bird's eye view of the trading desks and I could hear them tutting as the swearing became louder. I didn't like it either but I had to laugh when they shook their heads in disgust all the time. I mean, you'd think they would have got used to it, having both worked near the trading room for so many years. Sometimes I saw a more secretive language emerge between them as signs took over from words. I knew that nothing would happen in the trading room that would not be revealed in greater detail much later to anyone who would listen. The story would be embellished because they didn't understand the full detail of what was going on. To anyone in the know, these stories didn't make a great deal of sense and could even be dangerous in their implications. Gossip was always dangerous. I would try to get them to confide in me but they never would willingly and I had to extract the story out of them with a mixture of bribery and corruption.

During these early years, their story never changed. Sacha and Karen's complaint wasn't about job satisfaction, having a career, being professional, being happy or wanting more money, although these might have played a part in their dissatisfaction. No, it was something more fundamental. At the heart of their message was a hidden truth, a notion that they as women could run the business better than men. Men said stupid things – worse, *did* stupid things! Men could and did lie. The women's ode would start with a familiar line such as, 'Did you hear what he said?' or 'Why did he say it like that?' or 'If I was him I would have done that completely differently!' I would occasionally agree with them. At other times I would wonder at the energy they put into this and whether it was wisely spent in view of the amount of work they had left to do!

Earlier, Karen had tried to entice me to give up telexing and learn how to operate a switchboard. Stroking her PABX cords and pulling her lines as the plugs snapped and then sprang back into their holes, she would say, 'Gerry, why don't you have a proper training and become a telephonist? Then you can help me at lunchtimes!' Believing that honesty was the best policy and not wishing to mince my words, I said, 'I don't want to be a telephonist, Karen, that's why!' I'm afraid she took that as a personal insult and never really spoke to me again. Well, not as a friend.

When Karen was upset she would confide in Jan, her colleague, and often she would pay a visit to Sacha who had been relocated to the adjacent office. I would watch as she bent her head towards Sacha's ear, hiding her mouth with her cupped hand so that I couldn't hear her whispering the secret. As she spoke she would take a sideways glance to make sure no one was looking. It was daft really because I always was! The secret she was whispering was probably to my detriment. Karen knew everything there was to know since she sat on the switchboard. As most of my personal conversations were held when I was on lunchtime duty, I suspected that I was probably the source of many of her more unusual stories. Never mind, I thought, picking up the latest book I was reading and relaxing into my chair. Pulling up my sleeves, I took a slurp of coffee and, balancing my feet on a bar just under the desk, I leaned right back in the chair to read all about the Virgin Queen.

Queen Elizabeth the First was a smart woman who surrounded herself with clever and powerful men. She managed the intrigues of her court so well that she became one of the most successful monarchs this country had ever seen, despite being a woman. Part of her success was that before doing anything, she would make detailed plans and should anything go wrong she always had an exit strategy. Another thing I read was she was very shrewd when it came to choosing the right personalities, whether it was her Ministers, Courtiers or Captains. Despite her sex, most of the men around her stayed fiercely loyal to her. But if she hadn't been the Queen, would they have still have seen her as their equal? I don't think so. It was only because she was superior in ranking to them that they accepted her as their equal.

I read the book quite sure that I would benefit from the great Queen's story. After all, despite being the daughter of a King, her beginnings had been humbled and her life threatened when, as a very young woman, she was imprisoned in the Tower of London – the very same Tower that was just across the road from where I was now sitting! I smiled to myself as I thought about the three hundred and twenty years between us. If she could only see me here in the office, just a few hundred yards away from where she played as a child! What on earth would she make of it? Of course if she had reincarnated, she would not have done so on her own. Those who knew her before, the souls that had tried to destroy her or those that gave their lives to support her may have also reincarnated with her, albeit in another guise.

I dropped the book for a moment to ponder this important question. Do reincarnated souls recognise other souls that they have known in a past incarnation, even though the bodies are not the same? I considered the endless possibilities but came up with only one real conclusion, for which I make no excuses: Forewarned is forearmed, is it not?

It wasn't going to be easy for me to become a trader. I would have to play a clever game, bide my time, build trust, and work very hard before I would get a chance. Was there anything I could learn from this book? I wondered. The answer I was looking for might be on the next page. I looked up at the clock. How long had I got? I looked back at all the empty desks around me. There were many young men wanting their chance to become traders and all of them were well ahead of me in the stakes. I would have to make an opportunity for myself. I must have some initiative and show Henry that no matter how good a telex operator I was, I didn't want to stay one for the rest of my life! I comforted myself with the knowledge that the business was growing and new traders would be required. My time would surely come. Planning was very much a part of wielding control and managing circumstances to my advantage.

I didn't like to think of myself as a person who always liked to be in control because I thought that would make me selfish. Being selfish was not a quality I wanted attributed to me – not in this life at any rate. I instinctively knew that whoever we were in this life, there had been more lives before and there would be more afterwards. What you did in this life might affect what happened in the next life. Karma had to be considered before any action was taken. When I looked at someone I tried to see beyond the outer shell and I expected the same treatment.

My mother had a much simpler way of knowing people for who they really were. She would say, 'Actions speak louder than words.' Ah yes, action definitely speaks louder than words. Three hundred years ago, Elizabeth could not have imagined my office located just outside her home garden and certainly would not have understood typing on the telex. How times change and one could only hazard a guess as to where on earth we would all be in another three hundred years!

It was shortly after I had finished this book that a very strange incident occurred. It happened one night in my flat in Essex when I was woken up by the rapidly dropping temperature in my bedroom. It had become so cold that the blackness of a normal night had turned to blue. I tried to move my hands, my legs and my body but I couldn't move any part. I couldn't even move my head. Worse still, I could feel the water from my body draining onto the sheet. I was losing pints. I could hear my heart beating loudly but all I could do was open my eyes.

There at the bottom of the bed stood a woman wearing a nearly transparent gown that stretched to the floor. She was hundreds of years old and had long, white straight hair that fell past her shoulders. She stood rigidly, not moving. She appeared very tall indeed – so tall I could not see her eyes and yet I sensed they were blue. She had a bony grey face. I lay there helpless for what seemed an eternity, struck motionless by her terrifying appearance. I was awake but unable to move or speak. Freezing to death, I was sure I was going to die. My thoughts raced around my head while I tried to ascertain whether I had done something wrong to deserve this visitation. When I could bear it no longer, I shut my eyes, the only thing I had control over.

'Whatever your will is do it, since if you have the power you must use it.' I felt rather than said these words in sharp succession, all the while making sure my eyes remained closed until I felt the room warm up again. Relief! It was safe to open my eyes. She was gone. I breathed a great sigh and scrambled out of bed. I was so weak I could hardly stand. Looking back at the soaked bed sheet, I moved as swiftly as I could to put the light and radio on. I thanked God for my deliverance but after that experience I found it difficult to sleep without the light on and was always terrified that the woman would appear to me again. But it gave me a lot to think about. Who was she? What did she want from me? That night I learned an important lesson: that there is an ultimate power beyond our control that listens to us, and can help or hinder us.

A phone ringing tells me my lunch is over and I don't need to look at the clock to know it is half past two. 'Oh, hi Henry, is that the time already? Yes, I'm just moving now... Yes, the telex has enough paper in it... No, I didn't see that report yet... No, there weren't any phone calls for you... Yes it has been quiet today.' This is the response I give him at the end of every lunchtime; I sit in the same chair talking to the same man, saying exactly the same words. It never ceases to amaze me how many times we have to do the same things over and over again just to get somewhere!

Now the trading room that I am sitting in is a large, smoke-filled room with very little daylight on account of the need for privacy from the adjacent car park. On the walls are white boards with prices written in black ink. Against the wall is a row of twelve telex machines. Reuter reports litter surfaces around the room. The machines provide a constant buzz as they produce up-to-the-moment news and prices from around the world. Across a large, green carpeted floor there are long desks laid out in an H-formation, all quite independent from each other. The room looks like mission control with phones sunk into rising facades strategically located for easy reach by the traders. Between six and eight traders sit facing each other with a bank of phones separating them. They are constantly moving – first sitting then standing, waving their arms around as they shout at each other or down their phones. The desks are named after various commodities. Maurice and I run between the Sugar and Cocoa Desks, handing out appropriate reports, answering the phones if traders are busy and servicing the telexes.

Ah, I must introduce Maurice to you. He is a great friend and he treats me as his equal. Both of us are learning to trade at the same time. The only difference is that he is supposed to be learning and I'm not! He is tall with short, tight curly hair and a strong French accent. I find him quite attractive with his swashbuckling colonial-style moustache that makes him look like a famous explorer – which is funny, because that's exactly what he wants to be!

As juniors in the trading room, we have a steep learning curve. Learning the language of traders and different market rules and regulations. We pick information up as we go along, helping the traders, operating telexes, updating charts, and fetching coffees or teas for everyone. When the market is open, the trading room is extremely noisy. Looking back, I never felt any pressure to learn from the traders themselves, it was simply taken for granted that we would pick the job up as we went along.

Maurice and I desperately want to make our mark and impress the traders. One day we came up with a great idea of predicting the future movements of cocoa by charting past and current price movements. I mean, as if it was ever going to be that easy! During an exciting lunch hour we put together a chart showing the opening and closing prices during the last six months and tried to predict a pattern of future price movements. Every day Maurice and I would pore over the charts, discussing the possible outcome of the day's trading and agreeing where the next line should go.

The chart certainly took on some curious patterns and to us it was easy to see where selling or buying pressure might be building up. However, we were about to get the shock of our lives when suddenly the market closed at limit up (the maximum movement allowed for the day) for ten days in a row! The chart that had started on the wall with intricate wavy lines took on a straight upward line that, apart from the odd break, rose twenty foot into the air and then travelled halfway along the ceiling towards the trading desks on the other side of the office! Of course, we felt like idiots and were subjected to much laughing from the traders, until we were finally obliged to remove the chart and search for another way to impress the traders. You will understand when I tell you that I always believed it was possible to predict the markets and to make money. The system was out there. You just had to find or design it.

Sometimes during the trading day traders lost money and on others a great cheer would go up as they would make a small fortune. At lunchtime the markets in London closed and the office emptied of its din-makers. Henry knew I had nowhere in particular to go and so was not afraid to ask me to keep an eye on the phones. But now, instead of reading novels, I had something more to keep me interested. Half-listening and watching for the bank of phones to light up, I studied all about how to trade on the Chicago Board of Trade. Henry had said that I should learn about the Chicago Markets because 'we might want to start trading pork bellies in the future', adding as he left, 'Please also watch the phones, I'm expecting an important call from Nigeria.' By 2.30 most of the traders would return from lunch to their desks or they would make their way to the markets a few streets away from our office. The afternoons were always so full of excitement as the noise level and temperature in the trading room rose when the New York markets opened.

There are about forty-five of us in the trading room, some sitting, some standing, but all at their trading positions and nearly all talking. There are phones on loudspeakers on each of the trading desks.

What makes a successful trader? I can't say, but even in these early days I notice they are quite different from ordinary men. Of course they are rich, good-looking, always wearing very smart suits and for the most part smelling of expensive aftershave. Generally they have rather loud and flamboyant personalities. Something important and exciting is always happening in their lives. They have busy weekends full of parties and shopping trips. Pictures of their girlfriends and wives sporadically appear along with various stories of break-ups, reunions, or family visits.

At this time London is primed for the opening of New York and everyone is ready to make a fortune on arbitrage. The noise in the office is loud, almost deafening as all the different markets open at the same time. So it's busy on Cocoa, busy on Sugar, and busy on Coffee! TV monitors around the office display the markets' opening prices in New York and by three o'clock they are all frantically trading. My job is to man the telexes, which I do with the aid of a pair of headphones, a loud voice and very fast fingers. Clive, our floor trader, takes me through the opening call, shouting out the prices for sugar, which I then type as quickly and as accurately as I can, over to our New York office.

'Ack' is a word I type frequently, meaning 'acknowledged'. If I don't, New York will press a red button their end and a buzzer will go off very loudly on the telex next to me. So the time I take to 'ack' is a measure of how quickly I can react to the order being given. And there is no getting away with a mistake because the buzzer is so loud that it alerts the whole office to the notion that I may have missed an order from New York. Often I am late in seeing it, or the execution that comes back is not as good as expected, or the market has moved against me. Then there is hell to pay. I am usually at the end of Tony's verbal abuse and there is no one else I could pass it on to. Sometimes it is impossible to give Clive the order because he isn't always on the end of the phone. Then there are times when a new order is given and I forget about the first order. Being multi-skilled is important for profitable trading. Passing an order to Clive is never easy and I have to shout very loudly over the speaker to get his attention above the uproar of the Exchange floor. Office traders often look at me disapprovingly, covering one ear and straining with the other to hear their own telephone conversations.

Once trading opened in London, the call chairman of Sugar would read out the delivery months one by one, reporting on the bids and offers and matching them up before finally agreeing a closing price for the call. It would sound a bit like this: 'December 258, 260 - March 245, 247. May 240, 242', and so on. I would then type these prices as quickly as possible over the telex to our New York office, where the office traders would convert them into dollar prices and then trade if the differential between London and New York showed a profit. This process was known as 'arbitrage' and was tricky but very lucrative. In essence they were trading the currency since the position on Sugar would be square.

Regularly the phrase 'Fuck you' would appear on the telex, especially if they thought I'd missed an order. The first time it happened shocked me. 'Have I made a mistake?' I asked Henry with watery eyes and a red face. For support he would come over and stand behind me while I was seated at the telex. Comforting me, he would draw heavily on his pipe three of four times while he looked at the offending telex. He would then pat me on the shoulder. 'No, that's just Tony, he swears all the time, especially when he's angry. Uh huh, he probably doesn't like what the market's doing, ha ha ha!'

'Well, he shouldn't swear at me, it's not my fault.'

Henry looked down with genuine concern 'Don't get too upset, it's not personal.'

Henry was right. Tony, I found out later, was constantly swearing. Henry said it was because he was a cockney living in New York with a big reputation to maintain. But I thought he was just a bit of a bully; he swore because there was no one to say he couldn't. And it wasn't long before some of his traders started to copy him, swearing at any given opportunity. The swearing eventually took off in our office too and even though we women showed our disapproval, it continued unabated. Eventually I did complain to Henry. 'When will it stop? It's getting worse and worse! It might be OK in New York but it shouldn't be accepted here in London.' To my surprise, he agreed, and issued a decree that only in emergencies should we all be allowed to swear. At really difficult times traders would fly into rages and phones would be thrown down onto the desks, smashing into bits around us. The problem was they would then have to be put back together again. I found it really funny watching traders trying to screw in an earpiece and then, as the seconds ticked by, realizing that a garbled voice was trying to give them an order from the other end of the phone!

Occasionally Tony would visit us in London. I would watch him stride into the office, a larger-than-life character, and throw his arms around Mark. With tears in his eyes, he'd say, 'Ow are yer, me ol mate?' and then, turning to the rest of the office, he would add: 'Making loads and loads of money?' Ha ha ha...!' He thought he was really popular but in fact everyone was scared of him. He was known to sack on the spot without blinking an eyelid. Once he had sacked a trader who had worked for him for five years. 'Get out,' he had said brutally, 'and don't bother hanging around for your wages, you're fired mate.' Then, as if nothing had happened, he pointed at another trader. 'What's the arbitrage doing now?'

Oh yes, Tony was ruthless, make no mistake about that. Spotting me, he would say, 'Where's my little Penny? Oh yea she left to av a baibee... I hope you're not making a mess of fingz; Penny was so good... Ow I miss er!' I just looked at him on these occasions and wondered whether I should introduce myself to him but decided against the idea. The less he knew of me the better. I bet Penny doesn't miss you, I thought as I turned my back on him. Tony had always been volatile and excitable but deep down he was a good man – or so I was told!

On some occasions of over-excitement, Henry would say to Tony, 'All right, don't have a bloody thrombi!'

But Tony would always have the last say. 'I'll have a bloody thrombi if I want to!' And indeed, many years later he dropped dead on the trading floor in New York and they brought him back to London for the funeral. Mark always said Tony had had a sixth sense, being able to tell the future of the market, where it would go and even the day the movement would take place. Some thought that was rubbish but I think Mark was right. Tony was really able to tell the future and he always did just what he wanted to do.

The market was made up of two types of clients, speculators and trade customers. Our clients on the soft commodities – for instance, sugar, cocoa and coffee – were mainly trade customers and they took positions as a hedge to protect their physical purchases or sales. Speculating was the same as gambling. Traders would take a position with some prior knowledge or feeling about how the market might move. Jobbing the market was about taking a quick position or punt for, say, a five-pound profit. Usually this position would not be held overnight, only for the morning or afternoon market – unless of course it went wrong! Traders liked to job to make money. As much as £5000 could be made in a day by simply jobbing and trading on the back of the big orders. When I had first arrived in the city, I couldn't believe it; everyone would talk about making loads of money but I never actually saw any money passing hands. Yes, trading on a futures market was exciting and complicated but it was also a total enigma to me.

Arbitrage was not speculation or hedging. Arbitrage required speed and accuracy of calculation. Communication was of the essence. When the phone rang, it had to be answered immediately; when an order was given, it had to be executed and reported back swiftly. Tony was the expert arbitrage trader and he put the fear of God into everyone around him as he spotted opportunities. His fingers would rapidly dance over the calculator buttons and his face would get redder and redder the nearer he came to making a profit. The performance would finally end with a scream and a jump, and a fist banging on the telex behind me. 'Yes, a pony, yes!' Sometimes he would grab and kiss me, although thankfully not too often. Honestly, you would think he was the only one making money! On one occasion such as this, I noticed a bit fly off the telex. They were getting old and we needed to replace them with much faster and up-to-date models.

Henry had been thinking about putting some more direct lines in. We had a link from London to New York but now someone was opening an office in Amsterdam and Henry said we should have a direct link so that we could take orders from Amsterdam and give them to New York or London. So over the next few weeks, I was kept busy seeing in the new machines and interviewing telex operators. Surely now as a supervisor I should be earning more money? But when I approached Henry he said, 'Well, you're earning more than the new girls and in any case, with more staff you have less work to do!'

Returning home one Friday after a hard week, I poured myself a large whisky on the rocks, lit a cigarette and considered the evening ahead of me. Ten minutes later I emerged from the shower and, towelling my hair, I looked in the mirror. Staring back was a confident woman with blue/green, almond-shaped eyes, tall and slim with dark shoulder-length hair. My small features made me look quite feminine, even though my mouth was reasonably generous with a bottom lip that was slightly thicker than the top. This made me look quite determined, despite the dimple in my chin that I felt was an unnecessary 'girly' touch! I stared into the mirror, trying to be as objective as possible. Certainly I felt older than my years, though some thought my face quite young looking. Being charming was important and I liked to pay people compliments. Tonight I knew would be special. I could feel it. Humming to myself, I took a rust-coloured suit, consisting of a highly tailored jacket with flared trousers, out of the wardrobe and laid it on the bed. Stuffing £15 in my pocket, I grabbed the car keys and ran downstairs.

Fifteen minutes later, I was parking my blue, almost new car in Poland Street and heading towards the club. I knew the West End well and felt comfortable being out late at night, even when I was on my own. At this hour, all the revellers were happy – unlike later, when the squeals of delight would invariably turn to drunken tears!

I knocked on the door and within a second, a sliding screen opened up. A face peered through 'Yes?'

'Can I come in please?'

The bolt shot back and the door opened. It was all red inside: red lights, red carpets and red velvety benches. '*Oh my darling I... can't get enough of your love babe*' rang out across the dance floor. '*No I can't get enough of your love babe, oh you know, You know, You know... I can't get...*' Subconsciously, I started to move in time to the music with everyone else. The temperature was rising rapidly, and I considered taking my jacket off and looked around for somewhere to hang it. Not finding a suitable spot, I carried on wearing it and made my way over to the bar. Behind the bar was a mirror. I could just recognise myself lighting up a cigarette and I watched myself take a sip of lager. Yes, I looked fine. A movement to the side of me broke my concentration as I was passed a ticket.

'This is for your meal, it's free. Everyone must have a salad with their drinks tonight.'

I leaned over the winding staircase that led to a crowded dance floor, and smiled at a few people, who smiled back. There was plenty of action happening below! I tried not to feel conspicuous but I felt awkward not really knowing anyone. I comforted myself with the certain knowledge that I was blending in well in my orange suit!

Bob still hadn't arrived so I made my way down to the dance floor and joined in with the dancing '*Hot, hot, hot... yes it's hot, hot, feeling hot, hot, hot...*' Then I saw Bob smiling and battling his way through the crowd. I was well into the dance but decided for his sake to stop.

'Aren't you hot with that jacket on?' he asked me.

'Yes, but where should I put it?'

'Just put it on the stool over there, it'll be all right.' I took his advice. 'There that's better isn't it?'

'Yes much, thanks.'

The music was great and there were some interesting people around too, so we danced and chatted. Eventually we needed a rest. We climbed back up the stairs and sat down, both lighting up a cigarette. 'I'm just going to the loo,' Bob said, getting up. I was watching him disappear into the toilet when the door opposite opened and a woman with long dark hair and sapphire blue eyes walked towards me. She looked briefly at me, smiled and then looked the other way. She was casually dressed in a white shirt and blue jeans. Maybe I should have brought some gum, I thought, watching her chewing.

Sensing my gaze, she looked at me and raised an eyebrow, then looked away.

'Hi, I'm Gerry,' I ventured, 'you haven't got a spare piece of gum have you?'

'Sorry, this is all I've got,' she said, tugging at it before popping it back in her mouth. For a minute I thought she was going to share some with me but then luckily she turned to continue speaking with her friends. I hopped awkwardly from one foot to another before Bob thankfully returned. As he approached, the woman turned round again. 'Oh sorry, I'm Emily,' she smiled. 'And this is?'

'Bob, he's my brother.'

'Oh, nice to meet you.'

We all smiled again and waited for someone to break the silence. 'A drink perhaps?' I said finally. Emily, I noticed, had an empty glass in her hand.

She smiled, tossing her head to one side 'Oh, yes please. A Bacardi and Coke… thanks."

Occasionally I would catch her glancing behind me as if she

was expecting someone else to arrive. We walked back to the table and sat down, waving our tickets so as to take delivery of our free spam salads. Emily introduced me to her friend Paul, who was a waiter – a very useful contact as she later explained. He was great fun too, and in charge of distributing the spam salads. He told me that he collected all the half-empty glasses of Coke for Emily, so that when she ordered her next Bacardi, she didn't have to buy coke to go with it! How thoughtful he was.

Bob asked Emily if she lived in London and she replied, 'No, in Croydon.'

'Oh, that's a long way. Do you have a car?'

'No I get a lift with my friends.'

As we were all talking she kept looking round the room. 'Are you meeting someone?' I asked.

'No I'm just sussing out the talent.'

'Well, there's plenty here,' I said, pointing at myself. She made me laugh, especially when she gave a little wiggle to a favourite song. There was something different about Emily and I found it very appealing.

As the night came to an end around three am, we arranged to meet up with Emily and Paul the following night. I went shopping for something not so orange and ended up with a green flowered shirt. When we met, we had a great time planning a wild weekend in Brighton. One thing I noticed about Emily was that if she was impressed, she would never show it. It was as though you had to keep trying harder and harder to please her!

One weekend, after staying overnight at her house in Croydon, we headed off for the coast early one Saturday. We were both starving when we arrived and stopped off on the seafront for a fry-up. I noticed Emily appeared a little distracted, possibly after the hectic drive into town. As we ate breakfast I asked her if she was OK.

'Yes, I'm fine, why are you asking?'

'Oh, no reason in particular, it's just I think you're bored.'

'I'm not bored. Anyway, what are we going to do today?'

'I thought we could go down the Lanes this morning and then go for a drink at lunchtime.'

'Yes, the drink sounds good but why are we going down the Lanes? You know I don't have any money to spend.' I watched as she suddenly waved furiously at me.

'Well… we could just have a look, I thought if we went down the Lanes you might see something you like. Oh, come on! What else will we do before lunchtime? We'll have a laugh.'

But later, as we walked round the Lanes, I could see Emily was getting bored. 'I don't want to look at shops any more,' she said, 'let's go for a drink.'

Finally we found our way to a club along the seafront. 'Look, Emily, across the road is a club I thought we could try tonight when we meet up with Bob and his friend. It's The Palace and they play fantastic music.'

Emily frowned before agreeing reluctantly. 'Yea, OK, whatever. Come on now, can we have that drink, I'm gasping.'

That night, walking along the street, you could hear from a distance the music of Barry White followed by Abba blasting out onto the pavement, with the sole intention of attracting the punters. With music playing like that there was no competition: The Palace was clearly the best club in town. The following morning we grabbed a cooked breakfast in a small crowded café before going for a walk along the pier.

It was great being by the sea and I didn't want the weekend to end. But on our way back to the car, Emily stopped at a shop and peered into the window. 'Gerry, wait, look,' she said, 'isn't that lovely?'

I followed her finger and peered into the dark smudged glass window. 'What?'

'That ring, look see that silver ring with those clasped hands? It's lovely. I would love a ring like that.'

'Yes,' I said, 'it is unusual.'

'How much do you think it is?'

'I don't know but the shop is shut, we'll have to look at it another time.'

'No, Gerry, no… ring the bell – I must have a look at it.'

'I'll try but it's Sunday. I'm sure no one will answer.'

I rang the bell anyway and, to my surprise, the door opened and we were able to buy the ring..

'It's a lovely ring, don't you think, Gerry?'

'Yes, it certainly suits you and it's very unusual. Obviously a very old friendship ring.'

'Yes, that's right, it means that we are very good friends too, Gerry.'

It was a great weekend and we both hated the thought of going back to work all week. We arranged to meet up the following Wednesday to see Emmanuelle. 'I've heard the music is really sexy in it,' Emily said to me as I dropped her off.

Chapter Two

Tournament

Although the weekend with Emily had not been particularly expensive, it reminded me that I needed to increase my take-home pay. As I walked into the office on Monday, I decided that I would ask Henry about what the future held for me.

'Morning, Henry.'

'Morning, Gerry.'

'Henry, I wonder whether I could have a word later?'

'Yes, sure, Gerry. What's it about then?'

'Well, it's about my future.'

'You're not thinking of leaving us, are you?' I smiled at him, not saying anything. 'OK,' he said, 'come and see me in about one hour.'

Before trading started, Henry went into the boardroom next to the trading room for a couple of hours. Here he would catch up on some paperwork and open his mail. Normally this was not the time to disturb him, so I was grateful when he agreed to see me. As I tore off the overnight telexes and put the reports on the traders' desks, I was thinking about what I could say to him. I wanted to be a trader but most of all I needed to earn more money. Any job he could give me would help. I was even prepared to clean the offices for extra money if that's what it took. I was earning about £20 per week and, with overtime, I could earn an extra £8 per night.

Ten-thirty finally arrived and I knocked on the boardroom door. I could smell Henry's pipe burning so I knocked again. With my ear to the door I held my breath. Still no reply. I carried on listening, wondering what I should do next and then I heard

Henry speaking on the phone. Right, I thought, I'll come back later. I was just walking back into the trading room when Henry called me over to him. 'OK, Gerry, come in now, I've got a few moments.'

I walked into a plush but small wood-panelled room with a large oval table, green leather chairs and an enormous hand-carved African mural on the wall above where Henry was seated. I loved this room because this was where all the important decisions were made on rises and bonuses. I stood in front of Henry, waiting for him to look up from his papers. I tried to look as confident as possible. Henry was powerful and rich. One day I'll be as powerful and as rich as him, I thought.

'Right, Gerry, what can I do for you?'

'Well, Henry, you know I hate to ask about this, but I've been working for you for three years and I would like to know what my future is.'

'What do you mean, "your future"?'

'I want to be a trader and earn more money. I don't want to be a telex operator all my life. I can do much more and I'm sure I'd make a good trader.'

Henry stared at me, taking his pipe out of his mouth and glancing at the ceiling before re-adjusting his gaze. I was beginning to feel uncomfortable. I didn't want to beg but I knew I had to have this conversation with him.

Then I smiled as he broke the silence. 'Look, Gerry, you know it takes a very long time to be a trader and in any case, there are no vacancies. How much are you earning now?'

'One thousand pounds a year.'

'Yes and then at Christmas we pay you a bonus. How much was that?'

'Five hundred pounds,' I said.

'Five hundred pounds? Well, that's not to be sniffed at, is it?' I could feel myself getting angry. This was all going wrong. 'Frankly, Gerry, I think you're getting a bloody good screw.'

I looked at him incredulously. 'I beg your pardon?'

'I think you're getting **a** bloody good screw,' Henry repeated.

Suddenly I saw red and, without a word, swooped down on him, slapping his face so loudly that it rang out around the trading room. 'Bloody good screw'! Couldn't he have found more appropriate words to use? 'Bloody good screw' was not a term to be used about me.

I grabbed my coat and walked out. Now I'm in for it, I'll probably be sacked tomorrow, I thought. My only comfort was I would be free to move on – providing I could get a job. Unemployment was high and the agencies in the city were always full of prospective employees.

Then I thought of Emily and felt better. In times of crisis, life has a peculiar way of making you appreciate whatever it is you have and this moment was no exception for me as I suddenly recalled a job I'd had that had been even worse.

One upon a time I had been employed as a packer in a warehouse. I absolutely hated the job but had no choice since I had no other way of earning an honest living. Never had I seen so much poverty around me. All the lads and most of the older men that I worked with were extremely poor. By contrast, my boss was plump, well-suited with a constant smile on his face. His favourite saying was 'Oh come, on it's not that bad, is it?' But before you could answer, he was gone. He was not at all embarrassed about how much wealth he had compared to his struggling workforce.

At lunchtimes I would go to the local café frequented by the truck drivers. I was not well dressed but some of them were hardly dressed at all. When I walked in they would look at me and stare. I would always have to look away. As I brought my cup of tea to the table or, at lunchtimes, my pie and mushy peas, I could feel their eyes burning holes in my clothes.

'Ere, Joe, did I tell yer my latest joke about the bishop, the tart and the postman? Ha ha, Ha ha!'

On occasions such as these I would gulp my food down as quickly as possible and return to the freezing, damp, smelly warehouse. I never felt comfortable or safe working in the East End of London, surrounded by the prefabricated houses built during the Second World War. The sweatshops were full of migrant workers earning a pittance with hardly any teeth and torn clothing. This was a place with no joy, concrete with no sky, satanic mills, with their red black bricks and tall chimneys dominating the horizon. Their large gaping windows were fed sporadically by noisy wooden lifts accompanied by shouts from the men below as they were pulled into place for loading.

After six months' hard labour I was sacked. Not for pilfering – although I did quite a bit to substitute my income. No, it was for not agreeing to sleep with the boss. I told him straight I never would and he told me that I must be mad. Eventually he came to the end of his tether and said that if I didn't agree to the 'arrangement', he would have no alternative but to fire me! I asked him whether that was fair or wise and he told me to take it or leave it, so I left it.

And now, three years later, I'd probably gone and got myself into another mess!

That evening at the club I drank much more than I should have. The room was swaying or shaking, or was it me? People appeared a bit blurry but that was to be expected at that time of night. And where was Emily? Last time I'd seen her she was just popping to the loo, and I seemed to have been holding her drink forever. An hour later I was still sitting waiting for her, even though the club had almost emptied. I was getting worried and searched the toilets; no sign of her so I went downstairs where I spotted a fire-escape door that I opened. Emily was sitting in front of me on the stairs, a drink in her hand, talking intimately with someone else – or not exactly 'talking'.

'What's going on?' I cried. There was no reply as they continued unashamedly. I slammed the door shut in disgust, knocked back the drink and grabbed my car keys. Right, that was it, the end of what might have been a beautiful relationship.

The following morning, Henry, as I half expected, ignored me and the day passed uncomfortably slowly. I could sense his coolness. I wondered whether I should apologise but was scared to remind him of the incident just in case he decided to sack me. I was also worried that others in the room would sense that Henry was not pleased with me. Many traders would have liked me replaced by someone else, someone they knew privately or someone more amenable.

Clive had been angry with me for 'jobbing off his back' – his words not mine. Actually, he had taken it very personally, especially when at the end of the month I had made nearly as much as he had! Mark had said that I could take a view on the market and hold a position overnight. But I was too much of a coward. I didn't like taking risks with other people's money, especially my bosses'!

Sitting on the telex, I'd told Clive to buy fifteen lots of sugar instead of ten and then I did the same on the sale. However, it became obvious to me that New York didn't make money every time and this was a stupid thing to do. I would have to be cleverer than that. But I really didn't want to take a position overnight and it was important for me to show Mark that his trust in me was justified.

Picture the looks of astonishment, then, on some of the traders' faces when Mark told me that it was fine by him if I wanted to trade!

'Gerry, I'll let you trade with five lots of sugar and we'll see how you get on, eh?'

This was most unusual and it unnerved the traders. 'What does Gerry know about trading?' I heard one trader say to another.

If the market was particularly 'hairy' (volatile), all traders could lose large amounts of money. The sugar traders made it clear that they didn't want me to get ideas above my station. Perhaps they feared that Mark would be so pleased with my performance, he might wonder why he needed to have an expensive trader when a telex operator could do the same job just as well and at less than a tenth of the price!

I was amazed at the amount of trust that Mark and Henry put in their traders to make money. After all, this was virtually gambling. But their faith paid off because the traders would put in some astounding profits. Often end-of-week calculations would show in excess of £12 000 profit on sugar jobbing. Why on earth would anyone do a regular job when this amount of money could be made so easily?

The traders, of course, didn't want anyone to know their secrets. They explained to me that it wasn't that easy to make money; they were highly skilled and very few people could do what they did, which was why they were so well paid.

Henry was still not speaking to me so it was good that Mark was showing an interest in helping me develop my career. If I could show Mark my jobbing skills then he might allow me to become a blue button and go down on the Sugar or Cocoa Floor. The market was about to start so I sat down at the telex machine and put on the head phones.

'Hi Clive.'

'OK!' he shouted down the phone. 'We're just about to start the call.'

He was never particularly friendly but he was not impolite either. As the bell sounded, he started to call out the prices as they traded and I typed them over to New York as fast as I could, which was at least one hundred words a minute on this new telex. It was, I knew, the speed of my typing that helped the traders make millions. After all, I was the fastest in the City. Just look at the steam coming off the keyboard! *Buzz, buzz, buzz!* the bell on the New York telex was flashing on and off as the sheet of paper spewed out of the machine at about sixty miles an hour.

'Ack the fucking order, will you? You stupid cow...!' *Buzz buzz buzz...*

'OK, Ack,' I belled back.

Yea. Let's give em a feel of what it's like. I press the button again, Yea... I too can get angry Yea... *Buzz, buzz, buzz.* I've bloody well got it OK...

'Clive, are you there? Buy twenty lots of March Sugar at market.'

'OK, Ack,' Clive replies 'But we have to wait. We are trading December at the moment.'

'Hang on, Clive.' The buzzer was going again from New York. I watched as the words were typed out on the opposite machine. Execution? Exe? Exe? Exe? Where's my fucking execution? Buy twenty lots of March at Market... Quick, I've got to trade the currency. Where is my fucking execution? Where is my forty lots...?

The NY buzzer was ringing again. I watched in horror at the words 'I'll fucking sack you! Where's my bloody execution you bloody asshole...? If I lose money I'll fucking kill you!'

The buzzer went off again. 'Clive... Clive!' I shouted, turning to see the whole office looking at me. 'Clive... cancel that order to buy twenty lots of March Sugar'...just cancel the order will you? NOW!' I screamed.

'OK, Gerry, keep your hair on! It's cancelled now, Gerry.'

I had to think fast. I know, I'd just book them out and buy them back later. So as Clive gave the commentary I typed 'Bought twenty lots of March at 158' and then a few seconds later I typed 'Bought another twenty lots at 158.50... Ack pse?'

I pressed the buzzer to get Tony's attention in New York and watched intently as 'A. C. K' was slowly typed out, telling me that Tony was typing and on the phone at the same time. I was now short forty lots of March Sugar and the market was moving up against me! I sat exhausted, desperately trying to relax as the opening call ended and free trading started up. It was going to be hectic because at this time, any delivery month could be traded. By now the market in New York had opened and I could see it moving higher. Shit! London will go higher and I've just sold forty lots at 158.25 on my own account! I'm losing money...Shit!'

The N.Y. buzzer goes off again. 'Buy fifty March at market.'

'OK ack,' I type. 'Clive... Clive...' No answer, he's not there. I frantically type 'Mom... mom...' while trying to get hold of him.

Then Mark shouts from across the other side of the room.. He's got Tony on the phone. 'Where's Tony's execution?'

I can see Mark holding the phone away from his ear as the verbal abuse increases. 'Tony is having a bloody thrombi, what's he done, Gerry?'

I look quickly at the screen and see the price trading at 163. 'Hang on a minute!' I shout. My heart is thumping, my stomach churning. 'Mark,' I hear myself saying, 'bought twenty lots at 162 for Tony.'

'Good. Tony... Yeah... You got twenty lots at 163.'

Blimey, I thought, Mark's just taken a pound on twenty lots. Obviously he's not shy of jobbing off Tony's back but then why should he be? After all, he is the boss. I can still hear Tony yelling at Mark, 'Where is the rest of my fucking execution...? Hell... go to fucking market on the balance will yer... get those thirty lots in now quick, dammit!'

Mark screams, 'Go to market on the balance, Gerry!'

'OK!' I shout. 'Clive, buy thirty lots of March at market.'

'Ack,' he answers.

I look at the screen and March is now trading at 165. Clive picks up the phone again. 'You bought thirty lots at 167.'

'It's not showing as traded on the screen, Clive.'

'Well the screen's never up to date anyway!' he shouts back. 'Look, it's trading at 168. Give the execution back now.'

But I have frozen and I watch as the market runs up to 173 trading. 'You got em all at 170!' I shout. No reason why I shouldn't do a little jobbing myself. Nothing wrong with taking a profit of three quid! I wait for the fall-out... but there isn't any. Wow! I got away with it.

Tony seems happy the market is racing upwards, knowing this will spark yet more arbitrage buying from New York traders in London. Limit up or limit down is the maximum move the market can make in a day before it is closed. Any orders left over would then go into a pool and the opening prices would be set during a special call.

Instinctively we all know that the market will go to limit up, squeezing those that have sold out of the market and forcing them to take massive losses.

As London closes, New York will stay open and continue trading higher. Of course I am feeling sick as I watch the orders pouring in from our New York office. The yelling in my earphones is more than matched by even louder yelling from the office. Above this noise Clive is shouting something but I can't hear what he is saying because I'm also trying to concentrate on what Mark is yelling across from the other side of the room.

'Buy another fifty lots at Market, Gerry... Gerry... Buy another fifty lots... Yes...'

I wave at Mark to acknowledge: that's one hundred lots now, is it? Yes... Hurry, one hundred lots...

I look at the screen. I'm feeling disorientated. It's 4.30 and I've been on the telex for a couple of hours. The market is still moving up and the last price on the screen is showing limit up at 183. 'Clive, Clive!' I shout but he can't hear me. It's pandemonium on the market now. Mark is screaming, 'Gerry... what's Tony done? Quick... You can't take this fucking long.'

Panicking because I am unable to get Clive to hear me, I book them out. 'Yea,' I reply, 'he's got them one hundred lots at 183. The market's closed now in London.' Suddenly it goes quiet on the Exchange. 'Clive, are you still there?'

'Yes, I'm here.' He sounds exhausted.

'Is the market closed now?'

'Yes, limit up, Gerry, it's closed.'

'It's gone very quiet down there,' I whisper.

'Sshhh! The call chairman is saying something.'

A minute or so passed and Clive was back on the phone. 'OK, tell Tony the markets closed in London now.'

'OK, are you coming back to the office now then?'

'No, I'm going for a bloody drink, I think I deserve it, don't you?'

'Yes OK, see you later.'

'Probably!' Clive didn't sound happy. But Mark was very pleased and Tony was all right too. 'Well done, Gerry, I know it was tough but we've done all right.'

37

'Oh good,' I smiled, but my head was beginning to spin as I hung up the earphones and checked the telex. Reams and reams of paper all over the floor with just a few words on them. What a waste! I thought.

'Mark, I'm sorry you had to have Tony on the line, we could have done it by telex.'

'No, Tony always like to be on the phone when he knows it's going to be busy,' Mark said, smiling and patting me on the shoulder.

'It's not because he thinks I'm too slow then?' I asked, hoping for a compliment.

'No, he just wants to make sure that his orders get in first.'

But I was worried about Tony. I sensed he didn't like me and didn't want me in the trading room. He was always threatening to sack me.

Meanwhile, where was Clive? He hadn't seemed very happy when he went; perhaps he had been left with a bad position. I knew that often the traders took positions because they felt they had no choice and were just trying to please the customer. That was one of Mark's favourite sayings. Bowing his head with his eyes half-closed, he would say with a smile, 'Gerry, you must always please the customer, the customer comes first – always.' Then, straightening up again, he would turn to face all the traders and say loudly, 'We look after the customer and the customer looks after us. Because? Because the customer pays commission and commission is how we earn our bread and butter. Remember, we make just the commission. We don't steal. We don't rob like the other brokers in town do. That's why we have so many good customers. That's why we are making so much money and that's why we are the best.' He would complete this 'speech' by pursing his lips together as he marched out of the room to the applause of all the traders in the room.

Thinking of the commission was right, but for now my thoughts turned to my position. I had exceeded my authority and Mark and Henry would go mad if they found out. I should have five lots instead of 160 lots! The market was limit up at

185 and I'd sold out at an average price of around 174. I was losing a lot of money for Mark – over £8000.

On my way home that evening, I pondered my future. Trading. What *was* trading? It was not all it was cracked up to be. I didn't like all the pressure and the screaming and if you weren't even earning money, what was the point?

Arriving at the underground, I'm relieved to find it warm, even though I have to queue to move down the stairs with lots of damp raincoats. God, I hate that damp smell! Still, rich or poor, we all have to take the same smelly journey home when it's raining.

The next morning after spending a sleepless night, I got into the office earlier than usual – even earlier than Henry, who normally got in around 7.30. I was keen to see what the market had done overnight and to make it up with Henry if I could.

Straight away the trading room felt different. There was no coffee, pipe or aftershave and the desks look strangely empty. The whole room felt like a ghost ship. I needed to have a coffee and a cigarette before I saw what New York had done overnight. I heard Henry come up behind me as I was peering over the Reuters.

'What are you doing in so early, Gerry?' he said.

'Oh, guess I just can't keep away. Ha ha!'

'Hmmm,' he mused as he pushed me out of the way to look at the Reuters. 'I wonder how New York closed last night?' he muttered, making his way over to the screens and switching them on. Normally that would have been my job. Clearly, Henry was not being his usual friendly self with me. But who could blame him? I regretted slapping his face. It was a stupid thing to have done.

I tried to get his attention. 'Would you like a coffee? I'm going across to Sylvios, I thought I might get a toasted marmalade. How about you, Henry?'

'No, just get me a coffee, that'll do.'

No money was forthcoming and I didn't feel I could ask

him, not after our row. Perhaps he would remember and give it to me later. This week I only had enough for my tube fare and one sandwich a day, plus my ration of fags. There was nothing to spare.

At ten o'clock Clive came in and I was able to tell by his face what kind of night he'd had. The pound had rallied against the dollar overnight and Henry was frantically working out where the markets should open in London. I relaxed when Clive started laughing and talking with the other traders. I watched as he lit his cigarette and winked at me.

'I'm very pleased I was left a position overnight. I mean I wasn't too happy at the time, Gerry, I can tell you, but now this morning it looks as though I'll clean up!'

I noticed he had washed his hair and had a new suit on. Perhaps that was making him feel good too. Against all the odds, the market had opened lower in London. 'Good,' I said. 'What's your position?'

'Short forty lots.'

'Oh,' I said, 'when are you going to buy them back?'

'Probably this afternoon, I think we'll just let London drop this morning. Yea, drop like a stone... Ha ha ha!'

Henry called Clive over. 'I've been going through the overnight trading position and it looks like we're short about a hundred and eighty lots. I've told you before not to exceed your trading position.'

'No, Henry, that can't be right' I heard Clive say. 'I'll check it out. I know I'm short forty lots. Some orders must have gone missing. We'll sort it out when Tony gets in.'

Clive came over to the telex to look at yesterday's messages almost as though he smelt a rat. 'Do you remember any large orders, Gerry?'

'Christ, we were so busy they were all at market and then Mark had Tony on the phone screaming at him all afternoon.' I spoke as fast as possible, waving my arms around, hoping that by ending on a funny face, I could get him to lighten up a bit. Had I convinced him? Yes, yes, at last he responded.

'I know what's happened. Tony's forgotten to put one side of the arbitrage down on his overnight position, he's always doing that.'

'Yes, he is,' I agreed, feeling immense relief. I hated lying but I knew what the consequences would be if I spoke up.

'Henry, don't worry,' said Clive, 'it'll come out in the wash… at least the market's going our way!'

Henry, who was never one for taking Clive's opinion very seriously, came over to me. 'I want to speak with you later. I'll give you a nod.'

I knew I had to get out of some of the position this morning and with the market in my favour, it made a lot of sense. It wouldn't do for Clive to have his conversation with Tony in the afternoon and find out that no mistake had been made! Obviously I would need to square the position and make a good profit as well.

During the rest of the morning, I answered the phones, hoping that one would be a trade client with a big order on sugar that I could book out against my position. The market had steadied a little after dropping on the opening call to 168. Then, just as I was wondering whether I would have to wait until the afternoon, I got my opportunity, booking out a customer order on a total of eighty lots at the prevailing market price of 169. So far, so good. I was in the money but I wasn't sure about unloading the rest of the position onto the market.

New York was fickle and the currency was moving around rather erratically. I was still short sixty lots of March Sugar at an average of 176.50 and the market was only £9 away. I decided to enter a buy stop with Clive to cover myself at 173. Now I could relax over the lunch period.

I leaned back in my chair, sipped a hot coffee and lit another cigarette. At last I was on the last chapter of my book but this didn't stop me subconsciously looking up at the screens. I was looking forward to the jobbing profits being calculated at the end of the month, when I might even own up to them! Mark should be pleased with the money and hopefully allow me to become a floor trader. I might even get a bigger bonus at Christmas like the rest of the traders. Three thousand pounds would be nice.

Henry poked his head around the corner and called me over. I got up from my desk and walked over to the boardroom. Not knowing what to expect, I felt apprehensive and he looked very serious.

'Gerry, you know I can't give you a rise at the moment but Bob needs help on the Foreign Exchange Desk and I'd like you to go over to him for a while. This is a good opportunity for you to learn more about trading.'

'Oh, what will I be doing?'

He puffed on his pipe. 'I don't know exactly but you'll be helping Jonathan.'

'Will I be trading?'

'No, not for a while. I thinks it's mainly an admin job, but you'll learn all about foreign exchange markets which will be good for you and, oh yes, filling out Bank of England E forms for the currency after it's traded.'

Of course I was disappointed and my words showed it. 'But anyone can do that! You don't need to use me to do that, do you?'

There was no change in his expression; obviously his mind was made up. Henry was a hard man and there was nothing left for me to do except capitulate. 'OK Henry when do I start?'

'Monday.'

'That soon?'

'Yup.' The reply was predictable.

But I didn't want to leave the trading room. 'What about the telexes? Who'll look after them and supervise the girls' work?'

Henry stared at the door behind me for a moment before adjusting his gaze back to me. 'Oh, you don't have to worry about them, they can look after themselves. No one's indispensable, Gerry, the sooner you learn that, the better!'

I walked out of the boardroom in a daze, closing the door slowly. I realised then as I stood in the corridor: this was my punishment for expecting too much in the first place!

The Foreign Exchange desk was in another office well away from the trading room and all the fun and noise that I had grown used to. My thoughts turned to my team and to Dave in particular. I had recently taken him on against my better judgement. I admit I much preferred to work with women but felt that it was wrong to discriminate against Dave because he was a very good telex operator. But his attitude was difficult to deal with on a daily basis.

He did not like me telling him what to do, and felt most uncomfortable at the thought of working for a woman. This, I surmised, was because he considered us as his natural inferiors and he was not ready to take orders from his inferiors!

It was only his second day when he asked me, 'Where did you learn to type and use the telex, Gerry?'

'I taught myself just like my girls did,' I replied.

'You should have been taught by the GPO like me and then you would have first learned on the T7 before moving on to T15. The GPO training is the best in the world and if you haven't had that training, you can't call yourself a real telex operator!'

'Oh, really?' I said

'Yes... really... *I* should be *your* boss. I'm the one who is more qualified.'

For heavens sake, I thought: not only will the traders not let me earn a trader's salary even though I'm trading, but now this boy thinks I shouldn't be earning a telex supervisor's salary either, even though I'm practically doing two jobs!

I stared at him, pursing my lips, and thought: I'll have to nip this one in the bud. 'Ah,' I said, leaning a little closer to him, 'but you can't type a hundred words a minute and when you try, I've seen you make mistakes. You see, Dave, one of the reasons we make so much money in this office is because of the speed that we all type at. We get our prices to New York quicker than other companies in the City and—'

'Yes, I know,' he interrupted, 'but they type with two fingers, that's not proper typing, is it?'

43

'It gets the job done, Dave!' I snapped as I got up to walk away from the discussion.

The next day I heard him talking to Martin, our senior Cocoa Trader. 'I want to be a trader on cocoa. Can you let me know when there's a vacancy on the floor please?'

'Yes,' I heard Martin say, 'no problem mate.'

Later that day I approached Martin. 'Martin, you know I want to be a trader?'

'Yes,' he replied.

'Well, I hope you wouldn't consider Dave before me. After all, I've been waiting for three years to trade.'

'But you're trading in the office,' he replied.

'No, Martin, it's not the same, no one knows I'm trading. I don't have a proper qualification as a trader, and I'm not mixing with the traders on the floor. Therefore no one thinks of me as a trader and I'm not paid as a trader!' I was almost screaming out the words at him. I checked myself and apologised. 'Sorry Martin.'

'Oh, that's OK.' He was laughing. 'Now look, don't you worry about it, Gerry,' he said as he patted me on the back, and pushed me away from his desk. But I was worried, I feared Martin would give Dave an opportunity to trade before he gave me one, afterall, he was a man and I was just a girl! surely Martin would see sense and help me become a trader.

Dave would be very happy if he could successfully take over my old job as a telex supervisor. I consoled myself the best way I could – by thinking that I still had some trading to do and when Mark saw how much money I'd made, he might want me to stay. Perhaps all was not lost.

Jan, one of the telex operators, came back from lunch and I told her of my new duties. I had the feeling she already knew but she just grinned and said, 'Don't worry, we'll manage!'

'I know you will,' I replied, feeling emotional, 'but quite honestly I really don't want to go.' I squeezed her arm and she smiled back at me. 'By the way,' I added, 'I think Dave thinks he's going to be the supervisor!'

'Yeah, right...!' she replied, laughing, and gave me a knowing look as she rolled her eyes upwards. I sat down at the desk, my face in my hands, feeling quite despondent. Then, as if by a strange coincidence, the words of a song I didn't know particularly well came into my mind: '*And did those feet in ancient times...*'

That afternoon the market opened sharply higher as a rumour that the Soviet Union would buy even more sugar that year began to circulate. Luckily I got my stop loss order entered so I felt I could relax, having made a substantial amount of money for Mark. In fact, that month I had made over £10 000 for him. Surely he would want me to become a trader now?

The next day was to be my last day in the trading room – unless I could convince Mark that he needed me. This would involve going behind Henry's back, something I didn't really want to do – but hey, the ends should justify the means? I resolved to make sure that Mark realised that some of the jobbing profits were down to me, but like many plans I had in those days it backfired on me.

I was busy filing some reports when Mark shouted out, 'I'm very pleased sugar trading profits are well up on last month!'

I looked at Clive and he was smiling. 'Well, come on, how much did we make?'

Mark smiled. 'Sixty-three thousand pounds, our best ever, well done!'

Everyone clapped and it was great. Then Clive said, 'Are you sure of those figures, Mark? I only make it £52 000.'

'Of course I'm sure,' Mark responded and then, looking at me, he laughed loudly. 'You're not the only one making money in sugar. you know. Clive!'

Clive's face went white, then red. Looking straight at me, he asked Who? Who else is then?'

'Why, Gerry, of course,' Mark said, pointing at me.

'Gerry? What's Gerry doing with a book, jobbing off my fucking back?'

'No, Clive it's not like that,' I said trying to calm him down, 'it's not like that.'

But he continued to glare at me 'Of course it's like that! You're doing nothing but stealing, you're supposed to be a bloody telex operator, not a trader. It's easy stealing money, you wanna try making it!' He shuffled some papers on the desk before lifting his head and showing his mad red face. 'That's it, I've had enough, I'm leaving!' He grabbed his jacket and strode out of the room.

Mark frowned and then smiled across to me. 'Don't worry, we've upset Clive for now but we'll put it right tomorrow, eh?'

'Yes,' I agreed, because what else could I say? In any case, by Monday I would be banished from the trading room, helping out on the Foreign Exchange Desk – whatever that meant. In some dim office away from all the action and excitement. I was not happy, but change it I could not. I would have to do what I was told and tow the line.

The next eighteen months went as predicted and, try as I might to make the job interesting, I could not stop myself from wanting to get back into the trading room. I had set my heart on becoming a trader and I wasn't going to give up that easily. And so it was that as soon as I heard of a trading vacancy I would go and speak to the appropriate director.

On this particular occasion I gathered enough courage to speak to one of the directors for whom I had done some work in the past. It was lunchtime when I approached him and perhaps this wasn't the best of times.

'Desmond, I understand there's a vacancy on the Coffee Exchange for a Coffee Trader. Please can you consider me?'

'Don't be ridiculous, Gerry, no one would hear your voice, it's open outcry down there!' Clearly astonished, he shook his head from side to side, as though he couldn't believe I'd had the balls to ask.

I walked away from him. I couldn't bear to spend time away from the trading room. Hardly any of the traders spoke to me these days and I had even lost touch with my old friend Maurice, who had been promoted and was due to fly to the Cameroon shortly. Lucky Maurice, purchasing cocoa beans directly from the producers! How exciting for him! How exciting everyone's job was except mine! Here I was, stuck in this miserable job, filling out E forms! I felt I was in the wilderness, wandering aimlessly up and down the corridor under the pretence of getting forms signed, just so that I could hear the excitement in the trading room. If I was really lucky, a trader might run past me and I would take the opportunity to strike up a half-sensible conversation. 'How's the market?' I would say, feigning a perplexed look. Or: 'Oh, I heard you made a fortune yesterday. Congratulations!' OK, there was some consolation along the way; at least the telex girls still provided me with the latest gossip, some of it quite pleasing – such as the news that Dave had left the company. I may have been exiled but I was still well informed.

Afterwards I would pass the boardroom and the door would invariably be firmly shut. Henry didn't bother to look at me these days. Even when I passed him in the hall or corridor, he would conveniently look the other way! Mark on the other hand was still friendly to me. I'd been given a small rise and a good bonus, which brought my earnings up to about £3000 a year, which I knew was not bad, but I'd never be able to afford to buy a car or a house on that salary.

It was obvious to me that no one had any intention whatsoever of letting me be a foreign exchange dealer. It was the same old story: when Jonathan was at lunch, I covered for him and put a few deals together on D. Marks, US Dollars or French Francs for the traders. It was so easy dealing, but quite another thing to become a registered Foreign Exchange Dealer. Later, I spoke to Jonathan about my ambitions, but all he could do was laugh and look up at his favourite topless model sitting astride a large motorbike hanging on the wall opposite! This made me feel very stupid and I wanted to punch him. I reminded myself that he had never been particularly generous to other young employees wanting to climb the ladder of success, so why should he be any different with me? I had to learn to be patient. for heaven's sake!

One day, just as I had become resigned to my circumstances, Henry called me in. 'Morning, Gerry, why don't you come and speak to me later. I might have something for you.'

'Really?' I said. 'What, in the trading room?'

'Yes, quite possibly... see me later, about 12.30?'

I was excited and the morning passed slowly under Jonathan's watchful gaze. I noticed that he kept looking up at me to see what I was doing. Was I looking particularly happy today? I wondered. Jonathan usually treated everything I did with suspicion although I wasn't the one sipping whisky all day! Today, I thought, I would take extra delight in letting him see that I was watching the clock.

'It's a long time till lunchtime!' he shouted across to me.

'Yes, I know.'

'Well, get on with your work then, or haven't you got anything to do?'

I smiled at him. 'I've got plenty to do thanks, how about you?' He ignored me as he lit a cigar.

At 12.30, I made my way to the boardroom to find the door closed. I knocked three times and could hear Henry and Mark arguing. Now was clearly not a good time to see Henry. I started to walk away from the door and down the corridor. What should I do? Stay, go, hang around? Perhaps I should get some lunch.

Just then Mark opened the boardroom door, making me jump. Hoping he didn't think I was listening, I smiled confidently at him and walked past into the room. As I did, I gave a little shiver, even though the room was warmer than the corridor.

'Ah yes, Gerry.' Henry looked up from his papers. 'How about you coming back into the trading room? One of my metal traders is leaving. Think you can do it?'

'Of course, you know I would love to.'

He smiled at me for the first time in about twelve months. 'Well of course you know nothing about metals.'

'No, but I can learn! When can I start?'

'Shortly.' Henry looked at me firmly and I knew not to push it any further.

Happier than I have been for a long time, I march back down to the corridor with a spring in my step. By the time I get to my office I can barely contain my grin. Jonathan, of course, notices and he's right to be suspicious on this occasion but he says nothing. I get on with my work, expecting that Henry will walk in at any moment to tell Jonathan, but he doesn't.

Five-thirty arrives and there is still no sign of Henry. 'Right, I'm off home,' I say. They all look up at the clock in unison, disturbed that I am leaving before them. Tough.

On the way home, I consider my zilch knowledge about metals. Sure, I know about trading sugar and cocoa and now about foreign exchange, but metals… well, that's a whole new ball game. I make a note to find out more and get some books and information on the subject.

The next day was as boring as ever as I waited for Henry to speak to Jonathan. Why, I wondered, was he taking so long? God damn it! Why don't people do what they say they will do? I looked around the office; there was nothing in it to delight my eyes, not even the nude calendar on the wall! Jonathan smiled at me as if reading my thoughts. He must be just as bored, even though he earned well. I felt sorry for him having to sit in an office full of old furniture all his life, like me stuck, stuck at my old desk, too big for the chair, with drawers that didn't open properly and locks that keys couldn't open. How could anyone stay in such an environment and still have the will to live? The sooner I got out of here the better! But for now I'd concentrate on positive thoughts to keep me happy and forget about the pay that took forever to improve. After all, I would soon be sitting in a new trading room full of the latest designs and technology.

Henry didn't speak to Jonathan that day or the next and I was getting worried so I decided to go and see him. That was a brave decision and one I took after considering the possibility that Henry might well criticise me for nagging him. It was easy: all I had to do was think like a man. I knew that the other dealers would have considered it good form to keep the pressure on until you got what you wanted. They were always saying, 'Go for it, I would if I were you.' They always had the confidence to go for it. It was expected of them.

Satisfied then that this was the right approach, I knocked on Henry's door.

'Henry, you haven't forgotten have you?'

He looked up at me from his papers and took his glasses off. 'Forgotten what?'

'You know, the trading job.'

'Oh, that. Em… well no I haven't, leave it with me for a bit, will you.'

Here we go again, I thought as I wandered back to the office.

The next morning Henry came straight in to see me. 'I've spoken to Jonathan and you can join the team on Monday.'

'Oh great, thanks Henry, I can't wait!'

'Now don't worry about anything, I'll explain it all to you on the day,' he said, leaving the room with a smile. I breathed a sigh of relief, at last!

After lunch I started to pack up my desk. Jonathan seemed genuinely sad to see me go. Jonathan was so busy trying to find out what my new job would be that he had not even noticed I had hidden his favourite calendar, and that it was no longer on the wall but in my bin!

Over the next few nights I worked late, reading up on the London Metal Exchange. A lot of business went on in the old coffee houses and apparently the Jerusalem in Cowper Court played a special part in the establishment of the market. By January 1877, The London Metal Exchange Company had been established and I read that its original home was Lombard Court, just off Gracechurch Street. Apparently in 1897 it moved again to Whittington Avenue. Whoever made this decision made it wisely, because the market was now placed in exactly the right location to prosper. This I believed, since it was in the tale of Dick Whittington, who became the first Lord Mayor of London. The streets of London were paved with gold, it was said, and by simply walking down them, a man could become rich. I wondered whether it was true for a woman too.

I carried on reading. Apparently, The London Metal Exchange was different from other futures markets. Firstly, trading was confined to a specific cash date and to a three months date, with up to seven months allowed for silver, whereas other markets traded up to a year in advance in delivery months such as March, May, July, and September. Secondly, the metals market had no Clearing-House. So every deal struck through the Exchange would have to be backed by a Principles contract. In other words, each trading member was responsible for financially backing and honouring every deal made. Some argued that the Exchange was not significantly important in terms of world trade, since the vast majority of trade in copper, tin, lead, zinc, aluminium, nickel and silver took place directly between producer and consumer. However, the market remained crucial for providing a transparent method of price fixing and the ability to hedge metal against future delivery. Consequently, consumers and producers would use the quoted prices on the Exchange to fix their contracts at the closing price of the Ring. Often they would hedge their purchases and sales and significant volume would be traded within the closing minute before the bell rang. For good delivery, each contract of metal had to have a minimum standard of quality and be delivered to one of fourteen registered warehouses.

Now I'm not giving you all this information because I am trying to turn you into a metal dealer, but only so you will understand my story better. As I read, I realised how important it was to understand some of the rituals of the market. Only then, I felt, would I become accepted. The history of the Exchange was quite meticulous in its detail. Apparently one member, probably a copper merchant, took a piece of chalk from his pocket and drew a circle on the ground. This formed a ring. Traders would step into the ring to do business. Today the ring was a huge copper dish in the centre of a circle. Traders had transacted business there for the last hundred years and they had used the copper dish as an ash-tray for their cigars and cigarettes. Deals were struck by open outcry with all bids and offers shouted across the ring to the other brokers and merchants who would sit in their seats in a ring. After the ring closed and the bell rang, the clerks would check the deals verbally on the Exchange floor. Contracts would then be prepared by the office clerks, signed sealed and delivered later in the week.

It was clear to me that the whole business was based on an extraordinary level of trust between the dealers, who were critical to the business of trading on the Exchange. For members of the Ring, their word was their bond. A hundred years ago, trading outside of the official dealing hours took place on the kerb of the pavement. Here, hasty last-minute deals would be struck. Now kerb trading occurs inside the Exchange after the official rings have ended but traders are still allowed to smoke during this time!

All of this I now understood, but I knew from the other traders that the Metal Exchange was considered the most complicated market to trade because prices for cash delivery (the next day known as 'prompt') and a three-month date were the most frequent delivery dates traded. Every day the three-month price would be a different day, so you could end up with a position on your card for every weekday of any given month. These positions would have to be settled and dealers were renowned for spending huge amounts of their time doing level carries to tidy up their card. If you didn't square your card, the company would be committed to taking up the warrants of metal or delivering against them and this could be a very costly business indeed, especially if it had not been planned for! Obviously being good at mathematics would be useful!

Other commodity markets in London traded a monthly

delivery system, so for example say Sugar and Cocoa or Coffee traded in delivery periods of March, May and July. Therefore there were no dates to carry over or tidy up and no costs to worry about.

Also different metals had an impact on other metals. If you were a sugar trader you had to read sugar reports, but if you were a metal trader you might have to read seven different metal reports just to ensure that what had affected one metal producer had not affected another. As a metal dealer, you needed to be on the ball, absorbing all the required information and more whilst at the same time being able to critically analyse it for its relevance and impact on the market.

I was learning that a market in a backwardation could be very costly and it would be dangerous to be short in one. All the big historic losses had happened in that type of a market because there was no limit to how much you could lose. Generally, the market was in a contango or the cash price was at a discount to the forward price and the spread was always controlled by the prevailing rates of interest. Trading the spreads was called 'doing a carry'. Carries enabled traders to square their position. These trades were carried out at the beginning of each Metal Ring.

It was becoming abundantly clear to me that my knowledge of trading would have to be sharply expanded and built upon if I was to understand any of what I was reading.

Imagine the market in 1876, with the traders looking so very different from today. In those days they would have worn black silk top hats and long coats, most with beards and moustaches or at the very least, very bushy sideburns. Horse-drawn carriages would pull up outside the buildings and the street would be full of bustling pedestrians and even cyclists on their odd-looking Penny Farthing bicycles! Picture the horse-drawn buses or perhaps trams running down Grace-church St, the underground still under construction and the whole city lit by those round Victorian gas lamps. What an eerie place it must have been!

On Saturday I bought myself some smarter clothes ready for my new job and hurried down to Kensington High St to C&A. I couldn't afford anything expensive and needed to make sure that whatever I bought matched the rest of my wardrobe, which was for one reason or another predominantly orange or lime green! Luckily I found something that suited and hurried back home to get ready for a good night out. I was meeting a whole load of friends, including Tanya, a pretty dark-haired girl who read a lot.

We went to Hampton Court for dinner, visiting a very good Italian restaurant and then on Sunday I wanted to take some photos of the deer in Richmond Park. While Tanya and I walked, we talked about the furniture we would need for the new flat my mother had promised us. I had only a large double bed when I'd moved back home from Essex, having auctioned off everything else. We both agreed we were lucky to have more money coming in because even though Tanya worked as a telephonist for a big American company in Baker Street, she did not earn very much at all. I also had some savings, having recently sold a car and that money would also go towards buying new furniture for the flat. We were so excited at the thought of furnishing our own home and being able to purchase a big settee that we had seen in Habitat, one of those that follow the corners of the room, and have an integral coffee table.

On the way home, I noticed a leaf fall from a tree and I thought of Emily who had left England sometime ago. I shouldn't have been surprised really. Emily was well known for preferring foreign partners, and she had met a good-looking photographer and moved to Austria. As the traffic came to a standstill, I thought back to our last meeting. I had teased her about leaving us. I would miss her, I said; was she thinking of spending her whole life over there? How could she leave us all? Wouldn't she miss the nights out when six or ten of us would go out on the town until three or four in the morning? Could she see herself coming back?

'I don't know,' she had replied, half-smiling with her head

on one side, and then added, 'but of course I'll visit from time to time!'

'From time to time? Well, I hope I'm around. It's so easy to lose touch, people move and phone numbers change.'

'You'll be around, Gerry, won't you?'

I took a sip of my beer before answering. 'Yes, of course. I'm not going anywhere, am I?' I laughed, though I didn't really feel that happy. 'Anyway. I must say you do look very happy.'

'I am!' Emily smiled back at me and, looking around the room, glanced briefly at Tanya before returning her gaze to me with one eyebrow raised.

'Well, cheers then and have a good trip!' I raised my glass and smiled at her as she raised hers silently in return. It won't be the same without her, I thought. Yes, of course, I had many good friends but Emily was special. She was my oldest friend and though we'd had our differences, there was still a bond between us.

I walked over to Tanya smiling at her. 'Ready for another drink?' I said before realising that her glass was still half full.

'No, not yet' she replied in her quiet northern accent. As I went to the bar, I considered how different Tanya and Emily were, like chalk and cheese.

By Monday morning the events of the weekend had made me feel quite a bit stronger. I knew that my lifestyle had and would continue to put me at a disadvantage because I didn't discuss my private life in the way that other people did. Men thought of me as being shy and open to persuasion and pressure, while women just thought of me as not quite normal, which of course was ridiculous. More tolerance and acceptance would make society a better place for everyone. So I was proud to be different, proud to be rebellious too.

Only by frequenting the clubs could people like me, Tanya and Emily all meet, and we did regularly. So when Emily decided to leave, it was a big deal for all of us. Back then, people didn't speak up for their rights in the way that we do today and we relied on each other for support. But now I had decided everything would be different because from now on, I was going to be different. No longer was I going to give in to the marching army behind me. I was going to be marching ahead – with the same determination of any man around me.

Henry looked up as I walked into the office 'You're early, Gerry.'

'Am I? Oh well, just ignore me. Er, would you like a coffee?' I asked hesitantly.

'No, I've got one thanks.'

I shuffle a few papers on the desk. I don't really know what to do; it's early and the traders won't be in for at least another half-hour. Sipping my coffee, I look at the long narrow trading desk. I light a cigarette, take a deep drag, and count the places. Eight desks for the traders, and Henry's at the end makes nine.

I notice papers are thrown all over the place and rows of phones are hanging from the pyramid section running the whole width of the desk. At each trading position there is a bank of coloured square panels with numbers that light up when the phone rings.

'Answer that can you, Gerry?'

I put my coffee down, half spilling it, and quickly pick the phone up. I've forgotten what to say and mumble something into the receiver, looking at Henry to make sure he can't hear! The voice on the other end is breaking up and all I can hear is a disjointed, scrambled noise. 'Hello? Hear me…? Give Hen…. is… en…ry there…?'

'Yes, hello is that you, Mark?'

'Yes… I… in…t…car.'

'Henry, it's Mark, it's not a good line. I think he's in the car.' I pass the phone over to Henry and wonder how on earth they can have a conversation. Henry is speaking with his pipe in his mouth, probably making similar noises to the car phone that keeps breaking up. If Laurel and Hardy were alive today they would love this sketch! And it reminds me of Mark's favourite story.

One day he was on his way to work in his chauffeur-driven Rolls Royce and needed to speak to Robert Maxwell. So he phoned him on his car phone and Robert's chauffeur answered it. Mark said, 'Give me Bob please' and the chauffeur said, 'I'm afraid he's on the other line to New York. 'Can he call you back sir?' But Mark was not a man to be outdone. So the next time Robert Maxwell phoned, Mark told his chauffeur, 'Tell him I'm engaged on the phone to New York and I've got two other calls waiting!'

Mark used to tell this story often, especially to new visitors to the office who didn't always understand the joke because they were not aware of the friendly rivalry that existed between the bosses of major international companies operating within the City.

Henry hands me back the phone. 'Right, first thing you can do, Gerry, is see if there are any overnight orders on the telex from New York.' He points to a couple of telexes near the trading desk. 'Your job will be to look after them. Do you remember when you were on Sugar? Well, it'll be a similar thing, so at two o'clock I want you get on that telex machine and stay on it until the market closes in London, OK?'

'Yes, OK, Henry,' I say, eyeing the machine with contempt. I thought I was going to be a trader! What's happening? I consider it best not to say a word. I really don't want to fall out with Henry again. I'll just see how today goes.

I light a cigarette and wander over to the telex. Reams of paper need organising and before long I see columns of orders. There must be forty in total in the first column of scale-down buying and then another forty in a column of scale up selling for silver. Then there are the words 'IF DONE' in large letters and another column of orders with stop loss orders covering the executed orders. I tear off the telex sheets, handing them to Henry 'There are loads of orders here,' I say.

'Yes, every day we get these from New York for the London morning session only.'

I feel a bit confused. 'But this is not arbitrage, is it?'

'No, of course not, these are trade hedges,' Henry responds impatiently.

It's now nine o'clock and the traders are coming in. I haven't sat down yet because I don't know where to. Obviously these traders have their own desks. There is a chair on the telex machine so I can sit there for a moment. I watch a little nervously as they come in one by one with their coffees and bacon rolls. They seem quite boisterous, laughing and joking despite Henry sitting in the midst of them. I wonder whether they know why I am here and whether they mind having a woman on the desk.

By 9.30 the phones are ringing and I notice one chair is still empty so I take it. It's to Henry's left and directly opposite the head trader, Ryan, who is shortly due to leave. It is also the nearest desk to the metal telex. If I'm going to learn anything about metals, I will have to listen and watch what they say and do. Understanding the trading vernacular will be crucial, as it is different from the other markets I have worked on. I will have to get to know the clients and also understand the New York markets for Silver and Copper.

For the rest of the morning, I listen and help answer the phones, learning as I go. At about 11.40 all the traders except David and Henry get ready to leave for The Metal Exchange, which is a ten minute walk from the office. I wonder why David and Henry never go to the Exchange. Is it better to be an office trader or a floor trader? There are many questions I want to ask but now is not the right time.

David passes me a list of numbers before the Copper Ring starts 'Vee need to vone these numbers and see if they vanna listen, OK?' He speaks with a strong Austrian accent that, although difficult for me to understand, did mean he was able to cover most of the eastern European customers. Henry spoke fluent German, so I felt at a distinct disadvantage. Then I hit on the idea of learning Russian, because it was a notoriously difficult language that no one else could speak – besides Chinese, that is!

The morning market closed at 1.30 in London, much later than other terminal markets. Traders could then go for a long lunch until about 3.30. Henry and David usually had a bagel with salt beef from Blooms and often they bought me one, which was very generous. During the afternoon I would sit on the telex and feed orders backwards and forwards from New York to the Exchange floor via a network of earphones, just as I had done in my sugar trading days.

In fact the whole experience was surprisingly similar, almost a repetition, especially as the trader in New York, Jim, was a red-headed Irishman with a very lively temper, rather like his boss Tony. Simon, our Silver Trader in London, was the complete opposite to Jim. He was a quiet and generally polite bloke who nevertheless could be quite moody. Being stuck between the two of them arguing was a bit of a daily nightmare. Luckily, my voice tended to be louder than theirs and when I screamed they shut up… usually!

During an afternoon trading session, Jim would start his usual bout of screaming and shouting on the telex or phone and Simon would politely tell him through me to 'wait a minute, because the Silver Market hasn't opened yet'. I would pass the comment on and it would be ignored. The telex would start to rattle as a madman started to type frantically words that didn't make any sense, and then the buzzer would start buzzing. Ten times it would buzz and then it would all go quiet for a moment. I would wait for the phone to ring and pick it up quickly before Henry got to it. I'd look at Henry with a glance that said 'Don't worry, I'll handle this' and hope that he couldn't hear Jim screaming his head off on the telephone as I put it to my ear.

'What have I done? We've only got fucking five minutes to trade this fucking stuff! Hurry up will yer… come on, what's happening…? Shit, shit, shit…!'

I try to ignore the rantings while I speak to Simon. 'Simon, are you there?'

'Yes, we haven't started yet, now calm him down, I'll tell you when we do!'

But it was as if Jim had heard it direct and the response was swift from New York. 'No… I'm bloody not… calming down, it's too fucking late, the customer' hung up! He's gone! I tell you I'm not fucking going to lose him over this stupid order! I'll have to phone him back and give him a bloody good execution. I can't wait for you lazy bastards to get a move on! I've had to book him out and so you better get your fucking act together otherwise I'm going to change my bloody broker.'

Then just as I thought he had stopped, he started again, shouting even louder this time. 'And tell Simon we are short bloody fifteen lots of silver and he better buy em back! Tell him he can take the fucking loss, it's his fucking fault, not mine. OK, and tell him he can go fuck himself, I'm going home now, I've fucking had enough!' As he slammed the phone down, I felt the shock reverberate through the headphones.

Screwball or what? I thought. Finally the telex went quiet. Thank God, he was gone this time. The shouting had been so bad that Simon could hear it through my earphones on the other side of my head!

'Simon, we're short fifteen lots of silver. Jim hasn't told me at what price, but I suggest we buy them back now unless you have a different view… and oh, by the way, he's gone home now!'

By 5.30 I was ready for a nice cold beer. I smiled at the boys as they came back from the market. My first day was over. Simon looked at me and shook his head before sitting down to work out his position. He then came over to me and looked at the telex machine.

'Is Jim always like that?' I asked.

'Only when he's in a good mood,' Simon replied, smiling to himself, then added, 'He's a good trader though.'

'That's doesn't give him the right to behave like that though, does it?' I answered. I heard Trevor, our Zinc Trader, laughing the other side of the desk. I could almost hear what he was thinking: 'If you can't stand the heat, get out of the kitchen.' I glanced at him to show I knew what was on his mind.

My experience of dealing with young men who liked to scream and swear was that if you allowed them to get away with that sort of behaviour, all you did was guarantee a repeat performance. Just look at Jim. But it was not my place to stop his behaviour. Why didn't Henry reprimand him? I wondered.

It was now time to go home so I grabbed by coat and scarf. 'See you tomorrow!' I shouted as I left the trading room.

Walking down Mark Lane, I couldn't help but feel unhappy with the way my day had gone. Why didn't I feel any closer to being a trader? After all, Henry had said I would take the place of the trader leaving, but that was clearly not the case.

Journeying home, I engrossed myself in making new plans to achieve my ambitions. I would forget about my previous failures; they had, after all, been based on false promises that had been given to me in return for my hard work. Turning away from the black bowlers and umbrellas, I noticed a castle tower reaching up to the sky. I don't know why I hadn't noticed it before since it had clearly been there for some time, perhaps since 1066! I love it when the past and the present come together like this, and I imagined myself surrounded by market traders of times gone by, doing business in the streets under a clear blue sky. I had passed the tower many times before, of course, and I now wondered why it was never open to the public.

What had it been part of, and what was its meaning? Was it used these days at all and if so, by whom, and for what reason? Musing on these possibilities took my mind off my job – a very welcome break.

I felt almost as if I had dropped into a time warp. I don't remember crossing the roads or entering the station. I don't remember who may have seen me and said hello. In fact, all I remember is looking at the clock and it confirming the usual journey time of twelve minutes. But once away from the tower, I began thinking of work again. I would have to work magic to become a trader. Wouldn't it be good if forces from the Middle Ages could come and help me? If I could walk into the tower and like King Arthur draw the sword from the stone and become empowered. Or, like Joan of Arc, hear the voice of an angel that would tell me what to do. What if the past and the people who had lived in the past could see us, even though they were dead? Perhaps they or their souls were watching, waiting to help us and all we had to do was call them. Would they hear and would they come to our aid? Would they use their power to access the underlying, unifying energy force that was there to be drawn on for such purposes?

Why was I thinking like this? I've no idea but I was on another quest, and my thoughts continued to focus on whether it is true that the mind controls the brain or the brain controls the mind. Nor could I understand the concept of a soul living within a body. Did the soul live forever? I wondered. Had I already met some souls? Are soul and mind the same thing? Is it possible to get to know your own soul? Could *I* get to know *my* own soul? I was sure I could and in any case, it would be easier than trying to become a trader! All I had to do now was find the correct password! Random ideas kept me going in a life where everything was controlled, managed, planned and synchronised to the eighth degree. Soon that would all change but for now everything was as it should be.

The next day I resolved to speak to Henry about his plans for me to become a trader. But he was in a bad mood. I decided to wait until Ryan left, and then speak with him. I felt like I was running a marathon. It shouldn't be this hard! Perhaps I should turn my back on it all and just be grateful for what I had? After all, I was convinced that when the time was right, I would receive my due in full!

Henry smiled at me. 'Good morning, Gerry, today is going to be interesting. I'm interviewing Ryan's replacement.'

'Oh, that's good.' I was trying not to act surprised. 'What time is he coming in?'

Henry looked up and smiled at me 'You're looking very smart today! James will be coming in about an hour or so. He's a very good trader and we're lucky to get him. He's in great demand, you know…'

'Oh,' I said, 'great. Let's hope we do then!'

Was I surprised? Not a bit. There I was, silly me, thinking I was to be Ryan's replacement, and Henry had changed his mind and not told me.

I'd never heard Henry say a trader wasn't good and when I heard this new man's name was James, I was not surprised. I could see that David was far from happy but the others liked their new head trader. When I met him, I was pleasantly surprised. He was a tall, dark-haired man from Essex. I noticed he smiled a lot. I was glad that he would be joining us in a week. He was familiar and reminded me of someone else, but I couldn't think who it was.

Henry was now in a good mood, so I thought this was an ideal time to appeal to his better nature. 'Henry?'

'Yes?'

'When can I become a metal trader?'

'Soon, Gerry, soon. Let's get James slotted in first and then I'll talk to you.'

I walked over towards All Hallows Church for lunch, determined to be upbeat. I felt that I had received a fair response from Henry. It was quite understandable that he would want to concentrate on getting James sorted out first.

Entering the church, I smelt the frankincense and felt the warmth of the stone wall around me. I was at home here, where I could forget about today, the awkward present and dream about life in the past instead. It was all around me, at least a thousand years of history. I took my mind back to 1066 and imagined what London would have looked like in those times. The Tower would have been here too, not the present one but the original – the White Tower built by William the Conqueror. I knew that a purported ancestor of mine, Walter de Douai, had been at the battle of Hastings with William. He had been granted a barony and had settled near the present town of Bridgwater in Somerset. I wondered whether he had ever set foot in this church. I looked around the stone tablets as if searching for a name I knew, but of course there was none.

Looking up through the stained-glass windows, I watched the sun move slowly behind the clouds. I must keep an eye on the time! I imagined what it would have been like outside all those centuries ago, with the green fields and grazing animals this side of the river – perhaps some trees, orchards, a selection of wooden huts around and a few sheep. The river would have been very busy with boats transporting people, animals and goods. It would have been the focus of the city and there were probably more activities taking place on the river than on the land. I felt the peace and quiet that must have reigned in those days and for a second compared it to the noise of our age. Then again, in those days it would have smelt more pungent! Horses for courses!

Ah yes, living in those times you would have heard a few human voices mingled with the sounds of many different animals. Goats and sheep, horses and chickens, rabbits and dogs all set against a background of splashing water as the boats of trade moved along the river. I could hear the sounds of craftsman carrying out their everyday work: wooden planks being moved or axes chopping a log; a cart rumbling along the cobblestones and women, some dressed in pretty gowns, shopping in the market; children running alongside the carts or cavorting as they played games. In the distance, a church bell now called the faithful to prayer. Strange to think how different this part of the City was a thousand years ago, just a small rural community.

I look up into the gallery and notice a man smiling just as the bells start to chime. It must be time to go and have something to eat.

I go to a café in the church grounds, choose the only free table and sit down with my tea and sandwich. Just as I take a mouthful, an old man asks if he can join me. 'Yes, do,' I smile.

He smiles back and touches his forehead briefly.

'Would you like a cup of tea?' I ask him. He nods and I get him one. Back at the table I pass him a small packet of biscuits.

His eyes start to water as he tucks in and I try not to look at his unwashed hair. His bottle-green woollen jumper has holes in it around the elbow and is frayed at the cuffs. I'm happy to spend time with him, not saying anything, just smiling every now and then, for his sake. He takes a sip of tea and then starts talking to me in a surprisingly educated voice. 'Do you like it here?' he asks me.

'Yes,' I say, 'it's beautiful.'

'But there's more, you know. Oh yes, there's much more to see.'

He looks deep into my eyes. 'If you would like, I can arrange for that to happen.'

I think for a moment. 'Can you?'

'Oh yes, when do you want to see it? Now?'

I looked at my watch. I only had fifteen minutes left. 'Well yes, I'd love to but it will have to be quick'

With that he jumps up. 'Follow me... follow me.'

We walked for ages and as we did, he seemed to become more and more hunched. Perhaps it was my imagination but his hair appeared longer too, I'm sure.

Finally we reached a stone stairwell and in the darkness I saw seven or eight tourists, probably American. The old man nudged me gently. 'Follow them. But be careful because it's dark and the stairs are steep and there's no rail.'

'OK, thank you. By the way, what's your name?'

He smiled and for the first time I noticed he had a few teeth missing. 'Charlie.'

'Well Charlie, thank you, and maybe we'll share another cup of tea next time I'm here?'

'Yes, or some hot soup. I'm always here at this time of day,' he replied.

He waved as I joined the group and a door in the floor opened up to reveal a stone staircase leading into the crypt. I smiled reassuringly at the tourists as we stepped down in single file. As we got near the bottom, I could see lights and then someone shouted at us to stop. 'Stay where you are for the moment while we shut the door!' It went quiet and very dark for a few seconds.

I could hear people breathing heavily as it started to get warmer.

As the lights came back on, a gasp went up into the air as we looked at what was in front of us. Straight ahead lay a fully tiled roof of a Roman house. Below it, excavations had unearthed the complete inside of a house with kitchen equipment, pottery dishes and jugs, dried herbs, even a fully working underground central heating system! I stood there utterly astonished as the guide and lead archaeologist explained what they were doing.

Parts of present-day London were built on top of a Roman City. The Roman City was nearly fifty feet below the foundations of the thousand-year-old Norman Church. I learned that much more work had still to be done but they were confident of finding many more houses and indeed of unearthing the whole site. I turned to my fellow visitors – there was now only one left.

'Wow!' she said to me.

I shook my head in agreement and looked at the archaeologist. 'I'm really sorry and I hate to go but I must return to work'

'Fine, that's fine, thank you for visiting,' he replied. 'Don't forget the site will officially open in January next year.'

January next year, had I heard right? Was I really so lucky to see all this before the site was officially opened? Two twinkling green eyes were watching me and I thought of Charlie. How kind of him to show me all this. Waving goodbye to the tourist and the archaeologist, I climbed back up the staircase in the dark. I stumbled just as I reached the top, expecting to see Charlie, and felt disappointed when I did not.

I hurried back to work to Henry's angry welcome 'Where have you been? You're late.'

'I'm sorry, Henry.'

'Well don't let it happen again. The markets have been open fifteen minutes and David and I have had to cope all on our own.'

I sat down on the telex and picked up the headphones. Well, at least it sounded like they needed me! Besides, I thought, few people have been where I have just been; that makes me a little different because I have the knowledge. Despite the fact that it had made me late, I was pleased I'd seen the excavations. And if I got bored, I could just think about what was in that crypt!

The next day I couldn't wait to see Charlie. I went back to the church café and bought him a cup of tea. 'Are you always here?'

'Yes, always. I'm the curator, I look after the church.'

'Hmm, must be very interesting for you,' I said, pouring another cup of tea.

'Yes, I suppose so, it's my home you see.'

I wondered whether there was anything else he could show me about the church but there didn't appear to be.

A few weeks later I went to the church to see Charlie. Sitting down at our usual table, I waited for him to arrive, but he didn't turn up and I began to worry that something might have happened to him. I had waited three-quarters of an hour and my lunch-hour was nearly over. Fearing that he was ill, I asked the tea lady, 'Do you know where Charlie is today?'

She looked at me blankly. 'Charlie? Sorry luv, I don't know Charlie!'

'You know, the old man I used to sit with at this table. He always wore a bottle-green jumper fraying at the sleeves. He was the curator – you know Charlie?'

'No, sorry, luv, I can't help you, I don't know who you mean.'

I stood up, confused. She was the same tea lady who had served us before, wasn't she? Surely she remembered Charlie? It couldn't be that difficult, there was only ever two or three of us in the café at this time anyway!

Shortly afterwards, I walked downstairs and across the church towards the excavation site. Perhaps he was there. But when I got there I couldn't see the doorway, it seemed to have been blocked up. Maybe they'd shut it all up until January. Strange how people appear as if out of nowhere and then just as easily disappear!

Chapter Three

Whittington Avenue

The next day I resolved to speak to our new head trader, James. He looked very approachable, a bit of a laugh and didn't seem to take himself too seriously, which I found quite refreshing. If Henry won't play ball, I thought to myself, then maybe I can convince James to let me have a go at trading.

Entering the office, James sauntered casually towards the trading desk, his coat slung over his shoulder. The rest of the traders were checking their trading positions behind a cloud of smoke, coming mainly from Henry's pipe. I smiled at James, as he had the air of a pirate about him today. Henry caught me out of the corner of his eye and checked his watch rather pointedly. This prompted James to wink at me.

'Morning, everyone,' he said, almost laughing as he sat down.

Henry puffed harder on his pipe. 'Bit late isn't it?'

James raised his eyebrows and laughed under his breath but said nothing. Secretly I was pleased at his rebellion but looked away to pretend I hadn't seen it.

There was clearly no love lost between Henry and James, and I wondered how the other traders felt about him. They were a quiet and sometimes moody bunch and it was difficult to know what they were feeling. James, on the other hand, was always laughing and happy; he was quite cheeky but no one said anything because he was the head trader. I was surprised to see that no one palled up with him. I suppose his manner was different from Ryan's, whom they all seemed to have worshipped.

I waited until Henry went into the boardroom to open his mail and went over to James's desk. He was feverishly rubbing out pencil marks on a card and muttering to himself.

I knelt down. 'James, have you got a moment?' I said as softly as possible. He looked at me sideways and frowned a bit and I could see he was slightly amused. 'You know, James, I would like to be a trader. I want to learn to trade properly and I would like you to teach me how to trade. I want to be a metal dealer – please?'

He looked at me, opened his mouth as if to speak and then closed it again abruptly, letting out air as he did so. 'Speak to me later about it, OK?' I stood up and walked back to my desk. Well at least he hadn't said no.

James was considered by nearly everyone to be the best Copper Dealer in the Ring. That's because he had worked for a copper producer and was always sure of executing big volume orders. The more shout you had, the more clout you had! Although he was smart in one sense, in another he wasn't. His suit was always creased, his shirts weren't always clean, and much to Henry's annoyance, he didn't like to wear a tie and would only agree to put it on as he entered the office or Exchange.

I loved watching him puffing deeply on a cigarette, his collar-length hair flowing behind him, trying to put his tie on with one hand. I noticed he had never untied it, obviously because it was so much easier to put a loop over your head! If he didn't want any hassle from Henry in the morning he would make sure his tie was on before he reached the trading area. I would watch him striding down the corridor and as he passed the boardroom he would reach into his pocket, pull out a screwed-up, half-knotted tie and slip it over his collar, tugging on one end so as to tighten it before he reached the trading desk. At about 11.15 he would look at the clock, close his trading card and slip it into his top pocket. 'Right I'm off… see you lot down there.'

David would look at Henry and then Henry would say to

James, 'It's a bit early, isn't it? You don't need to be down there until ten to twelve at the earliest.' James would stare back, a full insolent look, before leaving the room. After he had gone, Henry, shaking his head would mutter, 'I wish he'd have his hair cut', and David would nod in agreement, as he always did.

So James liked to have a couple of beers before the market opened. What's the big deal? I thought. As the days went on I could see James was not happy in the job, but despite that, he came back every night and announced at least a £2000 profit for the day. On these occasions Henry was always pleased. 'Well done,' he would say, then add, 'What's your position now?'

James would pretend to think for a minute and then say, 'Square, I think, or thereabouts.' Simon would stand behind and look unsure for a second as if he was about to disagree and this did not go unnoticed by David, who would shoot Henry a look to say as much. David missed nothing, he noticed every nod, every wink, and he knew exactly what it all meant too.

'Don't you want to become a floor trader, David?' I asked one day.

'No,' he said, 'why should I want to do that? I'm happy in the office. You know you can make just as much money up here as down there and besides, I can keep an eye on everything going on better from up here!'

James never had a square position. Regularly the following morning, the card would show we had a position of five hundred tons. Much of the time the overnight position would make money but if it didn't, James would say, 'So, it will come out of the profits I've already made. Can't win all the time, mate!'

Henry also liked to job and his favourite metal was silver. One afternoon as I was sitting on the telex, he leaned over to me. 'Have we started silver yet?'

'No,' I said.

'Right, tell me when we start I've got some business to do.'

A second or so later I shouted, 'Henry, we're starting in a moment!'

'OK, what's the market?'

'262.50 at 262.70 and 70 trading and bid 262.80 offered now.'

Henry grunted. 'Who's buying?' he asked aggressively and before I could answer him he added, 'Where's the market now?'

'262.90 at 263.00.' I could feel him behind me, making me nervous.

'OK, sell twenty lots for me if it goes to 263.10.' He went back to his desk and excitedly picked up his silver chart, stabbing the paper with his pipe as if to make his pencilled predictions come true.

Looking at the clock, I think we've got a minute or so and perhaps I'll hang on before giving the order, at least until the buying is over because the market looks as if it wants to go higher. I wonder who Henry is selling for. Perhaps he can be persuaded to postpone the selling, but seeing his determination, I realise not. Henry is looking at me and it prompts my response. 'Simon, has 263.10 traded yet?'

'Yes,' the voice on the end of the phone responds, 'but on the bell so I don't know how many lots.'

'OK, what did it close?'

'263.10 at 30.'

I decide then to book Henry out and surprisingly, I don't worry over the consequences of getting it wrong. Turning round to Henry I say, 'You sold twenty lots at the high of the day 263.10.'

During the afternoon the market rises further and Henry continues his scale-up selling. But because the market is so strong I just keep booking him out; I'm long and he is short. By the end of the afternoon session I have bought thirty-five lots of silver from Henry. I am making money and Henry's client is losing it. So I safeguarde my position by putting a stop loss order in to protect my profits.

Although it was reasonably easy to take a position because I could make up orders on the speaker or pretend I was putting orders in for New York, it was often quite difficult getting out of a position even though Henry and David were the only ones in the office with me for long periods of time. They couldn't possibly listen to everything I was saying or doing, could they? You may think this very dishonest but don't forget, I was working in a jobbing environment. Speculation was the name of the game and if you wanted to get ahead, you had to take a chance. Everyone was doing it!

The next morning I came in to find out that my stop had not been hit and that I was still long thirty-five lots of silver. The market had run up very fast and I could see New York had closed very strong indeed. I looked at Henry. 'Silver closed strong last night.'

'Hmm,' he grunted back, looking at his chart.

'Do you think the market will come down today?' I asked.

Henry was still looking at the silver chart and trying to make sense of where he had put the lines. He paused before replying. 'Well, it's still a bear market as far as I can see, this is just a blip and we should carry on selling short into it.'

'Yes,' I said. 'But don't you think there has been a lot of trade buying? Who do you think it could be, Bunker Hunt?'

Henry looked at me, still puffing on his pipe, and shrugged his shoulders. Then, looking at his chart, he said, 'I think they are probably covering their shorts', pointing to a line he had drawn a few weeks earlier. Now the name Bunker Hunt should have frightened the living daylights out of him and I was astonished at his calm reaction to my suggestion. But even if it wasn't just one big buyer, it could still be very dangerous and I wondered whether he had taken into account the currency fluctuations. London would look a lot cheaper today than it did yesterday and anyone who was short overnight in New York might want to cover in London this morning. But how could a telex operator tell him he might have got it wrong?

'I wonder what the dollar's doing this morning?' I asked, hoping to encourage him to think about its impact on the market. But it was to no avail. My words fell on deaf ears as I watched him walk towards the boardroom, seemingly unperturbed.

Later, a look at Henry's charts tells me everything I want to know. The lines drawn just don't make any sense. I can't fathom out what it is he's trying to do. All the profits James has made this month will be absorbed by Henry's losses. James will be furious. The whole team will be angry and worse still, our Christmas bonus might be affected!

By the afternoon the market had risen sharply and the selling had all but dried up except for Henry sporadically selling an extra five lots every penny higher. Henry had made a big mistake by bucking the trend. I wanted to say to him: it won't work, can't you see that? There must be some news that the trade knows and we don't. Why else would they be buying?

During the afternoon I watch as Henry's losses continue to mount as the market continues to move higher. I have already taken half his position but if he carries on selling at this rate, he is going to incur substantial losses for the company. The dealing is hectic and lots of orders are coming in from New York. This is now so glaringly obvious that even David has some clients who are considering getting in on the action and trading silver.

Henry leans over 'Sell another thirty lots at market, Gerry.'

I try not to show my concern. 'Don't you want to wait a bit, Henry? We've only got thirty seconds of the Ring left.'

'No, get them out now please.' He stands up and walks over to the boardroom, shaking his head.

I shout down the headphone to the clerk at the other end of the line, 'Sell thirty lots of silver at market!'

And then, faster than I can blink, the execution has come back to me.

'You've sold thirty lots at 293!' Simon shouts back down the phone as I hear the Exchange in uproar in the background.

'OK, and what's the market now please?' I ask.

'293.50 bid,' he says hesitantly. 'Any offers?'

'No the Ring has closed and we're going into the kerb.'

Simon comes to the phone. 'Gerry, who was that last order for? Was it New York?'

73

'No,' I reply, 'it was for Henry.'
'Henry?' I know he's surprised.
'Why?' I ask.
'Oh, no reason don't worry about it.'

It seemed ages before I heard the final bell. I didn't see Henry again as when I went to give him his execution, the boardroom door was shut so I left a note on his desk.

Before going home I raised my sell order to 289. Luckily Simon didn't ask who it was for, he was too concerned about Henry's position to enquire about any other business. 'Do we know who Henry's selling for?' he asked me.

I shrugged. 'No, I haven't a clue.

And then, as an afterthought, he asked, 'Us?'

I shrugged again but out of the corner of my eye I could see David watching me closely. I turned to Simon again. 'What's our position, do you know yet?'

'No, not yet, I'm just trying to work it out now.'

Time to go home, so I grab my coat and head for the door. I hope I can sleep OK. I'm making a big profit but it worries me that Henry is making even bigger losses. It's not looking good at all.

On the way home, I pass the Norman tower. My thoughts drift away from the market as curiosity gets the better of me. The large wooden door is still locked shut; surely it must be open sometimes? Walking up into Fenchurch Street, I imagine what the tower must look like from inside. I see myself standing in a round room with stone stairs rising to a second floor. Above would be a wooden balcony jutting out into the main room below. From here I can see the full layout of the room. There is a round wooden table set for a light meal with wine and bread on the table and a deep red velvet curtain hanging by the stone wall, reaching from floor to ceiling. I notice it is held in place by heavy gold brocade tie-backs – ideal for concealing an assassin, I think. The wooden table has a few chairs surrounding it and there is an odd-looking footstool. Just one simple candle-holder claims the centre of the table. Further down on the table, a clay goblet looks as though it has been hurriedly placed, and next to it a small vase of flowers – Lily of the Valley, I presume. I see monks and knights moving slowly around the table in some unrecognisable ritual of devotion.

A car just misses me as I unwittingly cross the road, bringing me swiftly back to the modern world and the welcome warmth of the underground again. Journeying home, I make a mental note to gain access to the Norman tower. The door may have been locked for a century or two but I want to know whether my vision is based in truth. What was it I once read? *'If you hear me knocking at your door, answer!'* So, answer! Who, I wonder, holds the keys and who should I phone up to arrange a visit?

The next day, unfortunately for Henry, saw the silver market move even higher and I hoped he wouldn't continue to sell scale-up. If I was him I would put a stop loss order in and fight the urge to sell more in this fast-rising market. What was it Mark had always said to me? 'Gerry, you always go with the trend, you understand?' I smiled to myself, thinking of Mark because what he said and what he did were often the exact opposite. Everyone knew that he had made millions by shorting a bull market. So maybe Henry was trying to make millions as well. Trouble was, in order to make millions you had to risk millions!

As the day wore on we watched in horror as the market continued to move higher on the rings. Poor Henry was looking increasingly disturbed and we knew then that he wasn't trading for a client. He didn't even bother looking at his charts any more, he just stood behind me, rigidly reading what New York was typing on the telex, searching for an answer or reason for the market's behaviour.

I had long given up trying to persuade him to stop trading or convince him that he should consider putting a stop loss on his position.

'What do you think about the market then?' I ventured after he had been particularly quiet one day.'

It'll come down of course!'

'Yes, but when?'

'Soon,' came the terse reply.

David didn't know who Henry was selling for either and when I asked he just looked at me as if considering why he should bother having this conversation with me. 'No, I don't know but I think it might be for the house,' he finally replied.

'Well, in that case the house is losing about £65 000!' He looked at me aghast, 'Yes,' I continued, 'so you'd better convince him not to sell any more because he won't listen to me.'

I couldn't tell whether David went white because he didn't like me telling him what to do or whether he was considering Henry's reaction. Eventually he agreed. 'I'll try,' he said shaking his head.

By the afternoon the market had become quieter but it was still very firm trading at around 294. Henry was watching the market carefully and I saw David lean over to him and say something.

'Gerry,' Henry called over to me.

'Yes, Henry?'

'Put in an order to buy thirty-five lots on stop at 296, will you please.'

'OK.' I put my hand over the microphone so the floor trader could not hear me and spoke into my arm as loudly as I could. 'Buy thirty-five lots on stop at 296.' I then ignored the mumbling clerk on the other end of the phone and made sure Henry had been convinced. Thankfully it looked as though he was. I watched him walk sadly back to his desk, my hand in front of my face. If only he knew what I had done! Well, wasn't that what the market was all about, the strong taking advantage of the weak?

'The market's carried on moving higher again, Henry!' I shout. 'It's 296 trading and bid, it's 296.30 bid, 296.50 bid, 297 trading and bid. It looks like they've started buying again.' Is he listening to me? I wonder.

'OK where's my execution then?' he finally asks.

'You bought thirty-five lots at 296.30 and it's trading at 296.50 now.' I try to make him feel a bit better even though I believe he is buying it all back at the top of the market!

He seems momentarily pleased. 'OK, put another order in to buy thirty-five lots at 299 on stop.'

This time I put the order in for real and cancel my own sell stop at 289, having squared my position. I lean back and let the tension release from my shoulders. I want to smile to myself for a job well done but I deny myself the luxury.

As luck would have it, later that night the market came off the boil and started to fall as profit taking emerged. In New York the market closed lower and by the time trading started the next day, the market had fallen back to around 275. Henry lowered his stop following the market and eventually bought the balance of his position at a more reasonable price of 273. It was still quite a hefty loss, but not as severe as it might have been.

The next day the traders were talking about the market. James had made loads of money buying copper, which had ridden up on the back of silver. He was laughing because Henry had lost money and he had made it. David was not amused. 'Don't be so stupid guys, you're so childish. why are you laughing? It's not funny,' he said, going redder and redder.

Henry, meanwhile, was in the boardroom working out his position. Here was a situation I might take advantage of because James was so pleased with himself that I thought now would be a good opportunity to speak to him about me becoming a floor dealer. I carefully picked my moment as he was getting ready to leave for the market.

'James, a word in your ear please?'

'Oh, I know what you want!' He raised his hands as if he was being held up by a gun.

'Well,' I said, 'what's your answer?'

'My answer is yes!' he blurted out.

'Yes what?'

'Yes please. Ha ha ha!'

He was joking with me but I decided to take him at his word. 'Great, thanks, when do I start?'

'When I've had a word with Henry.'

'And when will that be?'

'Soon.' I watched him bend over to tie a stray shoelace.

Later, I overheard Henry speaking with David. 'I just don't understand why the position doesn't work out. I reckon we should have lost over 50 000 on the week's silver trading but I can only find 5000.'

David shrugged his shoulders in response. Only profits excited him, and talking about losses was obviously boring. 'Well it must be somewhere—' I hear him say.

'Unless, of course,' Henry interrupts, 'Simon has been jobbing off my back.'

I have to keep quiet because I am sure he would sack me if he knew what I had done. It's one thing for him to lose face to the other traders but to lose face to me would be quite another. No dealer likes to be outdone by a telex operator, and no man outdone by a woman either!

My feeling of foreboding grows as I watch James speaking to Henry and Henry then shaking his head in response. Staying positive is difficult as James heads towards me. 'I've agreed you can visit the Metal Exchange to see what it's like down there. Then we can take it from there, OK?' He pats me on the shoulder, expecting me to be happy but I am not and this time I'm not pretending to be either.

'Looking is not the same as learning to deal is it?' I look him straight in the eye, waiting for him to respond in his predictably gentleman-like manner.

'Look, it's tough down there,' he tells me. 'When you see it you probably won't want to trade anyway. Why can't you be happy and do what David does, trade in the office? Why is it such a big deal to be a floor dealer anyway?'

I take a deep breath, tired of explaining my point of view to them. 'Because you say I can't.' I point at him. 'Because he says I can't' I point at Henry. 'And because I… yes I…' By now I am thumping my chest and shouting, 'I want to, OK?'

James's hands go up. 'OK! I hear you loud and clear. Ha ha!'

Around the desk they are all laughing. Even Henry is smiling.

'OK,' I say as I reach for my coat. I can sense that they are all staring at me as I leave the trading room. I've made more than £45 000 this month and still nobody takes me seriously. I'm still no nearer to becoming a dealer. Tomorrow I'll tell Henry why his losses are not showing and why it's about time he let me become a clerk on the Exchange.

Next morning I approach James, who smiles at me as he comes in with his coffee. 'Yes, OK, I haven't forgotten.' 'Today's the day you can go to the Metal Exchange, but to the visitor's gallery only and you are to keep very quiet.' He winked at me and, nudging me with his arm said, 'We'll leave a bit early for the market and then I can get your pass, all right?'

'Yes, great.' I was pleased. I glanced at Henry and David with a big grin on my face.

'I don't know what you are so happy about,' David sniped, rolling his eyes up in his head and then smiling as an after thought.

'Just am!' I responded with an even bigger grin.

Eleven-thirty could not come quickly enough for me but when it did it was a mad rush. James suddenly leapt up from his desk, grabbed his jacket and flung it over his shoulders, rather like a caped crusader, as he strode out of the door. I looked to see if anyone else followed but they were still working on their cards.

I rushed out after him. 'Wait for me!' I shouted.

'Come on then, hurry up!'

I ran up behind him but as we got to the door he abruptly stopped. 'Oh shit, it's raining! Go back and get my umbrella, will you.'

I rushed back through the lobby again, having collected the

requested item, but James had already left the building and was striding up Mark Lane. I ran after him but struggled to keep up with his long strides. 'James, can we slow down we've still got a few minutes?'

'No we haven't, I want my pint first!'

'Oh, shall I come with you?'

'Well of course, where else are you going to go?'

We practically ran across Fenchurch Street and through Lime Street, a part of the City I hadn't seen before. Luckily James knew all the shortcuts up through the back alleyways to save time! Even though he was in a hurry he still had time to say hello or nod to someone he knew. Despite his friendly manner, I felt at a distinct disadvantage to him because I was quite a bit shorter and he had a dark beard that hid his mouth. So it was difficult to see what mood he was in, though clearly he was in a rush. That's why I was always pleased to hear him laugh, because then I knew everything was OK with him.

As we came into Leadenhall Market the light became dull under a huge glass roof that protected the market traders who were selling all sorts of luxury products: cheeses and chocolates from around the world on one side of the road, and on the other were a variety of wet fish stalls muddled in with others that sold all kinds of vegetables and exotic fruits. As I hopped over the odd runaway potato or cabbage, I marvelled at what was before me, although James was not at all impressed. I had never seen anything like it nor smelt so many different aromas in one place, and all this on the way to the Metal Exchange!

Ahead and slightly raised above us hung dozens of whole pig and cattle carcasses, great metal hooks holding them within framed alcoves in the wall. The sound of shouting and whistling and the ringing of money tills as they opened and shut accompanied the clatter of cartwheels on cobbled stones. Was this 1976 or 1876, and was this where the Metal Market was?

James looked down at me. 'All right?' he enquired.

'Yes, I'm fine'

'Right, here we go then' He had a broad smile on his face as we pushed through large swing doors into a busy pub. It was dark and I noticed many white faces and dark suits standing by the small curved bar. 'What do you want' James asked.

'I'll have the same as you thanks.'

'OK, two pints of lager, mate!'

He passes me a glass and I make my way from the bar but there is no room to stand anywhere else. 'Don't try to move, Gerry, just start drinking, will you, we've only got five minutes before we go. Want a fag?'

'Thanks,' I say, juggling a lit cigarette, my tankard of beer and his umbrella. All around is constant murmuring and I'm trying to hear what James is saying about me to the other traders. I can see they like him and I'm pleased that he is treating me like a friend.

Within a few minutes I hear the thud of his beer glass on the bar and see him striding out of the bar. I rush out after him to see him turning the corner.'

'Is it that time now, are we going to the market?'

'Yup, we're here.'

There is nothing special about the building we are entering. In fact I would have easily missed it. I look across the road; the sign says Whittington Avenue but where's the Exchange building?

James has already passed through a half open door. As I follow him, I notice a small brass plaque on the wall that says The London Metal Exchange. 'Come here, Gerry. Right, stand here for a minute. Let him give you a badge, now put that on and go up those stairs and you'll see a corridor. Follow the corridor round until you see the Metal Ring from up there. If you stand by the window in the gallery you can watch. I'll see you down here afterwards at about 1.30, OK?'

I watched as he went through another door. I wanted to see where he had gone but the doorman was watching and pointed me in the direction I should go. Climbing the stairs, I could hear all the traders coming into the market. Chatting and laughing they all sounded very relaxed. At the top I found myself in a narrow, thickly-carpeted hallway. I followed the directions James had given me and slowly opened the door into the main gallery. The whole building smelt musty and old. I walked over to the balcony rail and looked down. James had told me on the way over that millions of pounds changed hands daily across the Ring. 'The Metal Exchange is different from the other commodity markets in London,' he'd said proudly to me. 'Casual visitors are not encouraged and entry is much more difficult. You are very lucky to see it. Usually visitors to the Exchange have to be guests of member companies.'

I wondered whether I was now standing behind soundproof or perhaps bulletproof glass! Below I could see the Exchange becoming more crowded and in the middle was an enormous copper bowl. Surrounding it at some distance across a shiny tiled floor were four long wooden curved benches, equally spaced out in a circle. I counted about two hundred and fifty traders and clerks on the Exchange floor itself. Some were standing with notepads in their hands other were checking off their cards. I jumped as the bell rang loudly, indicating the beginning of the Lead Ring. Traders flooded into the Ring and took their places on the benches. Some stood behind and still others were manning the phones at the back of the room, relaying the market information to their offices.

After five minutes the bell rang again and a sign lit up on the wall, saying it was time for zinc to start. Some traders I noticed had changed. Trevor was still seated in our seat because he traded both lead and zinc. James was milling around in the background. I was looking forward to him entering the Ring for copper. Towards the last minute of the Zinc Ring, I heard the muted voices get louder and watched as the dealing became more hectic. Trevor came forward in his seat, pointing to a trader sitting opposite who was opening his mouth very wide and shouting out loudly 'Fifty tonnes!'

The bell rang again, the zinc traders left and the copper traders entered. Copper, tin and silver were the prime metals traded in terms of volume on the London Metal Exchange. It was for this reason that only the best or most senior traders dealt in those metals. When they entered the Ring you could see the difference in their physical appearance, and their attitude was more arrogant.

They were the best because they were older and more experienced. I watched intently as some would come into the Ring with a smile on their face, while others hardly acknowledged anyone around them. Some would be staring at their cards while others would be taking down orders from their clerks or giving executions back. These dealers were powerful, strong, determined, and very rich. I noticed that some had quite intimidating behaviour, others appeared ruthless yet controlled. Some clearly frightened the living daylights out of their clerks, who could be seen scuttling around in the background like frightened rabbits! By now I was getting really excited. James was one of the best copper traders in London and now I had the opportunity to see his performance for myself.

As he made his entrance, I noticed with some disappointment that he looked the scruffiest and had the longest hair. James looked up and smiled at me. I returned his smile, not knowing whether he could see me but when he winked I realised I was clearly visible from behind the smoky glass. A few other traders looked up at the same time, but I stepped back a bit, not wanting to intrude further. The shouting was getting louder and louder as the five minutes progressed. James as usual was looking amazingly relaxed, sitting half on the side of his bottom, one arm stretched out towards the trader sitting next to him and one leg stretched out into the Ring. He was looking at his card and stroking his beard. I wondered when he was going to do something and then I heard him shout out, 'Three months?'

The Ring goes quiet for a second, then a dealer across the Ring says, 'I'll give 760 sell at 762.'

'I'll give £761' James shouts even louder.

'Yes!' another dealer shouts back, pointing at him. 'How much? Five hundred tonnes?'

'Yes.'

'One thousand tonnes?'

'Yes!' I hear James shout even louder. 'Make it fifteen hundred tonnes in total?'

'Done!' says the other dealer.

The Ring goes quiet again just for a second before another trader says, 'I'll give £761?' There is no response. 'OK, I'll give £762?'

Suddenly the whole Ring is shouting, 'Give £762!', with no seller in sight. Then a different louder voice says, 'I'll give £763 and sell at 765.'

'I'll give £764!' I hear James voice as the last before the bell rings. Well timed, I think. I see him slap his leg with his card before leaving the Ring, and know he is happy long before he smiles up at me. Wow, what a performance!

I knew that during the break he would run up the stairs to me, so I was not at all surprised to see him enter the gallery. 'Well, what did you think?'

I was pleased to see that it clearly mattered to him what I thought. 'It's amazing,' I said, 'and you did so well in the Ring, buying all that copper and at such a good price too.'

'Nah, it was nothing, I was just bored,' he smiled and walked out again.

I looked down at the floor. All those men! How on earth did they know what they were doing? Well at least I'd seen what the market looked like and now I understood what the dealer had to do when I gave an order from the office. From now on, I would be more patient with the floor traders.

I stayed for the rest of the session until 1.30 but didn't feel good about going with James again to the pub. So I grabbed a toasted cheese on the way back to the office and wondered whether I could ever become a floor trader. Somehow I couldn't see myself even clerking on the Exchange, let alone sitting in the Ring!

I got back to the office around two and David immediately jumped on me. 'Where have you been? You should have been back ages ago! You know New York's going to open in a minute!'

'I've been down the market.'

'What all this time?'

I didn't answer but sat down to eat my sandwich.

'I don't know why you want to go down there anyway,' David continued. 'It's not as if you'll ever trade!'

I glared at him with my mouth half full, barely containing my annoyance. 'Have you ever been to the Exchange then, David?' I asked.

'No, and I've no wish to either. I'll tell you what, Gerry, why don't you just concentrate on those reports of yours and forget about the trading.'

David was talking about my pre-market metal report that I sent to all our clients. It would consist of individual reports for copper, tin, lead, zinc, gold and silver, a summary of the political and economic news affecting the market as well as a view on the foreign exchange markets, usually the sterling dollar rates. Later, I added aluminium and nickel once those contracts had been introduced onto the Metal Exchange. At the end of each report I would give a recommendation to buy or sell and if a position had been held for a while I would recommend instating stops to protect the profits or limit the losses.

Normally I would start writing the report at about 8.30 am and send it to thirty clients around the world by telex before the markets opened in London. I told Henry and David that this would enhance our client service and might even bring in new business. But my main reason for doing the report was so that I could demonstrate that I had a good feel for the market and making money. At the end of every month I would total the profits and losses and publish those in an end-of-month report.

During this time I developed my own trading system. Some of our clients followed the system while others were just interested in reading the recommendations. As a broker, it wasn't necessary to have a view on the market at all times but I thought it was important to generate interest as well as a commentary on the day's proceedings. Of course, no system can guarantee profits all the time. The trick was to cut your losses and run your profits. Taking losses was never easy but it had to be seen as a step in the process of making profits. Like hopscotch, the next step taken depended entirely on the last one. I liked to think that my system took the emotion out of making difficult decisions. It did this by introducing signals to buy or sell which had been triggered by the direction of prices on the previous day, along with the volume traded. If something had not happened by such and such a time, a further rule would come into play. Having a trading system made me stick to the rules without the temptation to get greedy. Sometimes I would double up on the position but only after making a profit. If I had taken a loss I would stand back from the market for a day or so until my system showed a strong signal to re-enter again. Of course there were days when I took profits too early and ran losses more than I needed to, but when I followed my system to the letter, it was profitable for my clients.

Writing the report was not difficult but it was detailed work and took up nearly two hours of my time in the morning. Supporting my reports and recommendations were my own charts that had been developed over a number of years. These recorded activity and volume of opening and closing prices of the official rings in the morning and the unofficial rings of the afternoon.

I also recorded the kerb closing prices. The lines that formed in the chart would reveal highs and lows and points of pressure and resistance where speculative trading intermingled with hedging from trade clients. If the highs or lows were breached, this would in turn trigger stop loss buying or selling. Knowing this, some clients would try to force prices higher in order to trigger the stops. This would lead to a run with prices racing ahead or dropping like a stone. The volume of metal traded on the Exchange only represented a small amount of the physical metal traded between fabricators and producers around the world, but they would use the official Ring to base the price of their physical contracts on. Sometimes this would be at a premium and sometimes at a discount, depending on the grade of metal. I knew the reports were valued because if ever I didn't send them, the phone would ring and the client would be on the line, asking where the report was.

One of our sister companies was a scrap metal company and the managing director would often question my recommendations, especially if they were contrary to his opinions. One day he phoned me up. 'I don't agree with your recommendation to buy zinc, Gerry, especially as I'm going to give you an order to sell two thousand tonnes at the market close this morning!'

I wasn't sure what I should say to him, so I explained that my system had been demonstrated to work and even though I had the knowledge he was going to sell, it would not change my mind. At that he laughed. 'You must be mad,' he said, 'take the order anyway!' Just as I was about to put the phone down, he added, 'By the way, how do you think your clients are going to feel when they see you're selling two thousand tonnes of zinc and you have just told them all to buy at market?'

'I don't question my trading system. If it's right to buy then it's right to buy!' I replied.

'We'll see, call me for the Ring,' he said as he put the phone down. I called him for the Ring and he sold on the close. I thought: my system will register his sale and if it makes a difference my system will pick it up for tomorrow. But he had made me think and I was worried how my clients were responding to the news of our selling on the close.

I reasoned that my clients would understand that I was acting just as any broker would: taking orders, executing them and earning the commission in doing so. They might, however, wonder why I hadn't booked it out if I was so sure the market was going up! Well, my system didn't work on unlimited volume and I had already bought my quota. It was never the intention of my system to try and dominate the market because inwardly, however confident and sophisticated my forecasting system was (actually it was incredibly simple), I knew the markets had a will all of their own. But would my clients understand?

I resolved then to put a note at the bottom of my report stating that the recommendations made were my personal recommendations, based on my own trading system, and not those of the company or its clients. When David saw this he was unhappy that I had put my name to it but I said to him, 'So what if I've put my name on it? That's a good thing, isn't it? Now they will all know who's to blame if it all goes wrong.' This made him laugh and he seemed happier with the idea, although he said it would be embarrassing if we started to lose business because of my recommendations. I took his point on board but I was pretty relaxed about the whole thing because I knew the level of interest it was generating, even if clients did try to prove me wrong from time to time!

As I later said to James, 'What advantages do clients have by trading through us, other than cheaper commission rates, if it's not our view and recommendations on the market?' Henry had said that it was always dangerous to give a view in case you were wrong but I reckoned it was no worse that the odds you get on a roulette game – fifty-fifty, red or black. Besides I wasn't just guessing – I had a workable system based on logic! Anyway, I remember Mark always giving his view of the sugar or cocoa market. In fact, I can't remember a time when he didn't have a view and he was always phoning someone up telling them to buy or sell, 'cas they'd make a fortune'. Henry and David thought that the metal market was different from the soft commodities. In their eyes, it demanded more respect, more caution. I didn't see it that way and neither did James; he just used it the way it needed to be used – and sometimes, as I'll show later, with contempt.

During the afternoon markets New York would be very busy with arbitrage on silver. This gave me an opportunity to job a little but the Ring dealers were also jobbing and it seemed pointless for us all to be doing the same thing! It was then I realised that the only real opportunity I would have to put my dreams into action and become a recognised dealer was to get myself fully qualified as a floor dealer. I also knew that James would be supportive if Henry agreed. So I resolved that, the next morning, when the office was quiet, I would speak to Henry about finally becoming a Metal Exchange Dealer

I went home that night, thinking about what my options would be if Henry said no. I decided that I would have to leave and join another Commodity Broker – a more go-ahead broker might be prepared to give someone like me a chance.

The next morning I entered the office with a coffee in my hand. I was copying James and it made me feel quite powerful, swaggering in with a nonchalant attitude as if I was the most important person in the world. If Henry sensed anything, he gave nothing away.

'Henry,' I said abruptly, 'can I have a word about trading with you please?'

'Yes, what is it?' He didn't bother looking up at me.

I sat down opposite and leaned over towards him. 'I want to become a floor trader on the Metal Exchange.' He looked up with an absent look in his eye so I repeated myself. 'I want to become a metal trader, a metal trader in the Ring!'

He smiled and pulled his pipe out of his mouth, slowly and very deliberately. 'Do you indeed?'

Thinking I was in with a chance, I tried my best to convince him of the merit of my suggestion. 'Yes, you need another floor trader. What if James, Simon or Trevor are ill?'

'Gerry, you know that women are not allowed onto the floor of the London Metal Exchange. The markets would never allow it and that's because of the way they trade by open outcry. Who would hear your voice with all those men shouting and screaming? You wouldn't be strong enough and in any case, the environment isn't right for you down there. So no, I'm sorry, Gerry, it just can't happen, it won't work and that really does have to be an end to it, all right?'

'No,' I said, standing up, 'it's not all right. I want you to put my application in. Look in yesterday's paper: the Equal Opportunities Act has come into force. *They* can't say no to me, *you* can't say no, you cannot discriminate against me because I'm a woman!'

He put his pipe down on the desk and sighed. 'You're wrong, Gerry, I'm not discriminating against you – I just don't think you can do the job!'

'Please, Henry, you know I can do the job. Let me try, why won't you let me try? What harm can it do?'

He pursed his lips together and stared at me before smiling. 'I'll say this, you don't give up. Bring me the article on the Equal Opportunities Act and let me have a look at it.'

'I've got it right here,' I said, passing it over to him. 'Does that mean you'll consider it, Henry?'

He looked up from the paper. 'I'm making no promises, Gerry. Now say no more about it till I've had a chance to think.'

The day passed very slowly and I was incredibly helpful to everyone, especially Henry! I was wondering what my next move should be when, quite by chance, I got the opportunity to talk to Mark. I had always had a good relationship with him and so found it easy, when he asked me how things were going, to tell him. At first he seemed surprised and then he laughed, putting his head on one side and saying, 'Well, if you can get away with it, why not?' I knew he was no fan of the traditional establishment, but it felt good to have his support anyway. I wanted to raise the subject again with Henry but felt I might be nagging him too much.

Then I thought of way that might intrigue him. I waited until it was quiet – the traders had not yet come back from the afternoon market and David had left for the day. There were just the two of us sitting at the trading desk. 'Henry,' I said as quickly as possible, so he couldn't stop me, 'I just wanted to say that Mark thinks it's a good idea as well!'

Henry was silent for a second. 'Does he indeed?'

'Oh yes, you would definitely have his support because we would be the only broker to have a woman dealer!'

'I suppose so.' He responded as though bored with the subject, but then he looked up at me. 'OK, you just won't let it alone, will you? All right, we'll apply tomorrow for you to become a clerk, but I don't hold out a lot of hope. Really I don't.'

'Thank you, Henry, you won't regret it, I promise.' I stood up and grabbed my coat and scarf.

This was going to be an exciting journey; one I hoped would lead to me becoming the first woman dealer on the floor of the London Metal Exchange. Little did I know that very shortly, life was going to get a lot more difficult. But for now I simply wondered how the lads would react in the morning when I told them my news.

That night, travelling home, I had plenty to think about. On one hand I felt relief that at last some progress was being made; and on the other fear. Fear of the unknown fed my recurring visions of my last visit to the Metal Exchange. I recalled the scenes in flashes as they came upon me one by one: a busy market and men screaming at each other unintelligibly, with mysterious symbols flashing up on the wall behind them. I saw the knocking and the shoving and I realised that I would have to be both mentally and physically tough to survive on the floor of the London Metal Exchange and a cold shiver ran down my spine at the thought of dealing in that male-dominated environment.

I got out at Notting Hill Gate station and walked the rest of the way home to Holland Park. I enjoyed the fresh air of the tree-lined pavements and it gave me an opportunity to recall my not-so-happy schooldays, which in an odd way offered me some consolation when I considered how far I had come in the eight years since I'd left.

Back home, I kicked my shoes off and Tanya bought me a cup of tea. 'Had a busy day?' I asked.

'Yes. I'm pleased we don't have to cook tonight, we have some of that left over casserole,' she added with a smile.

'That's good,' I said. 'I'm going to have a soak now but I've something interesting to tell you over dinner!'

When I told Tanya she was very interested but I could tell

she didn't really understand what I was talking about. 'Will you get more money?' she asked finally.

'Well, I certainly hope so but it won't be for quite a while yet.' Then I added, 'The dealers earn loads of money but I won't be a dealer for quite a while, at least six months. First I have to be a clerk to a dealer and then I have to take The London Metal Exchange Floor Dealers' Examination. The Committee of The London Metal Exchange will then ask me some questions and if I pass them, they'll let me sit in the Ring. It's quite a complicated process and it's going to take a while but I don't mind because there is a lot to learn. The London Metal Exchange is a very intricate market and there are many rules and regulations governing the market and its members, and of course it has an international reputation to maintain.' As I finished speaking I glanced at the clock and realised I had been speaking for over half an hour. Tanya smiled, looking a little tired. 'Oh sorry, Tanya, just listen to me! Let's clear up.'

The next morning I was in the office bright and early. 'Morning, Henry.'

'You sound very chirpy this morning.'

'Yes, of course. I can't wait to start clerking. Will you speak to James or shall I?'

'I'll speak with him later, Gerry.'

James sauntered into the office around his usual time of 9.45. He took a glance at the clock and then at Henry before smiling at me as he sat down.

'James!' I grabbed him as soon as I could. 'Henry wants to talk to you later.'

'Oh yeah, what's that about then?'

'Not your position, don't worry!'

'Better not be!' he said.

'Well, it's about me and I need you to talk to him today, don't wait for him to call. You can tell him I said he wanted to talk to you.'

'All right, but what have you been up to then?'

'I want to be a clerk on the Metal Exchange and I need you to support the proposal.'

'It's not me that decides. It's the Committee of the Metal Exchange who will have to decide. It's not going to be easy at all, you've got to understand this is new and no woman has been allowed to work on the floor.'

'Yes, I know, but please just say yes, will you, to Henry when he asks?'

At lunchtime Henry called me over. 'Read this application I've made, I'm submitting your name as a clerk for us.'

'Oh great, I am pleased,' I said.

'Well, don't get your hopes up too much, we have to see what response we get from them.'

'OK, how long do you think it will be?'

'No idea, but we should hear something in the next week, or so I hope.'

By the following Monday there had been no response so I asked Henry to phone up, and of course he couldn't get a reply. We wrote again and still there was nothing. I was very grateful for the help and support from Mark, Henry and James but I was nervous that our application was going to sink into a black hole. I was aware that the traders knew about our application and were quietly pleased by the lack of response!

Then one day I had the idea of visiting the Exchange and trying to influence the outcome for myself. James was pretty laid back and so long as I had finished my morning duties and was back in the office during the afternoon for New York, no one really minded. I was lucky that I could visit the market as a visitor or messenger for James at any time so long as I could think of a good excuse to be there if I was stopped by anyone!

As I walked to the Exchange, I imagined treading the same pavements, doing this every day, getting richer, getting more powerful, getting cleverer. I envisaged how why and when it would happen. I saw it happening and I saw it happening to me. I would make it happen no matter what; no matter who tried to stop me, it would happen and it would happen soon!

I reached the Exchange just as the traders were starting kerb. Some of them were making their way across to the pub while others milled around in the foyer. They looked surprised to see me standing there. They would look away and then look back again. 'Are you after someone, luv?'

'Yes, em, it's OK, I'll just wait if I may?' I knew from my last visit that this was the time that some committee members left for lunch, and I was hoping to catch the attention of one. I practised my speech: 'Hey remember me, I'm still waiting for your reply!'

Just at that moment, three elderly gentleman came down the stairs. How old they looked, much older than the Ring dealers I was used to, and how Victorian they were in their appearance. One looked very severe, in fact quite frightening. He had huge bushy sideburns, dark-rimmed glasses and a pocket watch with a gold chain dropping down from his waistcoat pocket. He had wavy, thinning hair greased back and he wore pin-striped baggy trousers that appeared badly creased as if he had slept in them all night! His overall image was significantly smartened up by the addition of a black jacket. Alongside him was a very tall large smart man with silver hair and a silver-grey suit who smelt of aftershave. I noticed his face was red and shiny and he had a huge laugh that bounced around the hall. He smiled at me, nudged one of his colleagues and gave out another roar of laughter as he walked past me through the door.

I knew then that I had lost an opportunity and was wondering just what I should do when a voice behind me with a strong Irish accent said, 'And what are you doing, standing there all lost?'

I looked up to see someone who did not look like a trader standing in front of me. 'Oh, I'm waiting for someone.'

'Are you indeed! And do you work here in the city or are you just visiting?'

'No, I work for a Ring dealer. Well actually, I'm trying to become a clerk. I already trade in the office though!'

The man put a cupped hand over his ear as if he could not quite believe what it was I was saying. 'Ah now, let me see. Ah yes, you must be Geraldine, are you not?'

'Yes, I am, how did you know?'

'Well, let me introduce myself. I'm Edward, a journalist. Yes, that's what I am, yes so I am, and I've been working these markets for a very long time so I have!' And he laughed. 'I know everything there is to know about the market, and I do daily and weekly reports for the Exchange so I do, huh, huh, huh. Oh, and the papers and whoever else you know who wants it, so to speak.' He laughed again and nudged me.

'Well,' I said, 'why don't you do a report on me?'

He looked at me. 'My, we are forward, aren't we?' And he laughed, taking a drag of his cigarette. 'And why should I be doing that?'

'Because...' I said, thinking quickly '...because I need your help and all the help I can get. The committee hasn't responded to our application for me to become a clerk and what's more, we don't know when they ever will.'

'Well, there's a surprise!' he exclaimed sarcastically. 'Hmmm.' He rubbed his chin slowly. 'I'll just have to see what we can do. Cheerio!' He gave a short wave and stepped out into the street.

Once he had left I felt strangely alone, despite being surrounded by at least a hundred and fifty traders and clerks making their way to lunch.

As I walked back to the office, I wondered whether Edward would help me. Is that why I had gone to the Exchange? Was it Edward the journalist and not the Committee that I needed to influence? Edward was important to me and I intended to nurture this acquaintance if I could. For now, I needed to do no more.

Back at the office, I hoped that sooner or later the phone would ring or the post would bring good news. The call and the letter never came. But good news came later in an unexpected form. It was an article in the Metal Bulletin: Friday August 6th 1976 Hotline. I read excitedly, 'The latest *cause célèbre* on the London Metal Exchange is Geraldine Bridgewater, who would like to be the first Ring dealing lady; and the London Metal Exchange Committee, doubtless mindful of the Equal

Opportunities Act, is presumably not thinking of standing in her way. But it is worried about the unsuitability for Geraldine's purposes of certain London Metal Exchange facilities at the bottom of a twisty staircase.' I had mixed feelings about this article. This was the first we had heard of facilities not being appropriate for my needs but as I said to Henry, 'I can use the toilet across the road in the pub like the rest do.'

So far we had not heard from the committee as to how they viewed my application, although I knew who had been responsible for the article and I guessed he was closely connected with some of the committee members.

'Well,' I said to Henry, 'at least it's up for discussion. Something must happen soon.'

Chapter Four

The London Metal Exchange

Over the next couple of months I kept as quiet as possible whilst patiently waiting for news on our application. Every time I saw Henry I hoped he would say something and he knew that I was disappointed when he wasn't able to. Then one day he could bear it no longer. 'Don't they take us seriously?' he said in a fit of anger.

'Have they said nothing then, Henry?' I asked.

He drew on his pipe three or four times as he considered his reply. 'Well, I spoke to them on the phone and they said it was not possible at this moment in time and you saw the article – they feel that they have made their case for not accepting you.'

I looked down at my shoe and rubbed it along the floor several times 'What does that mean?' I asked as I watched him take a chart out of his brown leather case. He was quiet so I continued. 'We have to be persistent, let's keep on at them. It's against the law to deny our application.'

Henry sighed 'They're saying it's not comfortable down there for you. There are no toilets for women. And in any case, no one would hear your voice in the arena, it's not a women's job.'

Henry sounded almost convinced, but I was becoming irritated. 'Look, we're not going to give in, Henry, of course they'll hear my voice, it's probably higher than the rest!' Henry smirked, but I continued, hoping he wouldn't think I was nagging him. 'As for the facilities, I can go across the road to the pub can't I?'

Henry began to feel cornered. 'You seem very determined to go through with this. I'll be honest, Gerry, I really don't know where this is taking us.'

'Look Henry, I can't do this without your support. Let's try once more – please?'

'And then what?'

'Well, if they still won't accept my application then we'll have to consider other action, won't we?'

Henry puffed slowly on his pipe again before raising his eyebrows and turning his back on me. Clearly my last question didn't deserve a response. I watched him walk into the boardroom and hoped that I hadn't pushed my luck too far. Later I heard him on the phone and I hoped he hadn't given in to the decision

I need not have feared because the next day, as Henry was dishing out the mail to me, the Secretary of the Metal Exchange phoned. It was 9.15, surely too early in the day to have a decision. I listened eagerly, not worrying how close I put my head to Henry's. I searched his eyes for confirmation of what I thought I was hearing.

'Henry,' said the voice on the other end of the line, 'I thought I'd phone to let you know the committee of the London Metal Exchange has agreed to accept Geraldine as your clerk, but I hope you understand: if there are any problems we will have to review the situation.'

Henry smiled at me as I jumped up and down with delight rather hysterically. 'Yes, of course,' he said, 'and thank you for calling.' He put the phone down and gave me the thumbs-up.

'Brilliant, can I go down on Monday?' I pleaded.

'Yes, but let's first clear it with James.'

The following morning, James agreed that I could start on the Exchange. I watched as the moments ticked by, feeling more and more nervous. I would leave it right up until the last moment to go to the loo. Surrounded by so many men would be a very different experience, even though I was used to working in a predominantly male office. I would have to look very sure of myself and appear in control, no matter how scared I was feeling. Today was not a day for smiling because it would be too much of a familiar gesture and in any case, I doubted anyone would be in the mood for smiling back! Up in the toilet I took one last look at myself in the mirror and, checking that my long skirt was not tucked into my underwear, I left the security of the ladies' and skipped down the stairs.

I heard Trevor and James as they strode out of the trading room heading for the market. 'Hey!' I shouted. 'Wait for me, don't forget I'm coming with you today.'

'Well hurry up, we haven't got all day,' James said rolling his eyes up in his head.

I ran into the trading room, got my jacket and picked up a long blue book and pencil. Turning around, I bumped straight into David on the other side of the swing door. 'Where are you off to in such a hurry, young lady?' David always spoke to me as though I was much younger than him, even though we were practically the same age.

'To the market – I'm clerking today!'

'Well, you'd better get on your way then.' He pushed me on the shoulder and I ran out into the foyer. I ran up Mark Lane with the cold air hitting my lungs, thinking: this won't do, to be late and out of breath! I checked my watch as I waited to cross Fenchurch Street. Blimey, I thought, I've got ages yet, it's only 11.40! Walking hastily through Leadenhall Market, I could still see no sign of James, Trevor and Simon, even though I knew they were ahead of me, and for one silly moment, I wondered whether they were hiding! Where on earth, I wondered, could they have gone? Perhaps they were playing some trick on me. I didn't want to enter the market without them, but clearly they didn't want to go in with me!

Then I had a thought: I'll check the pub. James liked to go in for a quick pint before the market. I slowly pushed open the Victorian glass panelled door. The pub was packed but that didn't stop me squeezing past large bodies into a very smoky room. I could just make out James standing in his usual place at the bar. 'Oh, thank god I've found you!' I said, grabbing his arm.

He peered down at me and, laughing out loud, asked, 'Do you want a beer, Gerry?'

I wasn't sure whether he wanted to buy me a drink, or was just being friendly. But he seemed genuinely amused by me and I was pleased that Trevor and Simon weren't with him. 'Yes please, I'll have a lager.' What was I thinking of? I'd need to go to the loo again if I wasn't careful! But I had said yes and before I knew it, James was passing down a golden pint! Even before I took hold of it, I knew I would never have time to drink it all. Besides, I didn't want to leave James and walk into the Exchange on my own.

I sipped the beer, watching the clock and looking up at James, half-listening to his stories and half lost in my own thoughts. I had shocked myself that I had so quickly accepted that drink, and this my first day of clerking on the Exchange! I looked around at the other faces and made a mental note of them. James seemed to know about eight of them and I imagined that they were Ring dealers. I forgave myself for accepting the drink by providing myself with the perfect reason for doing so. Men ruled the world and everything in it and I realised that if I was going to succeed, then I could do nothing worthwhile without them. And to be accepted I would have to become one of the boys, even though having a drink before the market was, to me, showing a rebellious streak! But they all knew their place, their rank and position. When it came to it they were obedient within a framework established by ancient laws and order. There were peer groups, clubs and institutions, each with their own etiquette. 'My word is my bond.' Those five words meant so much. They were a gentleman's agreement that allowed millions of pounds to change hands in any one deal. I wondered whether a woman could be party to a gentleman's agreement. Would a man ever trust a woman enough?

I looked again at the large round black and white clock and nudged James. 'Shouldn't we be going now?'

'Yeah OK.' His beer glass made a loud thud as it hit the bar. I followed him as he strode out of the bar, determined not to be late for my first day.

Suddenly we were there. I smiled at someone who didn't

smile back before remembering that today I wasn't going to smile at all. I watched James's feet in front of me as he made his way through to the inner sanctum of the London Metal Exchange. Without looking up, I sensed several pairs of eyes watching me, which I avoided by looking straight ahead. The commissioner had tried to bar my way but James had taken control by striking out his hand in a gesture that meant 'leave alone', and I was able to walk in proudly without being stopped.

It was darker and more intimate that I had imagined, almost like a club. At last I had arrived for work on the floor of the Exchange. As I followed Trevor and Simon around to our seat, I ran my hand across the top of the long wooden bench where the leather joined the wood. A bell rang out, announcing the beginning of the Lead Ring, and I looked around for James who was nowhere to be seen. More eyes were upon me and I felt like a duck out of water, but that was to be expected. There were loud mutterings too. Were they being directed against me or was it the clerks just checking their deals? At one point I thought I heard some booing in the background, but I stood my ground, holding the back of the wooden bench where Trevor was now seated.

Finally the bell went again and I released my fingers slightly. Trevor hadn't traded so there were no deals to check. So far so good – the end of round one. Surely it must get better now! Trevor stood up and walked out of the Ring. I smiled at him but he didn't see me. Why had I done that? I said I wasn't going to smile today, and that was twice now I'd made that mistake! Simon was on the phone to the office. Zinc would be busier than lead, I had to make sure I didn't miss any of Trevor's trades.

I tucked my hair behind my ears and leaned forward, listening intently for the deals he struck. That's when I realised the strange noise continuing in the background was booing. I stopped, looking around the room in amazement as it became louder and louder. By now it was abundantly clear that it was me they were booing at. There seemed no way of avoiding the full force of anger from several hundred men. Wishing for the ground to open up and swallow me was one option, but that wasn't going to happen and besides, by now my heart was beating loudly as I watched the action around me unfold in slow motion, the booing turning into one monster roar of disapproval. I tried to calm myself down by singing in my head: *'Oh the grand old Duke of York, he had ten thousand men, he marched them up to the top of the hill and he marched them down again. And when they were up they were up and when they were down they were down.'* I stopped to listen; they were still at it. *'And when they were only halfway up they were neither up nor down!'*

I summoned what strength I had without the smile, which was hard because smiling was what I was prone to do in the face of adversity. I only had myself to blame for this show of animosity; after all, I was down here because I had chosen to be. No one had forced me. On the contrary, I had forced their hands so why should I be so surprised at their behaviour? Besides, I was fully confident that I could turn this situation around once they had a chance to see that I could be trusted. As the booing continued, I thought of all the other women who had been booed at through history and I called upon them to come to my aid now: Elizabeth the First and Joan of Arc. The list was short but powerful!

When the room stopped spinning and the booing started to fade, I watched James take his seat in the Copper Ring. He was smiling widely, playing to the audience, bowing ever so slightly before he sat down on the bench. I realised that he was pretending to thank everyone for his reception in the Ring and this encouraged some dealers to laugh. There was an eerie silence about the whole place. It was as if we were standing still in time or floating though space with no particular destination in mind. It was the calm before the storm, or the second before a boat goes down: that moment when everyone knows that things will never be the same again. And when the bell for the Copper Ring rang out it, was as though a herald had flown down and blown his trumpet!

I stood there, unsmiling and cold as though I had no feelings.

This was what they wanted and this was what they would get – until, that is, they got bored of booing. James was still laughing. I could tell because his back was shaking. I realised this was out of embarrassment and that he was doing the one thing I could not do. I tapped his shoulder because there was business to be done. I don't think he felt my touch, he was too absorbed in his private joke. Trevor, who had been standing next to me, had now moved away and was shaking his head slowly from side to side, occasionally looking at me as if he couldn't believe I was still there. Sooner or later they would just have to get used to seeing a woman's face about the place.

James looked up at me. 'Ah dear, don't worry,' he said, 'it'll be all right in a minute. I've got some copper to do before the end of the Ring!" Through the chorus I heard him shout, 'Three months?'

And of course I knew what to expect as I leaned forward over the bench to catch what was being said. A great roar ascended into the Exchange as I furiously scribbled something across my pad. Actually it was nothing at all, I was just testing my pencil but they didn't know that. *'AAAHH!* Get out! Get out! No women allowed – get out! Get *OUT!'*

James was still laughing and I was pleased he was. I should smile too, having inspired such a reaction in them. James leaned forward in the Ring 'Three months?' he shouted to the noisy din and again, even louder, 'Three months?'

I looked at the clock. Some of the booing had stopped and there were thirty seconds to go. I leaned forward to hear his final quote and then the bell went. James got out of the Ring, shaking his head. 'Well, that wasn't so bad was it? Ha ha ha!'

But Simon was not at all amused. 'Bloody ridiculous, bloody ridiculous!' he kept repeating as Trevor came over and nudged me on the shoulder.

'Henry's on the phone, he wants to speak to you. Take it in our box over there.'

I picked up a big, smelly, dusty black phone 'Yes?' I said

'What was all that about?' Henry demanded.

'What, the booing?' I said. 'I don't know, but it's stopped for the moment.'

'Hmmm, OK then. Now ask James what I've done on copper, will you?'

'Yes, OK, hang on a minute.' I dropped the phone as I looked around for James. To my horror he was across the other side of the Ring. This meant that I was going to have to walk past two hundred or so traders and clerks.

I squeezed my way through crowds of men who wouldn't move, or whose elbows were sticking out at odd angles, or who hissed as I went by. Some cast a look of disgust at me as I passed. I avoided their looks as I picked my way around the benches and through the assortment of telephone wires, arms and legs, aiming to create as little disturbance as possible. Feeling as self-conscious as I was, I couldn't help but hear that as I moved around the Exchange in my high heels, my feet made a very different sound to those of other traders. They could hear me coming! Hundreds of eyes were upon me and the temperature was rising in the room.

And then I felt a kick on my shin. I stared at two or three very close traders until they all looked away. I couldn't be sure who had kicked me but kicked I was, and painfully bruised.

James was close by and I signalled to him to come over. Rubbing my leg because it still hurt, I said, 'Henry wants to know what his execution is on copper. Oh, and by the way, I've just been kicked!'

James grabbed hold of my arm. 'Come with me,' he said, leading me away from the crowded part of Exchange. 'Look, give them a chance to get used to you. Why don't you just stand there on the other side of our seat and don't move if you can help it.'

I rubbed my leg again. 'Well, I think I've had enough now, I want to go back to the office.'

'No, definitely not, you're not going back until the market's closed!'

So I had no choice now but to knuckle under and involve

myself in what was going on in the rings. But it was challenging and, strain as I might to hear the individual words from traders' mouths, all I could hear was one loud noise. I couldn't work out who was trading and who was just shouting because they were all doing it so fast and I wasn't at all sure who had pointed at who and what they had said! How on earth was I going to pick any of this up? Clearly, clerking was not as easy as I had first thought and all this on top of learning what seat belonged to what company in the Ring, and who the individual traders were. Not only that, I would have to know the clerks by name since it would be with them that I'd have to check the trades. I took a reality check and a wave of despair washed over me. There was just so much to learn. I watched James light a cigarette and walk into the Ring. I really fancied a cigarette as well but I couldn't have one until we got outside the market. It just wasn't the right thing to do.

The rest of the session passed as a blur, with me trying to get involved and scribbling frantically in my book. After the kerb, I hung around waiting for James but he was busy. Trevor and Simon were doing their best to ignore me, so eventually I left the market. In any case, it was down to us clerks to work through the lunch-hour, checking deals, adjusting the position cards and picking up new orders for the afternoon market. The dealers, on the other hand, were able to spend at least two hours lunching at the best restaurants in town.

Making my way back to the office, I took a detour across the road to Sylvio's, where I ordered a toasted cheese and tomato sandwich and a cup of hot tomato soup. I decided to eat it in rather than take it back to the office, as I needed some time to myself, time to relax and think about what had just happened. Besides, I felt tired and cold and even though the damp rain reached halfway through to the seating area, the warm Italian atmosphere would help me to recover. Looking at the length of the queue that stretched half way down the road, I wondered why there were not more sandwich bars in the City.

After lunch I returned to the office, proud to have

successfully completed the morning session but also feeling a little despondent. But no sooner had I arrived when David asked me, 'Well, how was it down there then?'

'What you would expect really,' I said rather nonchalantly, taking a cigarette out of the packet.

'Are you going down there this afternoon?'

'No, I think I'll give it a break and go down tomorrow morning instead.'

David seemed relieved and for once I had to agree with him. It wasn't wise to return to another round of booing and I hoped the traders would now be thinking about their behaviour towards me. They might even regret some of their actions. Stupidly, I thought my absence would give them an opportunity to reconsider their feelings about my presence on the Exchange, and I knew Henry would let me stay in the office during the afternoon.

When he came back from lunch he walked over to where I was sitting with a rather concerned look on his face. 'I can't imagine what you have been through this morning but it's quite enough for one day, do you hear, Gerry? I want you to stay here this afternoon and then if you like we can review the situation tomorrow.' He then turned to David. 'Let's look after Gerry this afternoon. shall we?'

And of course I was relieved to stay in the office. I didn't want to seem weak but I was grateful for the breather.

That evening I went home and after Tanya had handed me a bowl of curry, I took a spoonful and burnt my mouth. 'Ow!' Then I added, 'This isn't the only punishment I've taken today. Huh!'

Waiting for the curry to cool, I started to tell her a little of what had happened on the Exchange.

'Well, what's the point of it all then?' she said when I had finished.

'The point is, why shouldn't a woman be able to sit in the Ring and deal?'

Tanya stirred the rice before serving. 'Because it doesn't seem right, you with all those men, that's why.'

'OK, so why does society differentiate so much between the role of men and women? Surely there are some jobs that are unisex, so to speak? Can we really say that we are getting the best out of men and women if we slot them into specific male and female roles?'

Tanya picked up her glass of wine and leaned over across the table. 'I can't answer that, but don't you think there is something about your nature that when a barrier is put up, you just want to knock it down? And when rules are made you want to show that they don't work or that they need to be improved?'

'Yes, but that's not why I'm trying to be a Ring dealer!'

She laughed. 'Oh come on, Gerry, you got expelled from school! You've always been a bit of rebel and look at you now, you're not exactly the norm, are you? I mean, do you think if you hadn't been the way you are that you would still have done this?'

I was shocked. What did she mean, the way I was?

'Anyway, if I hadn't been the way I am, maybe I would have been happier to accept my lot in life. I wouldn't have thought about it at all, I suppose. But on the other hand, I would still have been angry because women are not being treated as equal to men! It seems eminently unfair that I should be unequal in terms of what I can expect as far as opportunities are concerned just because I have been born a girl and not a boy. It just can't be right that being born a girl should affect the contribution I can make to society, the level of responsibility I have, the education or job that I have or the name I could make for myself – in short, my destiny. Besides, men seem to have so little respect for us. Why do you think that is? It can't be good for society!'

I took a sip of wine and dragged heavily on my cigarette, waiting for Tanya to reply, but she had gone quiet. I wondered at her silence. Was this the calm before the storm? Was she thinking about what I had said or did she just think I was talking rubbish? I decided to continue.

'So if all of this is to change, we women have to work hard to change it! Am I making any sense?'

Tanya nodded. 'Yes, of course, but what if a woman doesn't want to be equal with a man? What if I want to have doors opened for me and drinks bought for me and not to work when I'm married?'

'Well,' I said, 'no one is going to force you, are they? Surely it is about having options. I mean, what if your husband wants to stay at home and look after the children? What if you earn more money than him and it makes sense for you to stay in work? Perhaps in the future there will be many options. I can't say, but one thing I'm sure about is that it is right for me to fight for equal opportunity and equal rights and I think we have to build on the work of the Suffragettes and move things forward. Women need to know that they have something to contribute in the workplace and that they are valued, otherwise it won't be long before men are questioning why we need to be educated at all or whether we still need the vote, since our opinion will count for nothing!'

Tanya was still quiet and still listening. I was sounding passionate, maybe too aggressive, but I felt that was the only way to show her how earnest I was. 'Look, I know I sound melodramatic but in all the history of humanity, women have only had the vote and free education for the last fifty or so years. Why do you think it is so difficult to find a woman role model? Nearly everything done well has apparently been done by a man, so no wonder men think women are only good for one thing!'

Tanya protested, 'But that's not true, there are women archaeologists, poets, scientists and historians who have made a name for themselves.'

'I know, but how often do you hear about them? Oh come on, you have to admit that you never do!'

'OK,' said Tanya, 'I agree, men do have most of the opportunities to get on in this world and are always taken seriously, and I know that women don't have those same opportunities.'

'Well then, that's exactly my point!'

Tanya waved her hand in the air. 'Look, you're confusing me and not letting me say what I want to say! What I'm trying to say is, not all women want to be like you, Gerry! Most women are very happy to be looked after by a man and I know I am very happy for a man to open the door for me! Perhaps women don't want to have to work all their lives?'

I rubbed my head in frustration and reached out for another cigarette as Tanya got up from the table. 'More wine?' I asked her.

'No thanks, I think I'll make a coffee, do you want one?'

'Yes please.' I watched her put the kettle on. But there was something else I needed to say, so I carried on talking 'OK, perhaps some women don't want a career or to go to work, but that doesn't mean they should deny other women the opportunity for a career. And as far as opening doors are concerned, isn't that just good manners? I mean, why shouldn't a woman open the door for another woman? If I see a pregnant woman standing on the tube, or an old man, I always offer my seat. It's not about sexual identity, it's about having thought for others. It's simply about good manners, surely?

'Black or white, Gerry?' Tanya shouted through the kitchen door.

'White, please. Oh, and I'll have a Sambuca with it too, thanks!'

Tanya sat down and passed a cup of coffee over to me. 'I think you'll just cause a lot of unhappiness and you won't succeed. Plenty have tried before, Gerry.'

I watched as she poured out the Sambuca. 'OK, can we at least agree that if we are to be valued then, we need to be accepted as equals and we are not at the moment? If we don't act with dignity, then we won't be treated with any respect or taken at all seriously!' I was on a roll now and without so much as drawing a breath, I continued, spitting the words out between puffs on my cigarette. 'And women who parade themselves across newspapers for the sake of money make other women's lives, like mine, a bloody misery! They make my job harder because I'm fighting for respect for women from the very men who have pictures of naked women on their office walls! How demeaning is that? Recently I tore a Pirelli calendar off the wall and put it in the dustbin. When the guys in the office saw what had happened, a few of them asked me why would someone do that and I looked at them silently and they knew I had done it and they knew why I had done it. Because I said nothing, they said nothing, but still I knew they knew it was me! I mean, who else in the office would have done that?'

'But if you argue for freedom for yourself, isn't it right that other women should be free to choose how to earn money as well?'

Tanya was clever and she was talking about the oldest game in town. 'Ah, the root of all our troubles – the basic belief that a woman's real reason for existence is to satisfy a man and have his baby!' Ooooh, I was getting really angry now! I could feel it. I must be careful not to fly into a rage. 'Yes, of course individual choice is important, but in making individual choices we must also consider the impact on society as a whole and on our own future wellbeing.'

Tanya shook her head and went into the kitchen. 'I think you're too judgmental, Gerry.'

'Maybe. I don't want to be, I'm just trying to tell you why I am motivated to try and change all of this. If I didn't think it was worth it, why would I do it?'

Tanya's response was not what I expected and her words hurt me. She leaned forward. 'For money, Gerry, for money. That's why you do it.'

Well, if she thought that little of me, then she really didn't deserve to hear more. 'OK!' I shouted, getting up from the seat, 'I'm finished with arguing about this. Thanks for dinner, I've got an early start in the morning, goodnight.' And then I added, 'Oh, by the way, remind me to finish telling you what it was like today down on the Exchange.' I was furious. How could anybody think I was doing this just for money? To me the Metal

Exchange was simply a stage to perform on to help change the world into a better place for women. It could have been any market anywhere in the world. If other women before me had not already so bravely fought to change the laws of the land, well then, I would have done the same thing myself! I was quite clear in my mind that what I was doing was absolutely right and there were quite a few men who agreed with me too!

On my way to work the following morning, I thought about the previous night's conversation with Tanya. My mind just couldn't let it go and I continued to rehearse my arguments for a fairer world so that when we came to do battle again, I would have even more reasons to convince her that my views were justified. I mean, if I couldn't convince her, what chance did I have of convincing the men I worked with in the City?

I relaxed my walk. I heard the voices of Americans speaking behind me as I queued to get into Sylvio's sandwich bar. Peering through a steamed up window, I wondered why the United States was so much more advanced in women's rights. Women over there were free, encouraged to be independent and have careers, and they were rich to boot – or so it seemed to me. Was it because it was four hundred years ago that women pioneers on the Mayflower were given the equal opportunity to start afresh in a new land? And why were American men so much more comfortable with women's rights and equalities than British, European or Eastern men?

'Gerry, egg on toast, coffee? Come on, I'm not coming round. You want it to get cold eh?' grinned Sylvio.

I smiled, 'Sorry of course not.' I reached out to take the plate from him, 'Thank you.'

Despite the damp conditions, I enjoyed my breakfast and tried not to think of the day ahead. At 8.40, I realised I couldn't sit there any longer. Time to bite the bullet! But the combination of yesterday on the Exchange and the conversation with Tanya had made me feel despondent. Why was I bothering? I told myself I didn't really care any more, because in all of this I had

111

to earn a living, this was my job! I was beginning to feel trapped. I knew I couldn't escape and even if I didn't want to go down to the Exchange today and hear all that booing, I would still be expected to go. I was obligated because I had made such a fuss about equal rights and I could not back down now. Perhaps I would feel it was worth it if I earned more money. Then I was reminded of Tanya's comment last night. She was right, because here I was this early in the day, thinking about money when I was so strongly arguing on matters of principle last night! Come on, get your act together, you're weak, I said to myself as I waved goodbye to the staff behind the counter.

Crossing the road, I felt more determined than ever to make a go of it. Whatever happened I would keep a smile on my face and show that I was just as capable as the others.

'Well, good afternoon, Gerry!' Henry greeted me sarcastically. 'Good of you to come in today!'

I smiled, ignoring his comment. 'Morning Henry.' Start as you mean to go on and don't take anything that happens to you personally, I reminded myself as I grabbed a coffee and sat down to write the morning metals report.

Since I had been working on the Exchange, there had been a change in how I perceived the market. For a start, it now seemed more difficult to form a view as to which way it would move and as a result, I found I was unable to make confident recommendations. When I was working in the office all day, I had the opportunity of listening to a number of views and I was aware of orders coming in as well. I could see what the other markets were doing and how they were reacting to international news as it broke. So although I was at the centre of action when I was working on the Exchange, I realised I had quite a polarised view of what was going on. I couldn't see the wood for the trees. If I continued to work on the floor, how confident would I feel in providing a valued opinion to my clients? Would that opinion be as objective as it had been when I was working in the office?

So that morning I paid particular attention to ensure that my reports made sense and that my clients did not detect any weaknesses as a result of the time I spent away from the office on the Exchange. An hour and a half later I finished and I looked at my recommendations as they whizzed through a line of telexes to our customers around the world.

'Ready for today?' James shouted across the desk at me as I looked up and smiled.

'Yes, of course, certainly for the morning.'

'No, Gerry, that's not on,' he said, smiling and shaking his head at me 'Look, either you're learning to become a trader or you're not! So all day is what you have to do, do I make myself clear? And don't forget, even then you've got six months on the Exchange floor to complete before you can sit in the Ring. So you'd better remember that!'

'Yes, that's fine, James, but do I have to continually put up with their booing and hissing? It makes it very difficult.'

He appeared to be thinking for a moment. 'Well, I don't think you have to worry about that, I'm sure it will be different today!' He patted me on the shoulder, trying to reassure me.

We left for the market at the usual time and, after stopping at the pub first, we arrived, having missed the Lead Ring but just in time for zinc. 'You can clerk all the rings, Gerry – that way you'll get used to it quicker,' James had said as we entered the market. I had agreed to the suggestion nervously and welcomed the opportunity to look up at him instead of the hundred or so faces now surrounding me. But I was determined to keep a smile on my face.

As the Ring opened, Trevor turned towards me to whisper in my ear. I bent down towards him. 'Have I got any orders from the office?'

'No, are you expecting some?'

'Yes, Alan's long of cash and he needs to sell it or roll it over.'

'OK,' I said. 'I'll check with the office.'

'Yes, ask David.'

At first I wonder whether he means I should check now or

later - but I can't interrupt him as he has started trading with a dealer sitting opposite. I decide not to speak to the office on the phone but stay behind Trevor so that I can listen to him trading and record the details. But it's noisy and I've got myself into a muddle. Then thankfully the bell rings, announcing the end of trading. This should give me a chance to catch up! Then I realise that I haven't spoken to the office either. I must remember to do so before the next Zinc Ring.

'Trevor,' I ask, 'who was that you traded with just then?'

Trevor brushes past me, waving his hand in the air as he walks towards the office phone booth to report his execution to David. Feeling confused as to what I should be doing, I look around for advice from James but he's busy and again I feel that everyone is watching me.

I search the market for the dealer Trevor has traded with and spot him across the other side of the Ring talking to his young clerk. Most of the clerks are standing behind their dealers now as the Copper Ring has started, but I am rather foolishly still trying to check the zinc deal. Of course I should go back to James so I don't miss any of the trading he does, but if I don't get Trevor's zinc deal checked I know I will forget about it. I hesitate for a second before making my way across the floor to the other side of the Ring, passing several immovable bodies on the way, which means, of course, that I have to squeeze past them. Embarrassed, I hear myself repeating, 'Excuse me, sorry, excuse me, excuse me, sorry.' I can hear myself apologising profusely.

'Sorry for what, love?' one dealer responds as others laugh out loud at my obvious unease. Is he being friendly or nasty? Then I remember my mantra for the day: not to take it personally, even though I need to take it seriously!

Persevering, I finally get to the dealer in question and his clerk. The clerk is bending over, whispering into his ear. I assume that he is giving him an order and I feel awkward interrupting, but I have to. I tap the clerk on the shoulder. Softly as first and then again harder, and then even harder, as I continue to be ignored. 'Excuse me, excuse me.' Worried that I'll be done for grievious bodily harm, I try to get his notice by tapping my jobbing book loudly with my pencil. Are they ignoring me on purpose, and who is laughing? I decide to ignore it all. 'Right, look I'm just checking you bought one hundred tons of zinc at 493? Yes? Thank you.'

At last I am able to tick the trade as checked and walk back to James sitting in the Ring. Squeezing through the traders and clerks, I feel a firm hand on my shoulder and turn to see the clerk I had checked the deal with.

'Ere, you just tried to check a deal with me and I don't agree it, you must have got it wrong, it wasn't me.'

'OK,' I say, trying to recall the person with whom I saw Trevor trade. 'I'll check with my dealer and come back to you, but you are RCW, aren't you?'

'Yea, but we didn't buy any zinc from you!'

'Well, did you buy zinc from anyone else?'

'Yes, everyone. We were big buyers but we didn't buy from you.'

By now the Copper Ring had come to a close and I had missed all of James's trades! Looking across the Ring, I could see he was not at all happy with me and not only that, by now there were about six traders listening to my apparent mistake. I tried to keep my cool and even had the feeling that I might have been set up. I wanted the clerk to go away and I didn't feel it was my place to argue with him any longer, especially as the surrounding audience seemed to be getting larger!

'Look,' I say again, 'I'll have to get back to you.'

'No you won't, cos I'm not accepting the trade. It didn't happen, all right?' he shouts. turning on his feet and disappearing into the crowd. I blush and walk back to James as fast as possible. Fancy getting it wrong and everyone knowing it!

Now, back in the relative safety of our phone booth, I feel secure standing behind Trevor as he is on the phone to the office. James makes his way out of the Ring, looking at me with raised eyebrows. 'Trevor?' I tap him on the shoulder as he puts the phone down. 'I need to check if you bought one hundred tons from RCW at 493?'

'You tell me, you're supposed to be clerking for me!'

'Well, I thought you did and I went to agree it, and they don't agree the deal.'

Trevor looks at me for a moment and I sense something might be wrong. 'Well you see, Gerry, you are so confused you really don't know what you're doing, do you? I don't think you should be working down here.' I can here his voice getting louder. Is he saying this for my benefit or for someone else's? I wonder. 'I didn't buy the zinc, Gerry, I sold it!'

'Yes, of course, that's right I meant sold, Trevor, that's what I checked with them and they said they didn't buy any from you!'

'Did they, indeed?' He spins around on his heels and makes off in the direction of the clerk.

I followed as quickly as possible, not understanding how Trevor managed to get through the crowds without the struggle I had just encountered. I got there just in time to hear the clerk say, 'Sure, Trevor. No problem at all. Yes, we agree that, don't know what the girl is on about.'

Trevor turned to me, thrusting his hand up and down. 'It shouldn't be like this, you don't know the difference between buying and selling, Gerry, it's hopeless!' And he stormed off, leaving me once again in the middle of a large audience.

As I made my way back to the booth I thought it was difficult not to take this personally. Why had the clerk lied and why had Trevor helped make such an idiot out of me? Anyone, I thought, can make a mistake, after all that is why I am learning!

James, always so sensitive to my feelings, came over to me. 'Don't pay any attention to them.'

Now I could feel tears welling up. Oh Christ, I thought, I'm not going to start crying am I? They'd love that. I sort of wave at James because I can't speak to him as I fight back days of built-up emotion. I so wanted this day to be better than yesterday and it's not even the free-for-all of kerb yet!

The tears begin to flow freely, despite my attempts to hold them back, and I'm going to be forced to leave the Exchange floor in the middle of trading! Then I catch two very senior brokers, probably committee members, watching me. It's no good, I'll have to leave because I have no handkerchief to wipe my tears with. I will have to leave the Exchange because I doubt whether there are any tissues in the toilet either!

Composing myself in the foyer, I hear voices getting louder as the large wooden door starts to open. I really don't want anyone to come out and see me, so I make my way over to the winding staircase in the corner. I've never been down there to the men's toilets. I sniff loudly as two senior brokers emerge into the foyer, forcing me to duck down so they can't see me. How ridiculous it would be if they caught me cowering below the stairs! I can't help but see the funny side of things as I watch them head straight for me, leaving me no option but to creep further down the stairs and hide.

I find myself in the men's toilets. It's damp and dark and I can't see anything, but I can hear the men speaking. 'Oh, she won't last long, it can't be very pleasant for her. Shame – pretty little thing!' I hear them talking about me as I search for tissues, but of course there are none. Then I hear the kerb bell go and realise that other traders will probable come down the stairs before lunch, so I've got to get out of here!

Wiping my face on my sleeve and hoping my mascara hasn't run, I creep up the stairs but realise it's too late when I hear more voices and laughter as the foyer fills up. Hesitating a second, I plan my response should I be caught.

'Ere, what are you doing down there? Ha ha, you been cleaning the toilets out?'

A few dealers turned round to see me in the corner of the room I clearly should not be in! Ha ha ha! I laughed with them, trying to think of a witty response. Ha ha ha! 'Yes, big deal, ha ha ha,' I said, walking into the middle of the foyer and retrieving my coat. 'Right, well I'm off now.' Ha ha ha.

A few minutes later, I felt much better as I stood on the kerb in Whittington Avenue, taking a deep breath of fresh air. As it started to rain, I made my way back to the office as fast as possible, as I was desperate to go to the loo! As expected, my mascara had run down my face. I hoped no one had seen me. Then I remembered that it had been raining on the way back. No one would have to know that I had been so upset. I cleaned my face the best I could, not bothering to apply more make-up. Feeling hungry, I then crossed the road to the café for a toasted cheese.

Could I get through another afternoon session on the Metal Exchange? James had said that I had to do a full day, but did I really?

'Ello, dwarling, ow are you today?' The café manager was always able to cheer me up. He was so carefree and polite, yet those supposedly educated traders were so rude. What a contrast!

'I'm fine thank you,' I lied as best I could.

'Is it the usual then dwarling?'

'Yes please.'

'OK, luvvy, be with you in a moment.'

I relaxed and thought of myself cowering under the windy stairs. Still, I'd learned something new today: not to take myself so seriously. The funniest things can happen at the most serious of moments!

I didn't take long over lunch because the café was far too damp and cold. Walking back into the office, I noticed David was sitting at his desk. He looked up from his newspaper and scowled. 'Hi David, on your own?' I said.

'Mmmm.' He didn't appear to be in a good mood, but then he surprised me. 'Well, how was it today?' he asked, raising his head. 'Any better?'

I could sense he was missing me and he didn't like me being out of the office and away from his control.

'It was OK, thanks,' I lied. There was no benefit in going into detail with him.

'Well why don't you come straight back to the office when

you've finished? Why do you always go off?' he demanded to know, raising his arm towards the door. 'It's enough *they* do. You should come straight back to the office.'

'Well I've got to get something to eat, David, and then I do come straight back.'

'Mmm, but how long does it take you? You always take your time.' I can't quite believe David is getting so angry with me. What right has he got to say these things, especially when he doesn't even know what I have just had to go through on the morning market! He wouldn't dare speak to the others like that. Still, if he was going to get angry with me, then I would get angry with him.

'Well, David, for heaven's sake, it's only 2.15, I didn't leave until 1.30 and it takes fifteen minutes to walk back to Mark Lane. The market doesn't open for another hour, so what's your problem?'

David stood up and thumped the desk. 'The problem is that every day I'm the only one left in the office. When do *I* get a chance to get out?'

'Well look, you can go now, David. I'll cover for you, but remember I have to leave for the market at about ten past three.'

He stood up and attempted to smile. 'OK, I won't be long,' he muttered, grabbing his coat and black trilby.

Looking around the trading room, I realised I was the only one in. I suppose I'd better get used to this.

Half an hour later, Henry came into the office, just, as I was getting ready to leave. 'Ah Gerry how's it going then?'

'Oh, fine thanks, Henry, I've got a lot to learn but the boys are all really helpful,' I lied again.

He smiled. 'Good, so long as you're enjoying it, that's the main thing!' He puffed on his pipe, satisfied with my reply. There was no point in telling him anything different. I'd learned over the years to play my cards close to my chest and if I wanted to stay on the Exchange I would have to show that I didn't rely on his help, that I was perfectly capable of being independent! The last thing I wanted was for Henry to see that I couldn't cope. 'Is it raining still?' he asked as I reached for my coat.

'Yes, It's going to be miserable all day I think.'

I hurried out of the office with only ten minutes to get to the Exchange before the afternoon session started. I ran most of the way through the pouring rain and so by the time I arrived, I was soaked through and looking a mess. I didn't care because I assumed the afternoon session would probably be every bit as bad as the morning's!

Shaking my jacket off in the foyer, I opened the Exchange doors. It seemed warm in there and the atmosphere appeared a lot calmer compared to the hectic morning market. I noticed there were only a few dealers around for the lead and zinc rings. They were leaning back on the benches, messing about with each other. Some were laughing while others where shouting and swearing at each other. Their clerks were casually leaning over their own seats, watching the antics with amusement. When the bell went I looked over to our booth, expecting to see Trevor or Simon on the phone but it was empty. I looked over to our seat in the Ring and there was no sign of Trevor there either! So no one was back from lunch yet except me, and I could hear our phone ringing. I ran over to answer it but it stopped just as I got there. I heard a loud roar go up in the Ring and, presuming it was directed at me, ignored it. But nothing could have prepared me for what was about to happen next!

Our phone rang again and this time I picked it up. It was David back in the office. 'Hello, Gerry, New York wants to do some carries in copper, can you take these orders down?'

'Yes, sure, right I'm ready, fire away.'

As I wrote I could hear traders still jeering in the background and I hoped that David couldn't hear them too. 'What's that noise in the background?'

'Nothing, don't worry about it,' I replied impatiently.

'OK give me Trevor now, I've got some orders for him.'

I looked around but there was no sign of him. 'Trevor's not here at the moment, you can give me the orders if you like.' As I took the orders down with the phone stuck between my head and shoulder, the other phone started to ring. Answering it, I'm surprised to find out that it's our New York office phoning direct to the floor.

'Hi it's John, I wanna listen to the copper market.'

'OK, hang on a moment.' I drop the phone so it's just dangling from the shelf and look around for James or Trevor. I breathe a sigh of relief when I see them walking into the Exchange. I wave across to them as a few nearby drunk traders laugh. I laugh too and they laugh back with me.

'James, quick, it's New York for you and Trevor, here's an order on zinc from David.'

The bell goes and the Ring begins to fill up. Everyone seems in a much better mood this afternoon and I feel a lot more relaxed. Dare I say it, I am almost beginning to enjoy it! Of course I would much prefer to stay within the security of the telephone booth on the phone to the office but I know I must stand at the edge of the Ring and clerk for Trevor. This afternoon I will pay attention and be alert because I don't need to make another mistake today. I listen intently to what's going on in the Ring and I am pleased that I am picking up more of the deals than yesterday.

Now the Copper Ring has started and the dealers have changed. I know it's going to be busy because New York has given us a lot of orders and some carries to do as well.

Carries are usually done during the first three minutes of the Ring but James doesn't seem to be doing any! I lean over to him. 'Don't forget New York's carries,' I whisper into his ear.

'Tell them they're all done at 15.75 for the period and tell them I'll give them the basis price later.' I notice James likes to book out nearly everything after lunch and I also remember that our forward position in copper has grown significantly since he started.

James was, of course, the best dealer in town and on average he was making £20 000 to £30 000 a year on the forward book alone. He seemed to instinctively know when it was right to book out business and when it was right to trade it on the market.

As I watched him I hoped that one day I would have the skill and earn the respect that he had. Other dealers watched when I spoke with him and I knew it would not be doing me any harm for them to think that I was being personally trained by him!

Across the Ring one of the lads smiled at me, or was he smiling past me? I ignored him at first, looking away and then looking back to see if he smiled again. He did and then he winked as well. I remembered that he was a silver dealer although he was dressed more as a clerk and had, I thought, very greasy hair. I ignored him but then considered it wasn't right not to make friends and he seemed quite friendly. So I went to the other side to check a deal and as I passed, he grabbed my elbow. 'I'm Andy, you're Gerry,' he smiled at me, still holding on to my arm.

'That's very observant of you, Andy,' I responded, 'but if you don't mind I'm in the middle of checking a deal.' I tried to pull my arm free but with some difficulty.

Another dealer said, 'Oh come on, Randy, let her go! Ha ha ha!'

I managed to pull away and walked off as fast as I could. And then it happened. I felt my feet slip from under me as I crashed to the floor.

'Ha ha ha ha! Now look what you've gone and done to her, you'd better give her a hand! Ha ha ha!'

I looked up to see about three men offering their hands to me. I chose the nearest and was back up on my feet. I wiped down the back of my skirt.

'You don't want to wear high heels down here, love. Can't you see this is no place for a lady? Look at the floor, it's so polished and it gets rough down here with everyone running about and people won't be bothered to check to see if you're all right or whether it's a lady or a man they are bumping into!'

'Ha ha ha ha!'

'You could do yourself a lot of damage down here with us.'

'Ha ha ha!'

'At the very least you'll be covered in bumps and bruises!'

How right he was! Even after the first day, I had been hit in places that I didn't know could hurt so much. Well, I had been floored but I could still speak up for myself. 'I don't expect any special treatment but I do expect some respect.' I could feel the blood flowing to my head from embarrassment, or was it anger? When that happened there was little I could do about it except vent my feelings. I heard myself rant and witnessed their shocked faces, their mouths open and their eyes fixed in astonishment upon me. 'Well I'm not going anywhere until I've sat in that Ring and you'd better get used to it because if it's not me, then it will be someone even cleverer who will outwit the lot of you and then you'll bloody have something to worry about.'

'Oh look, the lady's upset! Oh dear, what a shame!' one of the traders said as he beckoned to the others to leave me alone.

I looked at the clock. I'd only got half an hour to go and I was not going to be beaten by this. At that moment a smart and jovial senior committee member approached me. 'Are you all right, my dear?' he asked, stretching his arm out towards me.

'Yes, Sir, thank you, I'm fine.'

'Good. Now don't you let them get you down, Geraldine, you're doing just fine.'

I immediately felt better and, turning towards the Ring, felt brave enough to resume clerking. As I started to jot deals down, I was aware that he was still behind me. The next thing I knew, he had slapped my bottom! Shocked, I turned around to see him winking and laughing at the traders opposite. It's not that he had particularly hurt me, but it was the familiarity I didn't like. What if every man in the room slapped my bottom as they passed me by? I would be very sore indeed. Anyway it made me feel cheap, as though I was his personal piece of property. Where was the respect from these people towards me?

I looked around the room and felt the malevolence everywhere, even over the Exchange walls! Male eyes were peering down at me from beneath their top hats just like vultures eyeing their prey! I looked at the committee member who had slapped me. He was an important person, one of a handful who would decide whether I could deal in the Ring. But I wasn't going to let him get away with slapping my bottom as he passed by. Surely, I thought, it was enough that I had a difficult job to learn, let alone have to teach some manners to these overgrown schoolboys. I hated them all except James. He was a man I could trust, a man I could believe in. A man who liked me, not because I was a woman, but because he thought I was brave, he loved my courage, even though he didn't say so. Yes, there were some men I admired and who I felt safe with – and then there were the others. The others who would, whenever they could, make my life a nightmare. Men who just couldn't be trusted to keep their promises!

Eventually the day was over and I was making my way back to the office – exhausted, quite emotional and with another lesson learned. It was all very well thinking I was doing well playing their game, but now I realised I would have to teach them some new rules if I was going to make them respect me or any other woman who came down on the floor to trade.

The next few days progressed without incident as the lads left me alone to clerk and learn how to do tic-tac. Tic-tac is a sign language we use to relay market prices back to the clerk in our phone booth, rather like the one used at racecourses. It involved shaking the correct number of fingers to reflect the price trading. If the fingers were facing up then that was a bid, and if they were facing down that was an offer. Somewhere in the middle meant the price was trading. Only the last part of the price was tic-tacked so us clerks needed to pay very close attention to the direction of the market so as to avoid making costly mistakes in erratic markets.

As a clerk, my day on the Metal Exchange would start with checking deals that had been done in the office during the early morning. Once the rings opened I would stand behind the seated dealer and record all his trades whilst giving prices back through tic-tac. When the market got really busy I didn't have time to do tic-tac as I was so busy trying to keep up with all the trades. On these occasions the clerk in the phone booth would have no option but to stretch the phone as far as he could to enable him to get closer to the Ring so he could hear what was going on. After the Ring closed I would go round to the other dealers and agree the trades with them.

As I was the only one wearing a skirt and the floor of the Exchange was quite hectic, every morning I would consider carefully what I should wear. I felt it was about striking a right balance and being able to do my job without embarrassing myself. It was not about looking attractive for the men. In any case, my day was spent rushing backwards and forwards in all types of weather.

On the Exchange the bell rang every five minutes. Market orders had to be executed quickly and that often meant running towards the clerk at breakneck speed and then running back to the dealer again whilst remembering the order accurately. So wearing a longish skirt was sensible. The Exchange floor was always crowded and sometimes it felt as though the great heaving mass of bodies could never be moved from out of my way before the bell went and I would have to return back to the dealer without having checked all the previous rings deals!

Gradually, as time went on, life got easier and I understood more of what was going on. Dealers and clerks either accepted me or ignored me. James was always helpful, teaching me the ways of the market, telling me who I could trust and who I couldn't. I watched him trade, hoping to learn his secrets and noticed he used to book a lot of carries out. One day I asked him why he didn't trade them on the Exchange. 'Look, Gerry, there's not a decent market price for this carry so I'll just take it on our books and give them a suitable rate.' Sometimes this worked in our favour but on other occasions we lost money. 'Horses for courses,' he called it and so long as the market stayed in a contango, meaning the forward price was always more than the cash price, then that was OK. But if cash went to a premium, which it sometimes did, then large losses would occur. I was never worried when he purchased metal and then sold it later in a contango market, because the rate he booked it out would normally cover the costs and so the company would be covered. But sometimes he would do level spreads across the forward book and this would involve him putting on a short spread at sometime in the future, perhaps as much as six months in advance.

I noticed that trade houses, those representing producers, liked to do these deals and because they were so far in the future and they could make anything happen, I didn't trust them. I wasn't sure that I agreed with the way we were valuing the forward card either, because forward losses would not show up against current profits. I spoke to James about my concerns, wanting to learn all the secrets he could teach me, but he waved his hands about as if he was floundering in a sea of stupidity. 'Ah, don't worry about it, it will all come out in the wash, Gerry!' he would say.

Often if the market was quiet I would look up into the public gallery while waiting for James to trade. I wondered whose clients they were and on some very crowded days in the gallery I couldn't help but smile at the number of men looking down and pointing at me because I was such a rare sight!

It was on one of these days, quite to my surprise, that I saw a few Chinese men all huddled together in a group. They looked unusual in their grey mandarin suits with buttoned up fronts and no collars. The more senior ones had grey caps on. There was no doubt they were Communists. I found them fascinating and I noticed one of them looked about a hundred years old, while some of the others were much younger. They were standing with their broker and seemed very interested in the copper market. 'That's a lucky broker,' I said to James, 'to have such important customers'

He looked up at them. 'Yea, we'll never get clients like them, Gerry. They always like to trade with the big producers.' I asked James why the Chinese believed that they could get the best price by trading through a producer. After all, this was a free market; surely we could all compete for the business this client had to give! 'They just do, Gerry,' he replied in a rather bored tone.

Most floor dealers seemed uninterested in attracting business and the job of keeping customers happy; that was the job of the office trader. A floor dealer was simply in the business of executing the order as quickly as possible. That's what David had meant when he said he preferred to be in the office. It was the job of the office trader to speak to customers and get new business in. Yes, the office and the Exchange were worlds apart and very different jobs altogether. But I wanted to be the best, or at least good in all areas of the business, and even though I had been working on the Exchange for six months I had missed talking to the clients. Who said you couldn't do both jobs? So from now on I would talk to our customers from the Exchange floor as well as sending them my report. After all, customers make orders and orders make money!

Watching the Chinese delegates, I notice one of the committee members standing with them in the gallery. He sees me looking and waves before leaving the balcony. I choose to ignore him while I'm clerking for James. A few minutes later, he is standing behind me, apparently watching the dealing before whispering in my ear, 'I must say, you look very pretty today, my dear.' As usual, I feel his hand patting my bottom. I push it away, still smiling at him. 'Thank you!' I am determined to be polite, especially with such important guests in the gallery, but once again out of the corner of my eye I catch him smiling to the Ring dealers across the room. I wonder then whether, before he approached me, he said to them, 'Watch this!' For all I know, the Chinese delegation has seen as well!

It was no good, I would have to do something about it. Anyway, I thought the Chinese looked out of place, communists in a democratic, capitalist environment! But however strange they appeared, I realised that we traders must have looked even stranger to them – a messy unruly crowd, shouting and screaming in apparent chaos. They must have wondered how we were able to hear each other. I had noticed that when I was tic-tacking, one of the younger members of the delegation had been watching me intently. I wondered at their philosophy. How could they believe communism was better than democracy, better than capitalism, when they were obliged to visit a capitalist free market to purchase their metals! I mean, how did they square up the inability of a communist regime to provide for its people's requirements when they needed us to do it for them? If communism was better – and surely they must think so – why were they here? Weren't they losing face just a little, standing here in the middle of the City of London, ready to do business with us capitalists? And what on earth did they think of the only woman standing on the Exchange? I really hope they hadn't seen the committee member slapping my bottom as he passed!

After the kerb, I made my way out into the foyer and could hear the delegation coming down the stairs. I hung around, hoping for a closer look and was not disappointed. To my surprise, they seemed a gentle race and I did not feel afraid of them; in fact I rather liked them. This must have showed on my face because I received a 'get lost' look from their broker, but not before one of the elderly Chinese men had pointed at me as he walked towards me, smiling. There were now several Chinese surrounding a red-faced broker who was explaining my presence in broken English

'Em... em... ah yes, this is the first woman to be allowed to work on the Exchange. She is... em... em... a junior clerk working for... em... and... em... company and... em... she hasn't been here very long and... em... we are all looking after her down here.' Then, looking at me and nodding his head up and down, he smiled, 'Aren't we, Geraldine?'

'Yes,' I smiled and held my hand out to the eldest member of the delegation. 'I'm so happy to meet you and welcome to London.' He took my hand and I noticed how rough his were.

He smiled. 'Thank you very much for your welcome.'

I smiled back and waved to them as I left the foyer. Standing outside the Exchange, I took a deep breath, I felt so proud to have met them. What an experience, I thought, to be working in the heart of London surrounded by typically British historic monuments and at the same time meet this ancient race of people from the other side of the world. Although I had met Chinese people before (one of my friends at school had been Chinese), I could see these Chinese men were different because they were not westernised. They were, as you would expect, very proud of their culture and not at all envious of ours, which I had expected them to be!

Walking back to the office, I thought that, despite the grey-uniformed appearance of each individual, they were as a group very powerful, and although each man appeared humble, there was an aura of superiority surrounding the delegation that was felt by any broker who spent time talking to them. Nearly a quarter of the world's population was Chinese and that meant that if China was in the market to purchase metal, the orders would be big – very big! I also wondered about how they treated women in China and whether women had equal status or were, as in so many countries, second-class citizens. I had heard about the unsustainable population increases and the rumoured steps that China was taking to reduce the births of little girls.

After arriving back in the office, I sat down to eat my lunch and thought about our customers. I was sure I could be of more help to them and I knew how important it was to make the business grow. Somehow I wanted to mix up my job a bit. I wanted to do client liaison work, writing my reports and giving my recommendations, as well as learning to trade on the floor. In short, I wanted it all!

As David was in the office, I spoke to him about it. 'It would be good, don't you think, David, if we could get the Chinese Government as a client?'

He laughed. 'Not likely!'

'Yes, James agrees with you,' I said.

'Well, he would know, wouldn't he?' David looked at me with one eyebrow raised.

'So how is business today?' I asked.

He tutted and shuffled a few papers in front of him 'Not so good, it could be better.'

'Is that the German business you're talking about?'

'Yes, I think they're putting their business elsewhere.'

'Mmmm.' I thought for a moment before offering up a sensible solution. 'Well, why don't we lower our commission rates? Maybe they're a bit high?'

'A quarter in and quarter out is not high,' he snarled back at me.

'No,' I said, 'not generally but for carries it *is* quite expensive. Perhaps you should think about lowering them a little, David?'

'Why? What do you know about it? Do you know what other brokers charge, then?' he glared at me, waiting for an answer.

'Of course I don't, but you have to think they may be charging less than us!'

He went quiet and looked at the report in his hand. 'Mmmm, it's a possibility, I suppose, I'll speak to Henry and see what he says about it.'

I was pleased, especially if the commission rates dropped because that would give me a better chance of getting some really big business in! I was having a very good day and at last, I felt that my horizons were broadening. That pleased me because now I had more than one objective to achieve. If David could argue successfully then Henry would agree to lowering the commission rates and this would naturally increase the brokerage. James might also benefit because he would be able to offset his forward copper position without losing money. I was excited at the prospects.

'David,' I said, 'I think I'll send my report to the Chinese. I wonder what their telex number is? I'll ring the embassy, I think.'

David looked up absently. 'Good luck.' He was smiling but I had the feeling that he was wondering why I was not concentrating on my job as a floor clerk.

The next morning James did not seem to be his usual cheerful self. In fact he was miserable, and try as I might I could not cheer him up. Even when we went for our beer before the market opened, he was still as downcast. As we stood by the bar and he lit my cigarette, I noticed that his shirt collar was dirty. 'James, what's wrong with you today?' I asked him.

'Nothing, nothing at all.' He took a deep drag on his cigarette and picked up his beer, gulping it down as if it was his last drink.

'Why won't you tell me?'

'It's nothing, really, Gerry, it's—' He paused mid-sentence. 'It's just Henry. he's always on my back about the position. It bloody gets on my nerves that he doesn't like me to have more than five hundred tons of copper overnight. At my last company I could have thousands of tonnes open, and I used to make loads of money. I mean. how does he expect me to make any money when I can't carry a bloody position overnight?' He grimaced and took another long drag of his cigarette before furiously stubbing it out. 'I'm not used to being restricted in this way. I mean, either he trusts me or he doesn't!'

'Of course he trusts you James,' I assured him, 'come on, cheer up, it's not so bad'

'Huh, that's what you think! I'm in this bloody mess because of him so he'd better not bloody start when the end of the month comes.'

I didn't know what he was talking about but I could see he was upset. Senior traders like James were often under pressure. Still, I reckoned that was why they got paid so well. I resolved to cheer James up as much as possible during the day.

As I clerked for him later, I noticed a dealer across the room winking at me. I ignored him as best I could but during one of my rounds to check a deal, he introduced himself. 'Hi, I'm Gary, do you fancy a drink at lunchtime?' I had been aware that some of the traders had been wondering whether I had a boyfriend or whether I was free to go out with them. For the most part, I ignored them. To me they were just colleagues and I wanted to be their equal. Of course I had heard rumours from Sasha that women used their sexuality to earn financial favours from men.

She'd said to me one day, 'You have to realise, Gerry, that any woman in the city who has a position of power only got it by sleeping with the boss, and that's what you will have to do if you want to get anywhere!' Well, some of the stories might have been true. Sexually predatory men were a problem and I had great difficulty in thwarting unwanted advances, so I knew some of these stories were probably true. Constant refusals could unfortunately lead to a sacking. But just because it had always been the case – 'nature's way', as some said – I didn't feel it was right. Why should young women continue to be thought of as if they had nothing better to do than to serve men's pleasure? I was determined to change these assumptions about the relationship between men and women. I wanted men to respect my mind, not my body. All these thoughts went through my head as I looked at my new admirer across the Ring.

I didn't fancy him in the least, but I thought I should behave in a reasonable manner. After all, I liked to have a drink with James, and he was just a friend, so there was no reason why I shouldn't have a drink with Gary. If it had been an evening drink I would not have gone but at lunchtime, what harm could it do? Besides, I needed friends on the Exchange so long as I could trust him! I smiled at him. 'Yes, I'd like to, what time and where?'

'Straight after kerb if you like, I'll meet you outside the Exchange and we'll take it from there,' he smiled and looked at the dealer standing next to him.

'OK, I'll meet you outside then,' I replied.

I walked back to where James was seated in the Ring, not knowing whether I had done the right thing in agreeing to the drink. James had his head in his hands and was rubbing his forehead fiercely.

'Are you OK, James?'

'No, I'm not. I'm going home. Tell Simon I need him to fill in for me, will you?'

I looked around for Simon and spotted him speaking with another dealer. I made my way over and patted him on the shoulder 'Simon, James is not well, can you fill in for him? He wants to go home.'

Simon turned round and looked at James, half-slumped in the Ring, and raised his eyebrows 'What's wrong with him?'

'He doesn't feel good.'

'I bet he bloody doesn't! OK, I'll be over in a second.'

I went back to James, not feeling happy about what Simon had said. James had always been good to me and I liked him. Simon thought he should be the head trader and now James was playing straight into his hands. I leaned over the trading bench to whisper in James's ear: 'Simon's on his way over.'

'OK, check to see whether there are any orders from the office, will you?'

His face was grey. He must be coming down with the flu, I thought, or perhaps it was just a bad hangover. Just then I felt a hand on my bottom and turned round to see the usual grinning committee member smiling at me. 'And how are you today, young lady?' he said, giving me a broad smile. His voice was so loud that I knew everyone would hear. I was annoyed at his intrusion and, having straightened up rather fast, I'd made myself dizzy. He moved his hand away from me and then slapped by bottom rather obviously. It hurt and I was furious. Without thinking of what the consequences might be, I slapped him back very loudly on his face. It was a surprising success, considering his height! Immediately the market was engulfed in an unprecedented silence as all eyes turned on me.

Tic-toc, tic-toc, I could hear the clock ticking. Tic-toc tic-toc. I bit my bottom lip and turned away from my victim, facing the Ring. Thankfully the silence was broken as the bell rang again and trading commenced. James said nothing; I don't think he had even noticed. I looked at the committee member, who was not sure what to do and was still standing next to me as if expecting an apology.

'Don't ever do that again,' I hissed. 'Don't slap or pinch my bottom, do you hear me?'

'Ha ha ha, it's just a bit of fun! You shouldn't take things so seriously, my dear.' He patted me on the shoulder gently. I was sure I had hurt him but when would he stop laughing? And how loud it was! 'Ha ha ha, you shouldn't take life so seriously, my dear,' he repeated. 'I didn't mean any harm, I was just being friendly because I think you're a very pretty girl!'

I ignored his comments. Why wouldn't he just go away and let me get on with clerking? He must be waiting for me to answer him, I thought. 'Well, don't touch me again. I think you should apologise to me and then I'll say no more about it.'

He straightened his back and I could see he was getting annoyed. 'Now look here, young lady, if you can't take the heat, you should get out of the kitchen!'

'I can take the heat and I'm staying in the kitchen, so please, just let me get on with my job, will you?'

He walked away and I turned round to see James emerging slowly from out of the Ring. He was smiling.

'See what I have to do to cheer you up?' I grinned.

'Cor blimey, yeah, you certainly did that but what's he going to do about it now?'

'Nothing, I hope.'

'You know he's one of the most important men on the committee? I don't fancy your chances of trading in the Ring if he's on the interviewing panel next week!'

Oh God, I thought, what have I done? I felt the blood drain from my face. I had completely forgotten about the interview. How fast the last six months had gone!

Simon was making his way over to the Ring and took James's place as I went over to the telephone booth to speak to David. 'I shan't be coming back to the office this lunchtime, David, as I'm going out for a drink' It was silent on the other end of the phone. 'David, are you there?'

'No, Gerry!' he screamed down the phone. 'No, you come back to the office now, I don't want you going out for a drink with those men. You come straight back to the office!'

'Don't tell me what to do!'

But he continued, 'Look, you are not a trader, you come back to the office now!'

'David, I spend practically every lunchtime in the office. If I'm going to become a trader on the Exchange, I have to get to know the other traders, don't I?'

David slammed the phone down. There was no way I was going to let Gary down, so David and anyone else, for that matter, had better get used to it.

Later I met Gary out on the kerb. It felt a bit like being back at school, all his mates watching and laughing. I asked him, 'Where are we going?'

His soulful brown eyes looked into mine. 'I know a nice little place where we can have a drink and sit outside by a fountain.'

'Oh, that sounds lovely, is that where all the traders usually go then?' I asked, thinking: I hope it's not too cold.

'No, not at all, we don't want to go where everyone can see us, do we?' he said, taking my arm as we walked down the street.

'Why not?' I said, removing my arm.

'Well it's just nice, the two of us, and you can tell me all about yourself and we won't get interrupted.'

Naive as it now sounds, I honestly hoped he didn't think I fancied him.

The lunchtime dragged as we smoked half a packet of cigarettes and both had a couple of lagers. I could see he was married and I wondered why he was bothering with me. Perhaps he had been sent out by others to scout the landscape, so to speak! In fact as I sat with him and mulled over the morning's events, I felt like some woman pioneer, rather like a pilgrim on the Mayflower heading out for the new land.

Watching the clock and only half-listening to Gary, I couldn't help but think about what a difficult time us women have had through the ages. So misunderstood. We have always had to be on the look-out. And some men just wouldn't take no for an answer. I replied to Gary's questions as little as possible and became aware of just how boring I must have sounded. But it was intentional and I had run out of questions to ask about the history of the Exchange. Besides, it quickly became obvious to me that I knew more than he did. I wondered whether single women on the Mayflower had found it difficult being on board the ship with men they didn't know. How would they have fought off unwanted advances whilst at the same time remaining one of the flock? I bet they didn't have to slap faces to get respect!

Garry was still talking, although by now it was more of a slurred mumble! I lit another cigarette. I was bored and cold. I interrupted him. 'Shall we go in? It's a little chilly.'

'No, we can't, they don't allow women in there.'

'But there must be women working behind the bar.'

'Yes, but they're not allowed to have a drink, it's a man's club.'

'Well, I don't want to be drinking outside, so let's go.'

I was angry again. As we walked back, Gary asked me if I would like to see him that evening 'We can go for a drink down the Savage if you like?'

'No thank you, Gary, I'm sorry, I don't go out with married men.'

He looked at me. 'It's only a drink,' he said, putting his arm around me.

'I know, but I'd rather not if you don't mind.'

We made our way back to the market and I kept wondering whether there would be any trouble from the committee members whose face I had slapped.

Simon was talking to Trevor and pointedly looked at the clock as I walked into the Exchange with Gary and a few of the other dealers. I felt alone now James had gone home. I didn't like working with Trevor or Simon, who I often found moody and unhelpful, and both of them had made it known that they didn't agree with me being on the Exchange. When they saw me approaching, they dropped their voices but I could still hear Simon say to Trevor, 'Well, there are more deals to come out, Henry will go mad when he sees James's position!' Oh dear, what were they talking about? I decided to keep my head down; after all, I had caused quite enough trouble for one day!

But just as I was beginning to feel relaxed, I saw the committee member whose face I had slapped speaking with another committee member and pointing rather obviously at me. They looked very serious so I put on a brave smile, just to show there were no hard feelings, and to my surprise, the other one smiled back. If only we could forget what had gone on before! They couldn't help it if they thought that's how you treat women you fancy in the work environment. They probably thought that I liked it! I'd often heard such comments as 'Never mind, she likes it really', or 'Don't pay any attention to what she says, she doesn't know what she's talking about half the time.' Some, I believed, thought my only reason for becoming a dealer was to find a husband or, as I'd heard said, 'get laid'! How crude. But I would always try and have the last word. So I used to go into great detail about how I felt.

Even over lunch I had said to Gary, 'Look, it's quite simple, I just want to be a dealer and have the same rights and freedoms as you. I don't want to have to ask permission before I'm able to do what you do. I want to be able to make suggestions and have opinions that are as valued. I don't want to be thought about as a woman before being accepted as a dealer! I mean, when I look at you I don't see a man and then a dealer, I see you as a dealer and that's it!'

I watched as his eyes glazed over. 'Oh, come on, Gerry, admit it – you're the same as any other woman, you see the man first! Come on, you can admit it to me, you fancy me really, don't you?'

No matter what I said, I wasn't believed. I just couldn't get my point across to any of them. Of course I realised that it sounded as if I was justifying my position the whole time. So I stopped the debate and in the end let them carry on thinking whatever they wanted. Action speaks louder than words anyway! At least I knew James and a few others didn't think like the vast majority, who just couldn't help telling their inane jokes about how stupid women drivers were!

Later that afternoon, David was looking very pleased with himself. 'Guess what, Gerry?'

'What?'

'I've just found the number for the Chinese, I have a contact for you,' he smiled. 'You owe me now, it was very difficult, but I managed to find the name, telephone and telex number!'

'Well that's brilliant, David! I'll call them first thing in the morning to see if they would like to receive our metals report.'

Just as I was leaving for the night, Henry came into the room puffing hard on his pipe. 'So, Gerry, how's it going down on the Exchange?' I immediately thought of the slapped face of the committee member and recalled in horror that I had also slapped his face some months earlier! So I couldn't tell him. Why was I always slapping men's faces? Perhaps it was something I had seen on the television when I was a kid, something that I thought was perfectly acceptable for a woman to do! I resolved there and then not to do it again. Henry was staring at me. 'Well?'

'Well what?'

'How are you getting on down the Exchange. Isn't it time they allowed you into the Ring?'

'Yes soon, next week I have an interview and if it goes well I can do six months as an unauthorised dealer.'

Henry smiled and took his pipe out of his mouth. 'Good, good, very good! Oh, by the way, I see there is an article in Metal Bulletin about you this week. I'm glad they're supportive.'

'Yes, we should be pleased with what they say about us.'

'Us? Not us, Gerry, You.' Henry laughed as he walked out of the trading room.

Two minutes later Simon followed Henry into the boardroom and as I passed, I heard Henry mention James's name. I delayed my steps long enough to hear.

'I've told him I won't stand for it any longer. I'm fed up with these six, eight and twelve-month carries. Why does he keep booking them out and putting them down on our books? Why doesn't he offload them in the market? We've got to find a way of valuing the forwards; it's no good having all these profits sitting on the three-month position when we don't know what our bloody forward position is!' Simon was nodding and looking concerned. I heard a trader coming down the corridor, and quickly resumed my walk towards the door.

It was about 6.30 when I arrived home in Holland Park and Tanya was not in. Perhaps she had gone out for a drink after work. I couldn't remember whether she had mentioned that she would be late that evening. I put the kettle on and ran a warm bath because it was cold in the flat, even though spring was well on its way.

About an hour later I heard her come in just as I was putting a pasta and salad together. 'Ah, good, just in time, have a glass of wine.'

She sat down and asked me how my day had gone. As I told her some of my stories we laughed, but she knew I was worried just the same. 'Don't worry, I'm sure it will be OK,' she said at one of my more serious moments. By now we had been speaking for quite some time and she had gone quiet. Her mind was elsewhere or perhaps she was just tired. I took the dishes out to the kitchen and changed the subject 'That's a new perfume, isn't it?' I asked, handing her a coffee?

'Yes, I thought I would give it a try. I don't usually like cheap perfumes but this smells quite nice, don't you think?'

I sniffed the air. 'Yes, it's OK but I don't think it would suit me. Oh, that reminds me, how was your evening with Mike, you went for a drink didn't you?'

'Yes, we went to the Monkey Puzzle just off Baker street. It was great, he's such as nice guy, we'll probably meet up for a drink towards the end of the week.'

'Oh good, good, I'm glad you had such a nice time. How's work going? You seem a bit preoccupied as if you're worried about something.'

Tanya pulled a face. 'So, so, they're making lots of redundancies, don't know how long I'll last!'

'Hmm, it's a worrying time with so much unemployment at

the moment. Still, I don't think you will have too much trouble finding another a job,' I said, trying to sound confident.

These were difficult times for everyone with the threat of redundancies, high inflation and even higher interest rates. I was worried about my job too, especially if what I had heard last night was right. James losing all that money could affect us all. It seemed to me that now was not the time to ask for more money even if I would soon be sitting in the Ring!

The next day at lunchtime I went to withdraw my week's money from the bank. Twenty-five pounds usually did until Friday. As I was queuing a young man standing behind me leaned forward and tapped me on the shoulder. 'Vud you like to buy a car?'

I gave him a dirty look for touching me but he ignored it and smiled. 'I'm sorry, are you speaking to me?' I said coolly.

'Yes. Vould you like to buy a car? I need to sell it. You see I av to go back to Germany and I don't av the air fare.' I frowned for a moment trying to make my mind up whether he was honest or not. I thought for a second, no harm in looking, 'Yes, OK.'

He smiled. 'Come vith me it's just outside, eer look,' he said, stretching his arm out towards the entrance. I took a look at the queue, decided that I didn't mind losing my place, and followed him out into Mincing Lane. Outside was parked a fantastic looking white BMW with rally stripes painted down each side. 'Wow' I said

'Ya,' he responded, 'it's vonderful – look!' And he opened the door inside. Soft blue upholstery and a thick, fully-fitted blue carpet completed the overall impression of a unique luxury car. But the steering wheel was on the left-hand side.

'Is this OK for this country?' I asked, pointing at the steering wheel.

'Ya, of corz I av just driven it from Germany, but it doezn't matter, you can drive it like dis over eer.' He pointed at the number plate. 'Look at zee very special number plate, it means Munich eighty-five and dis vas BMW's eighty-fifth rally car, it has von many races and in Germany, believe me, diz iz a very very famouz car!'

I had never seen anything so wonderful in my life. This was just what a young dealer like me should be driving. Just wait until they see me driving this car! I thought. That'll put all those silly women driver jokes to rest! Oh yes, I could just see the look on their faces whened I park at the offices in this humdinger of a car! That would shut them up.

He was smiling as if he had read my mind. Clearly he could see that I was impressed, even though I tried not to show it. 'Vould you like to take eet for a drive?' he said, jangling the keys in front of me.

I looked at my watch and realised that I didn't have much time left. 'Oh dear, I'm sorry, I don't have the time. Does it drive OK?' I asked.

'Of corz, I told you, I drove it from Germany all the vay yesterday, eet's fine.'

Well, this must be my lucky day! I needed a new car and, let's face it, I wasn't going to get an opportunity to buy a car like this again. 'OK,' I said 'How much do you want for it then?'

He fiddled around in his leather jacket, searching for papers. Then he stroked his chin with a shaky hand 'Five hundred?'

'Five hundred what?' I asked rather stupidly.

'Engleesh money pounds, ov course!'

I thought for a moment, long enough for him to look a little worried. 'OK, it's a deal, five hundred then, but I haven't got enough cash on me, can we meet tomorrow?'

'No, zorry, I av to be in Germany.'

'OK, come with me. Do you have the logbook and other papers? Has it an MOT?' I asked as we hurried back into the bank.

'Ya, ya, ya, of corz it has everything you need and more.'

I wasn't sure it did but he handed me a black leather wallet full of papers along with the keys.

I felt on top of the world as I opened my hand and looked at the key fob with its BMW disk glinting first this way then the other in the bright sunshine. I stared at it lovingly as we queued

141

for the money. In didn't matter to me that instead of withdrawing £25, I had withdrawn £500 from my savings because I reasoned it was great value. After all, I would be earning much more money as a metal dealer and I was so proud to be the owner of this beautiful car. I smiled as I thought about Tanya's reaction when she saw me arrive home in it. She would be so surprised when I parked outside and I'd be able to sell my other car and put the money back in the bank. So no need to worry about my savings going down.

I gave the German his money and shook his hand. 'Have a good trip back to Germany,' I said.

'Vell it vont be good, vill it? I vill miss da car so much!!'

I pulled a sad face, commiserating with him on his misfortune at having to sell the car to me.

Chapter Five

Chinese Whispers

On the drive home I considered James's position in the trading team and wondered why the other traders didn't seem to get on with him. I knew he was paid a great deal of money but I also knew that Henry had faith in him and was happy with the profits he had been making. James had even had his hair trimmed a bit, although it was never going to be short. I hoped that he would come back to work soon, I didn't want to do my first day in the Ring without his support and besides, I would miss our customary drink before the market started!

My new car tended to kangaroo across roundabouts and the engine sounded very loud. Even the exhaust was making a racket but I enjoyed playing with the electric windows at the traffic lights. Besides, it turned heads and I felt very proud of it.

Pleased as punch, I couldn't help but smile, as I'd known I would, when I parked it in Clarendon Road. The car still sounded embarrassingly loud as my mother appeared at the window, wondering what all the noise was about. I waved to her on my way down the basement steps. I had expected Tanya to be home already but then I remembered she was going for a drink after work again.

The following day I did the shopping and cleaned the flat. But I couldn't wait to test the car out over a long drive. So we drove to Hampton Court. I was very impressed and Tanya liked the comfort as well. 'It makes a very loud noise when we're driving, doesn't it?' she said, looking at me with concern.

'Yes, well, what do you expect?' I responded. 'Don't forget, it *is* a rally car!'

Luckily the music covered up the noise for most of the journey. In the evening we went to our favourite Italian restaurant in Hampton Court. I talked about the new car, the week's trading and the week ahead; she spoke about her new friend Mike and the lovely time they'd had the night before. Just as I was paying the bill, Tanya leaned torwards me. 'I haven't been home for such a long time, it must be well over a year. Can we go soon?'

'Home' was Barrow-in-Furness in Cumbria, about four hundred and fifty miles from London. I smiled. 'Yes, of course, now I've got this new car it'll be a doddle. We can go up on Friday night and stay with Patricia in Harrogate before going onto Barrow for the weekend if you like.'

Tanya nodded enthusiastically. 'That will be great.'

On Sunday I took the newspapers up with me to the Ladbroke Arms to read before going for a walk in Kensington Gardens. I always enjoyed looking at the paintings hanging on the railings of Hyde Park. I thought it must be such fun to paint for a living.

The next morning I noticed how quiet it was when I walked into the office. Henry was not at his desk, so I went across the road to get some cigarettes and a coffee to take away. Today was going to be an important day because I would sit in the Metal Ring as an unauthorised dealer for the first time. James had told me that all new traders start with lead or zinc because they were considered the easiest metals to trade. I had considered carefully what I should wear that day. Most days I wore a longish but modern skirt, usually with a jumper and a large belt over the top. But today I would also wear a jacket. All the dealers wore jackets in the Ring. This emphasis on my dress code was all about how secure it made me feel. Design, colour and material were important only in so much as they represented safety and comfort. I was not a person to attract unwanted comments or attention by what I wore. As I put my jacket on I pretended I was a knight putting on armour. Today

I felt would be an important battle and our side though small must win! '*Nec Temere, Nec Timide,*' I whispered as I dressed and brushed my hair.

Today would be very scary. I had seen what the traders were capable of and I knew that I must keep my dignity, whatever might occur. I looked at myself again in the mirror. 'No slapping faces today, Gerry,' I admonished myself.

What would those dealers be thinking when they saw a woman sitting opposite or next to them? Obviously I looked different, but I wanted my image to be pleasant, not distracting, not threatening. No chance of that, I thought! My hair was very dark and shoulder-length, and it turned under at the ends. It was convenient hair because, by having a parting in the middle, I could swing it either side across my face if I ever felt the need to! And just as I wore my clothes as armour, my hair was designed as a helmet. My make-up was always discreet: a little mascara, a little eyeliner and subdued lipstick. Finally I put on my pearl earrings and treated myself to a dab of Givenchy's latest perfume – called Metal!

I looked at my little gold watch, a twenty-first birthday present from my parents, and thought that it was not really big enough for a Ring dealer. I would have to change it.

I planned to leave the office at 11.30 and not go with James to the pub. If anything went wrong today, I didn't want to be accused of being drunk!

Just as I am leaving the office, I see James approaching. 'Thank God, I thought you weren't coming in today!' I said, relieved at the sight of him.

'Who me? I wouldn't miss this for the world!' he grinned and tapped me on the shoulder. 'Hang on a bit, let me just get my card, and I'll be with you.'

I hopped on one leg then the other, staring at the clock.

Soon we were on our way and as we walked up through Leadenhall Market I could feel the butterflies building in my stomach and my mouth was starting to go dry. 'You're very quiet, Gerry?'

'Hmm. Am I?' I knew he was expecting me to go for a drink with him before the market and I was thinking about how I would say no. But at the last moment, I couldn't say no, so when he pulled open the doors I followed him in. The lager tasted extra good that morning and I gulped it down like James.

'Cheers James!' I raised my glass to him and noticed that he had trimmed his beard and looked very smart indeed. He didn't say anything but I think he was quite proud of me. 'James, I just want to say that I hope one day to be as good a trader as you and thank you for all your help and support.'

'Cheers, Gerry, ha ha ha, and don't worry, you'll be fine, you might even surprise yourself!'

I lit another cigarette and glanced at the clock. 'Christ, James it's ten to twelve, we've got to go otherwise I'll be late for the Lead Ring!'

I rushed out the door with James following behind, and up into Whittington Avenue, through the wooden doors and onto the Exchange floor in no time at all.

Normally, at this time the market would only have a few dealers and clerks on the Exchange floor but today it was a full house. Everyone knew it would be my first time in the Ring and I presumed they had come to watch. I wondered whether I should brush my hair as I put an oblong black and white badge on my lapel. I was clearly labelled a 'Probationary Dealer' now.

The bell rang, announcing the beginning of the market and I followed some of the other dealers into the Ring through one of four rather narrow gaps between the wooden benches. Suddenly the room felt full and every seat was taken – except, of course, mine! I made my way in, turning my back on most of the Ring as I took my seat. There was a deathly hush over the market but as I sat down, a slow clapping started. I sat there with my arms relaxed in my lap, holding my order book, and managing to keep a straight face. I couldn't work out whether they were congratulating me or whether this was some way of them showing their disapproval. I didn't mind too much since they would run out of trading time if they didn't stop soon. James leaned over the bench and whispered in my ear, 'If we haven't got any orders for the first Zinc Ring, you must make a trade anyway. Once you've done a deal the worst will be over!'

Perhaps that's why they were insisting on cheering and clapping me – to stop me from trading! Part of me wanted to leave the Ring but I felt as though invisible hands were upon my shoulders, keeping me seated. By now some of the traders were even on their feet clapping. The thought of them welcoming me was too much and tears welled up in my eyes, so I looked up at the clock, hoping they would disappear. I could feel James behind me and even Trevor leaned forward and congratulated me. But I had to act quickly.

'Three months!' I shouted as loudly as I could to overcome the clapping. Silence followed as all the dealers focused on the new voice in the Ring. Even I thought it sounded strange! One dealer leaned over and, cupping his ear, shouted, 'Pardon?' before breaking out into laughter with everyone else.

'Three months!' I repeated, listening to my lone female voice echo around the Ring. I had practised getting my voice as deep and as clear as I could, and I listened to how it sounded as I watched the expressions on the faces opposite. How strange no one was competing with me! They were just sitting back and watching the show. Perhaps they wanted me to make the market. To provide a bid and offer to anyone who wanted to trade with me! It didn't seem right that I should have to do that; besides, it would have been a certain loss for me. I looked over to another probationary clerk who was keeping very quiet and still, almost as if he wasn't there. I would just have to be patient.

And then a dealer opposite smiled. I knew he was going to help me. 'I'll give 292, sell at 295.' He winked as he shouted across the Ring. I had to think fast. If I gave 293 he'd also bid 293 to try and get me to raise my bid. I looked at the clock, there was not long to go. I had an order to buy one hundred tons of zinc at market and there was no point in messing about with it.

'OK, one hundred tons,' I said, leaning forward in the Ring and pointing at him. I saw his clerk write down the deal and there, it was done, my first deal on the LME. A flash of lightbulbs went off and I realised that there were journalists on the Exchange as well.

The bell sounded and I left the Zinc Ring. Today I had done something to be proud of and I felt very happy. Within the half-hour I was again preparing to deal in the Ring. From now on, lead and zinc would be my metals. I would run the book and look after the positions. Even though I had six months to go before being a fully authorised dealer in the Metal Ring, I could at least think of myself as being a recognised trader. About half an hour later a committee member came over to congratulate me and then asked if I would like to go for lunch sometime. I accepted and we arranged for the following week.

Returning to the office, I felt exhausted, and then Henry called me into the boardroom. 'How was it today, Gerry?'

'Very good, well as good as can be expected, I think, but just because I'm dealing on the Exchange now doesn't mean I don't want to continue with client liaison. In fact, Henry, we have some new clients. I don't know whether David has told you but they're Chinese and I'd like to do some trading for them.'

Henry puffed on his pipe several times, while he thought for a moment.

'Well, shall I start with sending them my report?' I persisted.

'Yes, that's a good idea,' Henry smiled at me 'Good luck!' And then, as if it was an afterthought 'By the way, I think we need to get a new clerk if you're going to be sitting in the Ring from now on. How do you feel about us getting another woman to work on the floor with you as your clerk?'

What could I say? I was pleased, the more of us the better. 'That's a great idea, have you someone in mind?' I thought Henry might have picked out a girl from the offices or perhaps one of the telex operators. I wondered what his motivation had been in choosing another woman; was it because we worked hard and cost less in wages? Was it because we were pretty? Or was it because he just wanted to have more women around him? I really had no idea but I didn't think the rest of the team would be particularly happy about another woman sitting on the metals trading desk! Still, I was excited at the thought of her joining us. I was also aware that I would not have quite the same level of attention as before. How much luckier she would be not to have to go through what I had been through. All the hard work in becoming accepted had been done and in any case, she would have me to teach and protect her!

In retrospect, I think Henry enjoyed my insecurity. He knew that I would be concerned with the petty things such as the seating arrangements around the trading desk and he did nothing to alleviate my worry. He was watching my face closely and I was hoping I was giving nothing away. Eventually I asked, 'Where will she sit?'

Henry smiled. 'Well, in the morning, when you're on the telex writing your reports for the Chinese, she can sit in your seat! Otherwise she can just make do like the rest of us. We all sit in different seats most of the time anyway!'

'No we don't, we all have our own seats and no one ever sits in your chair, Henry,' I responded quickly,

He puffed on his pipe and waved his hand to dismiss the conversation. 'It doesn't matter does it?'

But to me of course it did and I resolved to sort the problem out by speaking to the others.

I argued that we should have more space if we were expanding and perhaps we needed to have a bigger trading desk anyway. James agreed it was always a mess – with David and everyone's papers on it he couldn't find anything any more, not even his cards, so no wonder he didn't know what his position was and no wonder he was losing money!

Henry took a dim view of this. 'James, I have to speak with you later, there are some irregularities showing up.'

'Irregularities!' James repeated. 'Not irregularities? I made about £15 000 last week. You haven't got all the picture, part of the position must be missing. I'll check it out when I get back from the market tonight.'

'Yes, will you please. I did ask you to do that yesterday and you didn't even bother to come back from the market.'

'OK, I'll definitely do it tonight, Henry, promise!' James always ended his sentences with a smile but Henry was not amused.

As we walked down to the market I asked James what was going on with the position. Why did Henry think it was losing money? James shook his head. 'Because he doesn't understand how the market works, Gerry, he doesn't understand that sometimes you have to take losses. You have to take the good with the bad and you have to wait your time. Henry doesn't understand any of that because he has never been a floor trader.' He looked at me wearily; he seemed exhausted.

In the pub we sipped our lager slowly at the bar. 'You understand, don't you, Gerry?' he said to me as he lit a cigarette.

'Yes, of course I do, but I still think you should know what your outright position is, otherwise how can you take corrective action if the market starts to go against you? And after all, James, it is Henry and Mark's money, isn't it?'

James stared at me with his mouth open for a little longer than necessary. He knew then that if push came to shove I would be on Henry's side. Sure, I thought he was a good trader but there was no excuse for him to be taking advantage of everyone's naivety. After all, it could affect all of our jobs and I told him so. He wiped his head with his hand, and I realised then that not all was right with him. He was depressed and I wished I could help him.

Later, James did not come back to the office and Henry got very angry. 'Right, that's it, I've had enough!'

I looked at David who was shaking a card and saying repeatedly, 'It's ridiculous!'

I couldn't be bothered to ask but I could see the whole trading team was in a flap. I decided to distance myself and leave for the day. 'Goodnight everyone!' I shouted.

'Night Gerry!' a chorus responded.

'Oh, Gerry, before you go…' Henry stopped me '…I should

tell you, Debbie will be starting on Monday.'
'Good, I look forward to meeting her.'

I was glad it was the weekend until I remembered I had promised Tanya that we would go up to Barrow and visit her parents. I was looking forward to how the car would perform over a long journey but I had no idea just how eventful a time it would give us.

As we left London, I decided to step on the accelerator. After all, this was a famous rally car. But cruising at over ninety miles an hour on the outside lane of the M1, we had a front wheel blow out and hit the crash barrier. The car then went into a fast spin, moving rapidly into the central reservation before hitting another that was rather stupidly trying to overtake on the inside lane.

Luckily neither Tanya nor I were injured but the car was badly damaged all along one side. The Police arrived – rather spookily, in the same BMW Coupe but with police stripes on instead of BMW rally stripes! They were very kind to us, towing us to the nearest garage. When I look back it seems as though that was all a dream and I remember thinking what a coincidence that the police car should be the same model as mine.

After a couple of hours we were on the road again with Tanya happily munching her way through the miles by eating freshly made sardine sandwiches, which stunk the car out. By late afternoon we had arrived in Leeds. As the traffic lights changed at the top of a very steep hill, I applied the handbrake, only to find out that it didn't work. Very quickly I slammed my foot onto the brake and screamed out loud to a shocked Tanya as boiling hot water from the tank poured directly onto my foot: 'Mind your foot, quick, Tanya, in case the water hits you! Shit, I can't move *my* foot! I wish the bloody traffic light would change! Shit, shit!'

Unbelievably Tanya was still eating her sandwiches 'Why can't you move your foot?' she asked.

'Don't be bloody stupid, we'll slide back and hit the car

behind if I do that. I wish the bloody traffic lights would change.' Steam was now covering all the windows and we wiped them down furiously. A good few minutes later the lights changed and we were able to straighten up. I stopped and put water into the radiator, even though I knew it would crack, and carried on driving to Harrogate. My foot was really sore but then it had been sore many times in my life before. Besides, I was looking forward to seeing Patricia – hopefully before it got dark.

Patricia ran a very popular restaurant in Harrogate with her husband and we spent the evening dining on good food and wine. Disappointingly, she had to work through part of the evening but afterwards we went back for drinks before setting off for Barrow-in-Furness at three in the morning! The weather was very stormy and I wondered whether or not to go, but Tanya's mother was expecting us the next morning, so after checking that we had enough petrol, we set off across the Yorkshire Dales.

It was misty, dark and still raining when the windscreen wipers packed up. This meant that we had to drive across the moors in the pouring rain with my head hanging out the window, since this was the only way I could see where we were going! Tanya was oblivious to all of this and had fallen asleep early on in the journey. By the time we arrived in Barrow the rain had turned to a fine drizzle. This was my first visit and Tanya directed me through the town. As we stopped at the roundabout it was six o'clock in the morning and surrounding the car were at least two hundred men on their bikes. I seemed to be the only car on the road! I sat there with my mouth open – I had never seen so many cyclists.

Tanya laughed. 'Welcome to Barrow, they are all on their way to the boatyard, it's like this every morning. They work over there,' she said pointing across to entrance gates across the other side of the bridge. It's always like this, Vickers is the main employer all my family work for them,' she added.

Across the roundabout I watched as a huge workforce made its way slowly but in an orderly fashion through the gates. It reminded me of a scene from Moscow or some other

Communist state. I couldn't believe that this was England and I said so to Tanya. Six o'clock in the morning and we were the only car on the road! I knew I had to drive carefully. As I approached the roundabout I had to stop to let them by and I could not help but smile as hundreds of boatyard workers tapped their caps and rang their bells. Once again we were in the thick of it but for once I didn't feel at all threatened. We smiled and waved back as I pulled gently out onto the roundabout in to a sea of bicycles and waving caps. Then just as I went to change gear, the gearstick came away in my hand and I found myself waiving it aimlessly around in the air!

'Oh my God, I can't believe it, what else is going to happen to this bloody car?' Tanya rolled her eyes up into her head.

'Well might you ask. What else *can* go wrong? I'm surprised we've come as far as we bloody well have!'

For once I was at a loss as to what to do next as we came to a standstill on the roundabout. I put the gearstick back into position and shook it around for a while, attempting to find neutral. Eventually I lodged it securely back in its socket but the engine had stalled. We sat there for a moment, wondering what on earth we could do, when a few men dropped their bicycles and thankfully came to our rescue. They were now pushing the car forward.

'Steer round, luv!' one shouted and then more men joined to push us faster and faster until I was able to jump-start the engine.

'How nice of them to help,' I said to Tanya watching them return to their bicycles and then winding the window down I shouted: 'Thank you, thank you!' but they were already away on their bikes,

'Mustn't be late!' one shouted as I watched him cycle into the distance.

We arrived at Tanya's home just in time for breakfast, still laughing about the breakdown. 'I'm not sure that car is going to last too long, Gerry, I wonder what else is going to go wrong with it?'

As we drove round a narrow corner of small terraced houses

Tanya let out a howl of delight. 'We're here! Park here, park here!'

I parked, just managing to squeeze into a space behind a black Ford Zephyr. Tanya's mother came out of the front door to greet us and I couldn't help but notice the resemblance. This was the first time I had met her and I was keen to make an impression. Having made a fuss of Tanya, she turned her attention to me and smiled. I smiled back and had to stop myself from offering my hand in a greeting – something I had become very used to doing lately! I noticed that she seemed genuinely pleased to meet me, although I caught her casting a look of disapproval at the car and then at the orange suit I was wearing.

The day was spent in catch up conversation with the family and some good, home-cooked food. Later, as we were getting ready to meet up with Tanya's friends for a game of pool, she said, 'Don't make too much of a fuss about what you look like, we're only going to the pub round the corner!'

'Yes, I know, but I've never met your friends and I want to make a good impression.'

'You don't have to try so hard to make people like you, and you don't have to buy them drinks all night either.'

I looked at her, wondering where all this was coming from. 'So how much shall I take out, then? About £15 should do it, don't you think?'

Shortly after we left and drove round the corner to the pub. 'If I had known it was this close I wouldn't have taken the car'

'Well it's not very safe to walk home at night, besides we might go on somewhere afterwards.'

As we walked into the smoke-filled pub I heard the loud music and wondered whether I was going to enjoy myself. As Tanya introduced me, I noticed most of her friends were well accomplished in the art of chewing gum, smoking, and drinking pints of lager – all at the same time!

'Hiya!' Tanya shouted to a chorus of well-rehearsed 'Hi yas'. Some of her friends ran towards her, ready to give a hug, while other dropped their cues or stubbed cigarettes out. Some noticed me and gave an unimpressed look, realising I was from London, while others smiled a reluctant welcome. They seemed very different from me and I was quite sure that I wouldn't enjoy the evening. I thought Tanya was probably the prettiest and the most intelligent of them all, and at that moment I couldn't help but think of Emily and wonder how she was. Why had I thought of her just then? Perhaps it was because she was always talking about how people looked and what they wore. I knew that Emily would always be attracted to people by the way they looked. But there had to be more to it than just looks. Besides, wasn't beauty in the eye of the beholder? Everyone's idea of beauty couldn't be the same, surely? But according to Emily, everyone had the same idea of what beauty was; everyone always agreed on who was beautiful and who wasn't. You only had to look at magazines and films to see that. You didn't need a degree to see and appreciate beauty. So when I asked her: 'What about the personality, isn't it possible to fall in love with a personality or a mind or a soul?', my words fell on deaf ears. I think the reason was that Emily believed beauty reflected all these attributes. In other words, one couldn't be beautiful unless one already had a clever and good mind and an interesting personality. But I did not believe this was the case and from what I had read, there was no link whatsoever. It was perfectly possible to be beautiful on the outside and ugly on the inside. I remember trying to tell Emily about this but she thought I was stupid and said she didn't understand a word of what I was saying. 'Why do you always complicate things? Just keep it simple – either you fancy a person or you don't!'

Gazing into thin air, I felt a pool cue thrust into my hand 'Your turn!' I smiled awkwardly as I turned to take my go. Most of Tanya's friends were much better at the game than me and I could see I was on a hiding to nothing. To make things worse, I was dressed for a night out in London and felt like a fish out of water!

Later, a much boring later, someone suggested we go to the beach, where it was private. It was going to be a full moon and a clear sky, just right for romantic walks along the seaside, but I was not in the mood. 'What about my suit? I'm not dressed for this,' I said irritably, but I was persuaded that I would be a spoil-sport if I didn't join in.

The rest of the night was spent uncomfortably huddled behind the sand dunes under a silver moon. Early the next morning, we rose to find my car had sunk into the sand. A few hours more and it would have completely disappeared!

The sight of my car being hauled up from out of the beach with sand pouring through the gaping windows was too much to bare. This really had been an awful weekend.

Unbelievably, the engine was completely unaffected by the night in the sand and started almost first time, although it would need some tender loving care before we left for London. So I spent the rest of day cleaning yet more sand out, and checking the engine and tyres. Ever since I had bought the car I'd had trouble with it. Lookswise it was a stunner, everyone thought so, but then they didn't really know what was wrong with it! Appearances could certainly be deceiving. What you see is not always what you get. Still, I was determined to stick with it. Surely there couldn't be anything else that could go wrong? I just hoped it would get us back to London safely.

In London the following morning I resolved not to go to Barrow again. I hadn't enjoyed myself and I reasoned Tanya should learn to drive, so that she could go home whenever she wanted without me having to drive her there. Besides, work was becoming very demanding and the weekend had taken its toll on me. It should have been more relaxing.

I walked into the office with a coffee, sat down and lit a cigarette. Aahhh, the first was always the best! Henry came in and smiled. 'Don't forget we've got Debbie starting today, I hope you'll look after her.'

'Of course, Henry?' I am looking forward to meeting her. The phone rang and I picked it up. 'Ullo. Miss Gerry, please?'

'Speaking.'

'Oh, ello, Mr Hao ere.'

'Would you like to listen to the Copper Ring with me today, Sir?'

'Oh, yes, huhu. Also we get report from you please on wot yu think zinc will do to day?'

'Yes, OK, I will send report and phone you from Exchange for zinc then, Mr Hao.' I found myself bizarrely speaking in broken English but he seemed to understand anyway.

I was pleased, perhaps he would give some orders later in the day. I put the phone down and smiled, watching Debbie walk towards me. 'Allo mate, I'm Debbie, you must be Gerry?' she said, holding out her hand for me to shake.

I stood up. 'Very nice to meet you and welcome aboard.' I was pleasantly surprised, I found her very friendly, natural and full of confidence. I smiled as she turned away to speak to David. I looked up again as she started to move around the trading desk, meeting the traders one by one. She was vivacious with thick, wavy brown hair down to her shoulders. Her lipstick was red, redder than I was used to, but it suited her. We both had perfume on but that was OK because many of the dealers, including Henry, were covered in strong-smelling aftershave. I noticed a button was undone on her blouse and I wondered whether I should say something but decided against it. By now I couldn't help but compare my appearance to hers and she beat me hands down! There again, I reasoned, I didn't want to be too attractive to men. She obviously did and even though I had been asked out many times by some dealers in the trading room and a few on the Exchange, I had always replied that I couldn't as I already had a boyfriend. But I understood the importance of networking and so always accepted an invitation for lunch. Some of the men were persistent and were not prepared to trade dinner for lunch, but most did and I had no problems. I wondered how Debbie would be with all these good-looking, well-off dealers around. Looking at her now she seemed very happy and who could blame her!

Just then, as though she sensed my thoughts, she came over

and plonked herself down beside me. 'Phew! Ah, that's much better,' she said, taking a sip of coffee. 'Phew! Got a light mate?' I smiled and lit up a cigarette with her. 'So... what are you all up to today? Arry tells me that you gotta show me the ropes an all that?'

'Yes, I can do that, how much do you know about trading?'

'Next to nothing, mate, but you can teach me and I'll learn. Deal? Ha ha ha!'

I laughed too, I could see she was definitely one of us. 'Yes, you're a natural, believe me', and again we laughed. 'I'll tell you what I think – Henry probably wants you to stay in the office this week and learn the ropes. So I'll give you some books and reading to do and we'll see how we go? Is that OK with you?'

'Yea, whatever, I'm easy.' Again we laughed. I could see we were going to get on fine.

I smiled and stood up to move to the telex but my chair was obstructed by something. I looked down to see a large, black shiny handbag, half-open with a hairbrush protruding from it. This was the first time I had seen a handbag so near the trading desk. I froze for a moment, realising that I didn't use one and I wondered whether she had noticed. I got to thinking about other differences she might pick up on, like me not going all gaga every time a good-looking man came into the room – something I could see she was bound to do. It was one thing making various excuses to men who wanted much more; it was quite another doing the same with an intuitive woman who you wanted to be friends with! All this went through my mind as I bent down to clear the trapped handle of her bag from the foot of my chair.

'Oh, excuse me,' I said, lifting my chair.

She looked up and smiled again, waving her arm. 'Oh, sorry mate, was that in the way? I'll move it.'

The other dealers watched our newly-formed relationship closely. They were expecting trouble somewhere down the line, perhaps some bitchiness and competitiveness. Well, I was going to make sure that Debbie and I got on like a house on fire! Debbie swung herself up into her seat and flopped her handbag on the desk and out came a mirror and lipstick. We all watched as she applied a new layer and then, grabbing her brush, swept her hair first forwards and then backwards. We all looked in amazement as her hair immediately doubled in volume She was unaware of our attention because by the time she looked up again, we had all looked away in embarrassment. She flung her handbag to the ground and gave me a questioning look. In response, I rolled my eyes, which made her laugh out loud again.

Later, as I sat at the telex thinking about a zinc report for the Chinese, Debbie approached. 'What are you doing on the telex?'

'Well, some years ago I started writing a metals report for our clients and even though I'm training to be an authorised Ring dealer, I still do the report.'

Debbie looked confused. 'Sounds to me like you're doing two jobs, why don't someone else write the report? I mean why do you have to do it?'

'Well, I don't have to but no one else will write it. I like to write the report because it gives me an opportunity to show off my own trading system and besides, I think the clients value having recommendations, they use it as a guide, you see.'

She gave a smile as though participating in a great secret. 'System, what do you mean system? What, like how you write it or what?'

'No, not *how* I write it but *why* I write it! I have a trading system that I use to inform what recommendations to give at the end of the report. You see, look, at the end of the zinc report a recommendation says "take your profits today and sell short". I'm getting them to double up!'

Debbie turned slightly as if to look around the room and then, jabbing me in the side with her elbow, she said, 'Ere, you're aving a laugh aren't ye? Anyone can say take your profits! Ha ha ha!'

'Yes, but they do have profits to take because I recommended them to go long a hundred tonnes about three weeks ago!'

'Ow did ye do that then?'

'Well, that's where my system comes in, you see.' I started to explain, showing her my charts.

'I don't understand any of this,' she frowned.

'I know you don't, but you soon will. Of course it does take time to pick all this information up, but just you wait and see how much you'll understand after a week or so.'

'I bloody ope so, ha ha ha!'

'OK, Debbie, well, I must get on with this report as I have to send it out by eleven this morning'

'OK,' she said and got up. 'Ere, thanks, Gerry.'

I watched as she walked over to the trading desk. 'I could show her everything I knew about trading but I couldn't show her my trading system – that would always be my secret. It was, after all, the reason why I liked to trade and being a good floor dealer was only part of the deal. The heart of the business was helping clients to make as much money as possible because it was their orders that had the power to move the market. These would be my loyal clients, those that only traded through me, those that regularly gave one hundred ton orders for the Ring, sometimes at market and sometimes at limits; clients that traded my recommendations and had faith in my system. They paid their commission and believed in my reports. They visited the market just to watch me in action! Yet as I watched Debbie gesturing to the others, I knew she was born to trade and she would be a good dealer. I wanted her to be a success; after all, I didn't want to spend my whole life down on the Exchange! It was always important to me that other women followed. Debbie would be the second woman to be allowed to trade on the Exchange. I tried to impress on her the importance of the role but I don't think she saw it the way I did. How could she? Everything was just a laugh to her and I would often say, 'If we are to get other women down onto the Exchange, we have to be seen to be making a go of it.'

'And enjoying it!' she shouted back. 'Oh shut up and bloody stop naggin me, will ye, Gerry?' And as if to emphasise her point, she slammed her trading book down in her frustration.

She was right. It was not my duty to nag her but to train her! But as I said to her later, 'You're a born natural that needs very little training in the art of bullshitting, which is one of the main skills you're required to have to be a successful dealer.' I laughed as I said it and she laughed back, proud of it!

As for me, my ambition to be the first woman dealer on the Metal Exchange was about to be realised. In the beginning I had never planned for it. It had just happened that way because there were no women on the Exchange before me. All I had wanted to do was be able to trade and earn the same as the men. Now I was thinking ahead and doing what all ambitious people do: I was planning my next goal of building up a successful client base. I already had a successful trading system in place that enabled me to confidently make recommendations to my clients on all metals traded on the Exchange. But now I needed to secure one of the really big customers and trade for them across the Ring.

I was enthralled with the idea of securing the Chinese business and I would do everything in my power to get it. China was known to be interested in purchasing large amounts of copper but for as long as I could remember, it had always just been a rumour. Often if the copper market moved up significantly, it was rumoured the Chinese were buying. Traders would look expectantly at each other saying ,'Hope so!' or 'That will be good for the market.' Opinions on the subject were always optimistic but never seemed to amount to anything. The Chinese were doing a lot of listening but not much trading and I noticed they seemed to have a relationship with everyone!

I sat there with my pen in my mouth, watching the telex report tape run smoothly through a bank of five telexes, wondering how I could persuade them to trade through me. The only conclusion that I could come to was if my trading system could predict advantageous moments for them to buy or sell. I knew they didn't want to control the market, they just wanted to buy at a good price. But as I'd said to Mr Hao once, how do you know when you have a good price? Is it by the next day's price, the next year's price? I mean, surely getting a good price for copper depended on the volume you intended to buy. But he thought I was always trying to trick him into telling me how much he wanted to buy. 'Ah, Miss Gerry, I no stupid!' and we would laugh together.

I released a tape from the telex and signed off what I hoped was another good report. Working on the market and clerking for James had provided me with the opportunity to see who was buying but as I said to Mr Hao, just because a producer is buying on the market, it doesn't mean it's trade business, it could still be speculative! He laughed. 'Ow you know what goes on, Gerry?'

I replied, 'I don't, I'm just guessing' and he seemed to like my honesty. He knew I was trying to get him to trust me more. But I did believe that we would do the best for them. I would make sure of that.

Having finished sending my report, I made my way down to the market. The phone was already ringing when I arrived in our office telephone booth. 'Gerry, quick, take an order, buy five hundred tonnes zinc at close of second, OK?'

'Yes, who is that for, is it New York?'

'No, Mr Hao'

'Great, that's brilliant, does he want to be phoned for the Ring?'

'No, I don't think so.' I thought for a moment, I wanted him to have the very best service we could give and this was our opportunity to impress him. 'Well, can you check with him please, David, it's important. I want him to have the best service ever!'

Later, I walked into the Ring feeling great and trying to suppress the smile on my face. I was never very good at hiding my feelings and I was as pleased as Punch! There was nothing worse than having to sit with no orders to do and although I had none for this Ring, I would probably buy a hundred tons for the book, just so I had something in hand if the market went haywire. After all, they could give the same order to everyone in the Ring and then where would I be! James had told me that closing Ring orders could be tricky, especially if they were at market, that's because I couldn't be sure to secure the total tonnage requested at less than or at the same price as the closing price, and if the market continued to run higher on the kerb I would lose money. It was a difficult decision because it could go either way and the commission wouldn't cover the costs.

As I sat in the Ring, it occurred to me that I had been thinking they were going to give me a great big copper order and instead I got a zinc order! Just imagine if they want to buy thousands of tonnes, and all through me! The Ring had gradually filled up and I felt a tense, exciting atmosphere. This was an atmosphere with a difference. I could hear the other dealers breathing and I saw their eyes dart away from the looks of others. All of them were trying not to move their heads. A couple of coughs unnerved us all, followed by some shoe-shuffling as the silence became quite unbearable. No one was moving so I leaned forward, waiting for three months to start trading. Traders were nervously looking at each other; some were smiling and others were more serious. Now they all thought I had something to do. Oh dear, I'd blown my cover, that was stupid. I leaned back against the wooden bench and relaxed my arms, hoping to confuse them all. It was then that the trader next to me moved forward in his seat. 'Three months!' he shouted and then, before waiting for an answer, screamed, 'I'll give 298, sell at 301.'

That was a bit wide! 'I'll give 299!' I shouted as loud as I could, hoping they could all hear. Uproar descended upon the Exchange with everyone leaning forward in their seats, some almost having one knee on the floor while others, nervously looked at the clock 'I'll give 301...'

'I'll give 302...'
'I'll give 305, sell at 310!'
'I'll give 306.'
'Yes... How much?'
'Five hundred tons?'

'Yes and I'll take more, give 306, give 306.50…' The trader just kept shouting as I watched the second hand moved towards the close of the Ring.

'Another five hundred tonnes?'

'Yes.'

'One thousand tonnes?'

'Yes.'

'Two thousand tonnes?'

'Yes.'

The bell heralded the end of the Ring and I had frozen. I had said nothing other than ask for a three month quote. I had started it and they had finished it! I was hopeless, what on earth was it going to be like in the next Ring? And I had a difficult order to execute. I should have been better prepared and I should have come away with at least a hundred tons of zinc under my belt. Now look at the market, it had rocketed. How would the Chinese ever be happy with me now? I walked out of the Ring disappointed and already getting nervous ahead of the next Zinc Ring. I needed a cigarette fast. After indicating to Trevor that I was going out, I lit up on the pavement.

Ah, that's better! Still shaking, I revisited the scene in my mind again and again. I saw myself sitting in the Ring and doing nothing, absolutely nothing at all. Why had I frozen, was it with fear? Was it the ferocity of all those men shouting into the Ring? Was it because I felt that I wouldn't be able to compete against all those male voices at once? It was one thing to shout across the Ring to your opposite number in a one-off deal, quite another to fill your lungs with air and open your mouth as wide as possible and yell at the very top of your voice. Hardly ladylike! Trust me to get myself into such a ridiculous situation!

I took a deep drag on the cigarette and walked back into a quiet Copper Ring. There was an eerie silence as I went over to the telephone to speak to the office. 'Hi, David, any more orders for the Zinc Ring?'

'No new orders, but the Chinese have phoned and they want to cancel that order to buy five hundred tonnes on the close of the second.'

'Huh? That's a bit strange. OK, it's cancelled then'

Well, to tell the truth I was quite relieved as I walked back to the Ring. Lucky I hadn't bought a hundred tonnes in the first Ring. Then I wondered if they had taken the order away from me to give to another broker. If they had I would be disappointed; obviously that would have meant they didn't trust a woman to do a proper job!

I comforted myself in the certain knowledge that Debbie would make a great trader. Her voice would be at least as loud as mine and it would be good to have her down here on the Exchange with me. I couldn't tell her how scared I was because I didn't want to put her off the experience, but I knew I would be braver with another woman watching me.

Now it was time for the second Zinc Ring and I felt calmer knowing that I didn't have an order to execute and that I wouldn't have to compete against the other dealers in the Ring. Still, I couldn't show anyone that I had nothing to do, otherwise what was the point in me being here? Besides they would think it was because I was a woman and no one trusted me enough to give an order! So I would lean forward, like the men, looking like I was going to trade but not actually doing any trading. These quite mad actions kept me sane. What a way to earn a living!

The bell rang and suddenly the market erupted. The noise was ear-bursting. Surely the whole city must be able to hear the price of zinc soaring through the roof! I leaned forward, partly in the pretence of having something to do, partly to hear above the uproar. I needed to mentally note the deals taking place, at what price and between whom. One minute to go, and I felt an arm on my shoulder. It was Trevor pulling me back towards him. 'Gerry, Gerry, sell five hundred tonnes of zinc at market!'

I looked at the clock again – forty seconds to go. I strained to hear where the bid was and who was first buyer in. Thirty seconds to go and Trevor grabbed me again. 'Make it a thousand tonnes at market!' he shouted loudly in my ear. Twenty seconds to go and I'd said nothing.

Then, as the second hand approached ten seconds to go, I heard myself shout, 'Yes!' at the top of my voice and everyone looked at me.

'Five hundred tonnes?'

'Yes!' I shouted again, pointing to another dealer. 'Five hundred tonnes.'

I heard the bell go and I sat back, exhausted. Were my yesses loud enough? I wondered. Had they heard me? I turned to Trevor, who had been clerking for me. 'Did you get all that?' I asked nervously.

'Yes, of course, I'm just going to check that last one but it looks like you sold one thousand tonnes at an average of £305.50!'

Although I would have to wait for the official price to be agreed by the committee, I was confident that I could give them a closing price of £305 and still make fifty pence for the house. I rose from my seat and caught some movement in the gallery. Someone had been watching. I was not sure who it was but I guessed who it might be. They would have to have the best possible price now if I wanted more business from them. I phoned the Chinese from the Exchange with their execution and was greedily hoping for another order, but instead they just wanted to listen to the Copper Ring. Halfway through the Ring the phone went dead and when I redialled, the line was engaged. That didn't surprise me. Other brokers were providing a service to them as well.

I returned to the office at lunchtime to pick up my report and charts so that I could remind myself at what level I had recommended clients to put their stop loss orders in. The markets had been more volatile than usual and I had noticed that the foreign exchange markets were behaving erratically as well. Something was going on and I needed to know what.

Debbie smiled as I rushed into the trading room. 'How was it down there today?'

'Busy, very busy'

She smiled again. I liked her expressive bouncy personality.

She told me she came from Essex. I knew some of the places she spoke about since I had lived there for a very short while.

'I dunno how ya do it, talk to the clients on the phone and trade as well,' she told me.

'Not easy, not easy at all,' I replied, searching for the right chart.

'Well then, maybe I should do that while I'm still up ere?'

'Thanks but no, I've only just got them to give us an order and I need to look after them personally, but there are other clients of mine you can give a commentary on the rings if you like?'

'Yeah, no problem, just give me their names and numbers and I'll call them.' I could see Debbie had bags of confidence and nothing would be too difficult for her. 'Oh, by the way, Gerry,' she added, 'can you phone Mr Hao? He wants to speak to you?'

I phoned right away and was surprised when Mr Hao answered. I reasoned then that it couldn't have been him watching me from the gallery on the Exchange. 'Now you listen carefully, Gerry, we have an important man coming from Beijing next week. You come to lunch and meet him, yes?'

'Yes, I would be delighted.'

'OK, I make arrangements but first you make me a visit to Metal Exchange and to your office, OK?'

'Yes, of course, what day suits you, Mr Hao?'

'I will tell you later, OK?'

'Yes, of course that's fine, Sir.' I put the phone down, feeling that I should do some research on China and the extra knowledge of their culture would probably pay off. Nothing was too much trouble for me because I wanted the Chinese to be the best account we had. In any case, by now I had already invested large amounts of time on them and had received the equivalent amount of criticism from David. The other traders were also rightly annoyed at my commitment to a customer who hardly ever gave an order. But I hoped to prove them all wrong and was quite religious about looking after them, spending many hours on the phone to them.

'We never get any bloody orders from them. I don't know why you bother, Gerry,' David would say to a chorus of agreement from the desk.

But I would just smile, although I usually felt quite stupid. 'One day, one day, we're going to get a really big order and then you'll see that it was worth providing them with a service.'

'Ha ha! Don't be stupid, Gerry. Why would they give us an order, and why would they want you to trade the order anyway? It's a bloody joke, I need help with my clients and all you want to do is speak to people who never give us any business anyway. I should have more help with my clients. You know I've got the Germans and what about the Czechoslovakians? They're your clients too, you send out your report in the morning but you're never here to service all your clients, are you, Gerry? It's not bloody funny any more, not at all!'

'Well, David, the Chinese have an important delegation coming over from Beijing and they want to visit the office and the Metal Exchange. They have asked me to arrange something for them, so maybe we'll get a big order after all and the time we've put in will pay off!'

David glanced across the desk at Trevor, who was nodding his head in agreement, 'Yes it would be good if you were in the office and not on the Exchange floor, and soon, soon we gonna have some important tin business and no one bloody helps me and I'm always on my own in the office at lunchtimes!' His voice had reached screaming pitch.

'OK, David, but you know we can't speak to any more clients down on the floor, so we have to get more people into the office to help you speak to the clients. This is a growing business and we have to grow with it. In the meantime, why don't you make more use of Mick? He's very good with the clients and has a nice manner. Let him speak to more clients instead of just servicing New York all the time.'

David stood up and banged the desk 'Don't tell me what to do or how to run this fucking business! I told you, you should be spending more time up here.'

'Look!' I screamed back. 'You're not my boss, so stop telling me what to do all the time! If you have a problem, I suggest you speak to Henry.' As I shouted, I felt Debbie getting anxious as she started shuffling her legs around before reaching nervously for her handbag.

David's advice consisted of what he thought the client wanted to hear. He reckoned that he would get the maximum amount of orders from them because clients always liked to think they were right. He didn't believe you should argue with the client or express a different opinion because that would only lose the company client business. In short, he thought it right to play it safe and not have a personal opinion. 'I don't understand how you can know for sure which way the market is going,' he would say, 'and if you don't know for sure you shouldn't be telling the customers!'

But I would reply, 'Customers need to know what we think of the market and it's good to have an opinion. I'm not forcing them to agree, am I?'

'No, but don't you understand, Gerry, if you keep getting it wrong they're not going to listen to you and then we're going to lose them altogether!'

I laughed. 'But what if I get it right?'

'Don't be so bloody stupid, Gerry, no one gets it right all the time, do they?'

I laughed again, even though I was far from amused. 'Don't be so bloody stupid, David, no one gets it wrong all the time, do they? Honestly! Can we just stop this now, it's not getting us anywhere!'

David puffed and tutted with his tongue rather loudly. I noticed his face had gone red 'You know what? You're stupid, Gerry, bloody stupid! You're going to lose us money and clients!' He thumped the desk and spoke even louder. 'You're really stupid, because when you give your recommendations, you don't know what the clients' orders are going to be for the day! It's stupid because you tell them to buy and they're the biggest sellers ever, and they're laughing at you all the time, can't you see that?' He laughed like a maniac.

By this time the whole trading room had come to a halt as traders turned round from their desks to watch the show. So I had no option really but to continue trying to convince David that I was right. 'No, David, but I can see it's important that I don't decide what the market is doing on the basis of what each individual client is doing. How can I advise them if all the time I'm asking them what the market's doing? If they decide to sell when I say to buy or to hold a long position, then that's their business and time will tell whether it was wiser to sell or to hold off for a bit.'

Realising that nearly everyone was listening, David went quiet for a bit. Everyone knew he played it safe most of the time. He was not one for sticking his neck out. One morning I'd heard him say to a client, 'I'm one hundred per cent sure the zinc market is going up' and to another 'I'm absolutely sure the zinc market is going down the pan'.

'How can you give two different views on the same market?' I had asked him one day. 'I can't believe you tell the clients what it is you think they want to hear. Does it never occur to you that they may talk to each other and ask themselves: why is it that David tells me one thing and you another?'

Staring back at me, his mouth dropped open. 'How do you know what I do? You're never here to see it!'

'I know what you do and I know why you do it! You do it to make as much profit as possible for today and you don't worry about tomorrow! I, on the other hand, do worry about tomorrow. When I give advice to my clients it's impartial advice based on a tried and tested trading system that I designed and have belief in. If it's wrong this time, it will correct itself and be right next time! Clients can watch the system for themselves and they can make their own minds up as to what they should do. If they give me the business it's because they trust me and because I don't change my mind like the wind! That is why I write the reports and send them out before the market opens. What other broker does that, David?' I was screaming loudly now. 'None, and I'll tell you what you need to do, David, you need to read my reports and you need to sing the same message to your clients, it's no good what you're doing and it's not helpful to the companies business.'

The show was far from over and David's face was white with rage as he bent towards me across the trading desk and shook his finger violently at me. 'Don't you bloody tell me what to say! You know nothing about the business, you bloody make me sick, why don't you go home or something stupid like that!' He had picked up a large, leather-bound ledger and thumped the desk loudly with it spilling cold coffee from out of a plastic cup. I picked up a couple of position cards before they were soaked through. He was still ranting and raving and I wondered how long he was going to go on for. Surely he could see this was not getting us anywhere. Time to shut him up.

'The truth is, Gerry, you know nothing about anything that's the truth!'

'Well David nor do you, because there is no such thing as a truth. There is only your truth and my truth. My truth is not your truth and your truth is certainly not mine, and if you say something is true you lie, it's as simple as that! Comprendez vous?'

'What's all the bloody racket about?' Henry was standing at the entrance to the trading room. My heart missed a beat. Shit! How long had he been standing there? How much had he heard? He knew that David and I had very different ideas about how the business should progress, I smiled at David, whose face looked grey except for his brown eyes surrounded by black shadows, and his lips that had turned a deathly white.

Debbie spoke up. 'He,' she said, pointing at David, 'doesn't agree with her about the advice she's giving clients and he wants more help on the desk than he's getting at the moment. I think he wants her to stay in the office with him!' I couldn't make up my mind if I was happy or not with her interpretation of events. It was simple and to-the-point but whose side was she on?

'Well, keep the bloody noise down, will you?' said Henry. 'We have an important lunchtime meeting and we can't hear ourselves bloody think!' Turning , he slammed the boardroom door loudly.

David sat down slowly, cradling his head in his folded arms on the trading desk. 'David are you OK?' There was no answer. 'David, do you need some water?' Still no answer. I decided not to repeat the question and grabbed my coat and left. I worried about David speaking later with Henry, speaking with him while I was out of earshot. I worried that he would send Debbie on to the floor in my place and keep me in the office instead. But then I felt better when I reasoned that he had always intended for Debbie to clerk on the Exchange and in any case, it would be at least six months before she could take my place in the Ring. Hopefully Henry would allow me to continue my career both in the office and on the Exchange. But I would have to watch David. He would push for Debbie to come down onto the floor so that he could get me back in the office assisting him with his clients!

David quite clearly had no intention of letting me become a successful ring trader as well as a successful office trader, and his continued outbursts at me were probably because he feared just that. I had often heard him say to other traders, 'You're either good at one or the other but you can't be good at both!' The very best of dealers would have been someone who had traded in the Ring and then gone on to build up a massive client base in the office. Then you would get respect from everyone. But if you were just an office trader with no Ring dealing experience on the Exchange, then you would be like David. He was someone everyone laughed at behind his back. I thought it was sad. Besides, I knew they also laughed at me behind my back. Who cared?

Anyway, David wasn't completely alone. Mick had always been clear that he would never want to trade on the floor and even Henry, who was the company's named subscriber, had never dealt in the Ring on the London Metal Exchange. Although David and I had different approaches to the business, his one big advantage was his ability to speak many languages and he was fluent in English, German and Hebrew. I took my hat off to him in this respect. Much as I wanted to please the Chinese, I knew that I was never going to be able to speak Mandarin!

That evening I studied my reports and thought about how I might refine my system. Despite my shouting match with David, I knew that my system needed adjusting from time to time – not that I would admit that to anyone! I shut my eyes momentarily, envisioning solutions to the questions I pondered. No trading position could guarantee a positive outcome if harmony was being disrupted. Harmony is measured by the amount of times a certain level of expectation is met, or not as the case may be. In my trading system I searched for the rhythm of the market, like a breath of air or the beat of a good tune. It was at the very heart of learning how to make money. If expectations became disrupted, disharmony changed the mood of the market, making it erratic, unpredictable and dangerous. The market then starts to move about on very little volume as buyers and sellers become nervous and the orders dry up. In such times I would advocate liquidating the position and standing aside. The problem is that it was often in unpredictable markets that the really big profits could be made. I hated standing aside because it was always a precarious situation to be in. Reckoning when the market was ripe for re-entry could be hazardous and mistakes costly. Consistent losses incurred over a period of time would lead to a streak of bad luck. Bad luck, hit confidence hard. Once caught in a streak of bad luck, all sorts of demons had to be overcome. Fear, greed, vanity, pride and arrogance and, of course, those never-ending losses. That streak of bad luck could make us do stupid things – things that, at the time they were done were not stupid, but become stupid afterwards!

Emotions run high as you convince yourself that you are right. Then you shudder and go cold because you are not right at all. You are definitely wrong. But it's too late because the market is moving against you and because you are weak and don't have the strength to get out of the position, you just watch as the really big losses start to mount up. You get into a comfort zone where you tell yourself that the market will come right in the end but it only does once you have liquidated your position and have nothing more to gain.

I open my eyes. My system gives clear signals when to enter, when to liquidate and, most importantly, when to stand aside and not trade. There were no decisions to be made. The system, having made the decisions, would tell me when it was right to take the profits or the losses. It was working very well indeed! I could not help but make profits even when all those around me were losing money. It was almost too good to be true.

God, how I wanted that big Chinese order, the myth that everyone talked about but never got. I wanted it because in my mind the Chinese were like me – they needed to be given a chance and I was the only one that could be trusted to do their business. From now on everything I would do would bring me one step further to securing their trust. I thought again about David and how uptight I had made him feel. Was it my fault that he had got so angry? Why was it we kept having these fights? There was something, but I just couldn't put my finger on it and as for Debbie, well, she was a bit of an unknown quantity, wasn't she? I would just have to wait and see how she behaved in the future. Perhaps there was some action I could take to bring her more on board with my way of thinking. I wanted to influence her but I didn't want to stop her from developing in her own way. I sensed she knew there was something different about me. I decided I would speak to her soon about the office situation.

As I walked through Mark Lane the next morning, I smiled at an elderly woman sitting at a trestle table just outside the great arched wooden door of the Norman tower. On the table she had placed a notice saying the tower would be open for visitors at lunchtime and that all were welcome. There were a few old books on the green, felt-covered table and she warmed her hands around a white mug of hot tea as we spoke. Picking up a leaflet,

I said, 'I'm so pleased that you're here' and, laughing a little, added, 'Do you know how many years I've been waiting for this door to open?'

She smiled and tipped her head to one side, still looking at me. 'Not too many, I hope?'

I noticed that there was something of a gypsy about her and it was difficult to judge her age. She was a beautiful woman with wonderful warm brown eyes accompanying a thin but wide smile. 'I'd like to go inside but I don't have the time now, will you be here later?' I asked

She nodded slowly and retied her scarf under her chin. 'I'll be here to let you in.'

'Well, are you sure? I should be here about 1.30, I hope that's not too late? I'm afraid I can't get here any sooner, will you still be here?' I asked without stopping for breath.

'Yes, I'll be here,' she smiled and winked at me.

'Thank you, and what's your name?'

She stood up and moved to the other side of the table, picking up one of the books on her way round. She looked down at it before answering. 'Maggie.'

'Maggie? Well, thank you, Maggie. I'm Gerry and I look forward to seeing you later then, bye.'

'Yes I'll be here,' she repeated. As I left I noticed a moneybox on the side of the table and made a mental note to make sure that I had some change later.

Back in the office, I was so excited that I could barely contain myself and so I told the other traders while we were eating our bacon rolls. A couple of them seemed interested while others seemed confused as to why I would be so interested in an old tower. 'You know the Norman tower just before Plantation House opposite the turning to Fenchurch station, surely you must know it?'

'Yes, I may have seen it,' David said, shrugging his shoulders.

'Well, look, I'm going there at lunchtime, would you like to come with me, we could make a lunch-hour of it, go for a bite to eat if you like afterwards?' David stared at me with his mouth open. I was just trying to be friendly. 'Sorry, David, just if you were interested, that's all.'

'Ha ha, and what makes you think I would be interested in an old Norman tower?' He continued laughing as he turned to engage with the other traders, who all but ignored him. Why was it he was always trying to make me look stupid?

Debbie, meanwhile, was checking her make-up in the mirror. 'Don't look at me,' she said, laughing. I wanted to laugh with her but felt I couldn't, not after yesterday. I couldn't understand their attitude. After all, wasn't this an opportunity of a lifetime, to see inside a majestic tower that had not been open to the public for a very long time and probably would not be open again for a good many years?

At times likes this I felt like a fish out of water. Some of these people's ancestors might have been locked in that tower. They might have been knights or crusaders, monks or prisoners. Why not go inside and feel the vibes? Perhaps they had prayed in the tower before going abroad to do battle. I sipped aimlessly on my coffee, looking down at the ring on my finger with the family crest on it, a rampant stag holding a sword, or was it a cross? Shit, what did these people know about the past? Clearly they felt nothing for it. All that was important to them was the future and making loads of bloody money. Money, money, money! They are even writing songs about it.

I took another sip of coffee and turned towards Debbie, who had by now finished applying a thick coat of red lipstick and was smacking her lips together while she brushed her hair. 'How has your week in the office been?' I asked, watching her every move.

'Yea, good, I've really enjoyed it and David has been such a help, I'll miss him next week.'

'Why? What do you mean, he's not going anywhere, is he?'

'No, but I am. Henry says I can go down onto the Exchange and clerk for you! You've got your exam next week, haven't you?'

'Yes, on Monday.' I watched as she put her brush neatly into her bag

'Do you expect to pass?'

'Yes, of course, why shouldn't I?'

'Oh, I don't know, maybe they don't want women traders in the Ring or working on the floor. Maybe we should all be up in the office. I mean what must it be like to be working with all those men down there? Some of them are gorgeous, don't you think?'

'Um, yes, I suppose so, I hadn't really given it any thought.'

'What? some of them are real hunks! Come on, you're having me on, Gerry, surely, one of them must have asked you out?'

This was the conversation I'd been dreading having with Debbie. 'Well, I occasionally go for a drink at lunchtime with some of them but I don't socialise with any of them in the evening.'

'What do you mean, you don't socialise? Are you mad or something? I think you and me need to have a little chat or something. Gerry, are you shy or what?'

'No, I just like to get on with my work, that's all, and I don't want people to think that the only way I got down here was because I was easy and slept around. Look,' I said, 'a woman's brain is just as good as a man's. I believe women should have the same rights as men, that we're equal, what's so wrong with that?'

Debbie flung her head back and roared. 'Ha ha ha!'

Oh dear, this was awful! I had wanted her support and had hoped her arrival would make things easier. I had hoped that the men would accept us both as equals and treat us with a bit of respect, and not just see us as a bit of skirt! But apparently Debbie saw nothing wrong in their attitude towards us. On the contrary, she positively encouraged it! Now she was on their side, and didn't want me around. I wondered whether I should try further to convince her to come over to my way of thinking. After all, she didn't really know what it could be like down on the Exchange floor. They were nice to her now but as soon as she became a threat, their tune would change. But for now words did not come easily to me and after the feeling of betrayal had left me, I decided that laughing with her was the best method of defence.

Debbie looked at me and stopped laughing herself. 'Nah… seriously, Gerry, that's not how you really feel?' She had now raised her voice to such a pitch that it was clearly audible to those sitting around us. I knew instinctively what she was going to say next and I knew I could not stop the words reverberating around the room. 'I don't believe it! You're not a bloody feminist are you?' She shouted it out so loud that it sunk into the silence like a permanent fixture, the words now set in stone to be remembered by all. Now I saw all my progress, all my good work being underdone, second by second it was unravelling and I was helpless to stop it.

'Of course not,' I said, standing up to leave. I gave her a look of contempt, something I also felt for myself for not having the strength to tell it as it was. The betrayal I felt from her was the betrayal I now felt towards myself, to my knight and crusader who would have been so disappointed in me to see what a coward I had become, denying what I knew to be my truth.

How dare she do that to me! I thought as I went to get a coffee. I lit up a cigarette and stared blankly at my position card. I was so mad and I could feel David smirking behind me. I looked at him and as usual he turned away. The rest of the traders seemed to have ignored her comment and Henry was puffing on his pipe, staring into thin air. Sensing my attention, he smiled and his face warmed. He winked at me and puffed again on his pipe. I wanted to go down to the market but I wasn't happy leaving first. I shuffled my papers again, thinking about my next move.

Debbie moved closer, perhaps sensing my vulnerability. She stretched out her hand towards me and I smelt her perfume, a mixture of fruit and spice. Perhaps this was her way of saying sorry, perhaps there was some understanding there after all? But no, Debbie, as usual, was thinking of herself. 'Can I come down the market and watch today?' I remained silent as though I hadn't heard her. 'Can I come down the market this morning?'

she asked again. 'David says it will be all right.'

'Did he?' I responded nonchalantly. 'Well, I think it's best if you stay in the office this morning, Debbie, and help on the desk. We can think about your visit to the Exchange later, perhaps even this afternoon.'

To my surprise, David agreed. 'Yes, do as Gerry says. I need help in the office this morning so you stay up.'

Well at least I'd won that round! I left for the market feeling a little better with some of my credibility left in tact!

The morning market was quiet so afterwards I made my way to keep the appointment at the Norman tower. Maggie was, as she had promised, sitting at the table just outside the large arched wooden doors. Doors that I had never seen open and doors that even now remained closed 'Maggie,' I waved to her, 'I'm here now.'

She smiled and slowly rose from her chair. 'Ah, yes, hello,' she said as she searched for the key. 'Now where did I put it? It's always getting lost and I can never find it when I want it! You, I know, would like to have a look in here. If only I could find it.' Her hand stretched across to pat the green velvet tablecloth and I found mine joining hers in the search.

'I hope you don't mind? Only I'm short of time, I haven't got long.'

'No, no, of course not, we can't get in until we have the key, can we?'

Perhaps it was under the table. I dropped to my knees, ducked my head and stretched under the table to reach another wooden box. I hoped no one from work would see me crawling around on the corner of Mark Lane like this. Trust me to get myself into such an unexplainable situation!

'Do you think the key is in this box under the table?' I asked.

'I don't think so but let's have a look just in case, shall we?'

I took another impatient glance at my watch, then quickly placed the box on the table in front of Maggie. Time was marching on, but she didn't seem to be aware of just how short of time I was. She looked up before opening the box, smiling wistfully. I turned away not wanting to be nosy. She emptied the contents on the table; different coloured feathers fell out of the box, and some blew away. My nose felt tickly and she laughed, pointing to a blue feather stuck on my jacket. 'I don't think the key is in here. Can you come back tomorrow?' Then she tucked her hand into the side of her long brown skirt and pulled out a heavy iron key on a chain that was attached to a belt around her waist. 'This, you see, Gerry, is not the right key! I don't know why I was given it if they knew it wouldn't fit.'

'Are you sure? Can't we at least try? It might work.'

'Yes, it might, but I don't think so.' I followed her to the door and she stuck the key in, rattling it around with some difficulty.

'It's not working, it can't be the right key!'

I hadn't come all this way not to be able to get in. I felt sorry for Maggie, because I knew she had been looking forward to my return. I looked back at the table, hoping to see the key lying there. 'Maggie, what about your bag, is it safe just lying on the table like that?'

She turned. 'What can I be thinking of?' She gave a short laugh. I watched as she slipped the key back into her pocket and picked up a mug of cold tea from the table. Surely that was not going to be the end of it? I hadn't come all this way to fail! I went back to the door and grabbed hold of the handle. Shaking it violently, I turned it to the left and then again to the right and then, just for good measure, I gave it a really good shake in the middle that made the great door move on its hinges. By now my palm was quite sore from holding on so hard to the rusty twisted knocker. Clearly the door had not been opened for years. But I could open it, I knew I could!

And then, as though by magic, a loud click heralded some movement and the great arched wooden door slowly creaked open, revealing the secrets of the inner chamber. Maggie laughed out loud. 'Can you believe it? Can you believe it?' she said, sounding more Irish by the moment.

'Yes, I can believe it all right.'

'There,' she said, leaning forward to open the door even wider. 'Feel free to walk around, I shall be outside waiting, if you need anything just call.' She left, the door closing slowly behind her.

It was gone two o'clock as I looked around, absorbing the fine stonework and hanging wall tapestries around me. I assumed that once upon a time the tower must have been part of something much larger, and yet it was strangely complete in its current form. Just then I felt a presence. 'Maggie?' There was no answer. She must still be outside. The floor was laid out in numerous large flagstones except for an area that had been filled in with medieval clay tiles of black and red diagonals. One in the centre had the remnants of a white *fleur-de-lys* engraved in it. Further in, almost in the centre of the room, was a flagstone bearing a large cross, Templar, I imagined. Inlaid with brass was an inscription in Latin.

Rising in the corner was a winding wooden staircase that had small acorns carved into its balustrade. As I walked up the steps, I wondered why the stairs were wooden and not stone. Halfway up I turned, as you do, to admire the view below. The stairs creaked a little and for a second I worried they might give way. I continued on up and reached a small landing, noticing how much warmer the air had become, almost as warm as a greenhouse. How long had it been since the last visitor? I wondered.

I remained there for some time, looking into the auditorium, expecting to feel something special or be initiated into some great mystery. Perhaps I should say something, say words to make peace. Show I was friendly. Show that I was at one with the place, whoever it may be home to!

'I was here, but now I'm gone, long ago before you were born. The years of many have passed me by, but wherever I was still am I!' The words just seemed to come to me.

Silence followed as I waited for the happening, perhaps a vision, a voice, anything? I stood very still, motionless, adamant that if I was patient something indeed would happen. Now, with all my senses alerted to the slightest change in vibration, something would certainly happen. Slowly and steadily, the room got lighter as the sun shone stronger through a small, arched stained-glass window. I watched, inspired by its growing warm rays creeping along the floor, stopping just short of the fleur-de-lys tile, before rising in a circular movement around the tower walls. I was now engulfed by an array of rainbow colours moving slowly around the plain walls like a kaleidoscope. A sign indeed! How many times, I wondered, over the last two thousand years had this beautiful pageant taken place? And was the kaleidoscope intended? From my elevated position, I marvelled at the show as the words of the famous song came into my head. How did it go? *Like a wheel within a wheel, like a never-ending circle, like the circles that you find in the windmills of your mind!'*

Then the show was over the sun had gone behind a cloud and the tower became dull again. I made my way back down the wooden stairs, stopping half way to take in the view. Beautiful, simply beautiful! There were heavy red velvet curtains hung from a long brass pole that stretched from one end of the wall to the other and almost from the ceiling to the floor. Part of the curtain was lifted to the side by a gold-brocade tie-back attached to the wall. In the centre was a large, round wooden table and on it a clay jug and a candlestick. Two large gold and silver brocade banners, one crossed over the other, were clasped firmly to the opposite wall to the side of what I now saw to be a blue, red and white stained-glass window. I could just make out St George and the Dragon, or was it the Archangel Michael, on one of them.

Hush now… Listen to me. 'When I was born I saw the light and the light was with me all my life. And as I grew the light grew with me but I was moving in darkness. In a world of hate I heard people speak of love but I saw no love, I heard them speak of fair play, but I saw no fair play and they made me carry out their lies, knowing that I believed they were not so.

And then I saw that I was a liar, no better than they! I must escape, return to a more normal life, but how? I was not heard because the ears could not hear and the eyes could not see but even so the heart still feels. Many were strangers, yet others? I knew them well and they knew me well. There were some that only half knew me, some that thought they knew me, many who wanted to know me, given time I could know them all.'

The room was quiet again. The sun had by now completely vanished and it was cold, time to go. Au revoir! Lifting the heavy latch, I opened the door and made ready to step into the warm sunlight, taking a last look into the tower and the table, half-covered by the velvet curtain. I wondered if there was something behind the curtain, it seemed a strange place to hang it as there didn't seem to be a window behind it. Curiosity killed the cat but I couldn't help myself. I would have to take another look before leaving. Pulling the curtain aside, I was surprised to see a wooden, high-backed chair that, despite its age, looked as though it would be quite comfortable to sit on. Why hide a chair? And why was there only one? I pondered these questions on the way out and tried to imagine when it had been used and for what reason. One sat in a chair at the table to write or to eat. But who would have dinner alone at this table? And what would they eat? Surely only bread and wine could have been served from here. Anyway, there were no catering facilities and as far as I could see there wasn't even a loo! OK, this was silly, no one was having dinner here, so why the goblet and candlestick? Maybe they were writing. Writing what? What on earth would you write about? I found myself going round and round in circles again. What was the point in wondering how long it had been since someone had sat at the table? It was polished and there was no sign of dust anywhere, probably because Maggie had cleaned it before opening up. Well, that was a good explanation but it wasn't good enough for me. No, I preferred to consider the more romantic option. A Templar knight or some other crusader visited on special occasions to pay homage to his past. I imagined him standing there in chain mail, covered by a white tunic with a large cross stitched in red upon the front and back. He unsheathes his long sword from its scabbard, placing it gently on the floor beside him. Kneeling, he swears a secret oath of allegiance. Now with his mind, body and soul fully attuned, he lights a candle, sips some fortified wine and prays.

I stood on the corner of Mark lane with the image still quite clear in my mind. For heaven's sake, enough of this time travelling! After all, I was hungry and it was lunchtime! Outside, Maggie was nowhere to be seen. Traders were passing by and not even noticing that the tower was open to them or that the entrance fee cost nothing!

'Have you finished?' Maggie suddenly said, approaching from behind.

'Yes, thank you, it was very interesting, exactly how I imagined it!'

'Really, I'm so pleased.' She nodded her head and smiled, cupping her hand around the white mug she was still holding. Maggie was, I thought, a very peaceful-looking woman, and even though her clothes appeared shabby, I noticed they still held their colour. In fact the blue shawl she had around her shoulders matched the colour of her velvet bag that was now hanging on the back of her chair.

I dug around to find some loose change to put in the box. 'Don't worry about that,' she said, waving her hand rather impatiently as she made her way over to the tower door, locking it with some difficulty.

'Don't you think anyone else will visit today, then?' I asked, surprised she was closing up so early.

'I doubt it.'

'Well, thank-you for showing me around, I best get back to the office now.'

She waved at me 'Ah, now, don't you forget, if you want to make a return visit I shall be here for a good while yet.'

I moved closer to her. 'It's very kind of you but don't you get bored just sitting here waiting for people to show an interest?'

'No, not at all, I like to think of it like this. If you make a space then people will walk in and it's so interesting to see just who it is that walks in! You see, Gerry, if I wasn't here today making this new space, then you couldn't have walked into it, could you? You see the door is not always open,' she added, waving a long finger in the air, 'and you have to walk through it to know that and you have, haven't you?'

I nodded. 'Yes, I have!"

I would have stayed all day talking with her but now I really did have to leave. Checking my watch, I waved to her for the final time. Five to two, it must be later than that, I thought. I bet my watch has stopped. God knows what the time is and I've still got to check the position and orders and I haven't even eaten yet! Hurrying along, I think of a million things I need to do before the afternoon session and ah, yes, there's a conversation I need to finish with Debbie.

A few minutes later I was queuing at the sandwich bar. I checked my watch against the clock on the cafe wall. It was two after all so luckily I still had plenty of time to check the position cards.

Chapter Six

Win Some, Lose Some!

Unaccustomed to feeling relaxed at this time of day, I returned to the office in a relatively good mood. Debbie was sitting with a coffee and smoking a cigarette rather furiously. I knew she wanted an answer from me. Well, she would have to wait until I was ready. Why, I wondered, should she have life so easy when I had it so hard? Life wasn't at all fair. It seemed to me that the more you wanted something, the harder it was to get.

'All right?' she waved at me.

'Yes, I'm fine,' I smiled back at her, knowing what was coming next.

'Good morning, was it, down there on the Exchange?' she asked.

'Yes, it was OK.'

Debbie stubbed her cigarette out impatiently. Obviously she had something on her mind. 'OK, well… it might be a good idea if I come down this afternoon then, eh?'

'Yes, I thought we'd agreed on that already,' I said dismissively.

She tutted loudly. 'What on earth's the matter with you today?'

'Nothing, I'm just thinking about the zinc market, that's all.' Actually, I was thinking about telling her a secret. But I wasn't sure she could be trusted. She was a gossip and the last thing I wanted was the whole market to know my business. I decided it could wait – wait until I could trust her more. Perhaps next week, when I became a fully authorised dealer, perhaps then I could tell her.

As we made our way to the market, Debbie was, as usual, full of questions. Today she wanted to know all about the relationships in the office, who fancied who, and who was going out together. I tried to answer her as honestly as possible without gossiping. But in the end I had to say to her, 'Look, I really don't know anything. It doesn't matter to me at all. I just want to get on with my work. I'm not looking for a husband or a boyfriend at the moment.'

'Aren't you? Why ever not?'

'Because, because, I don't have the time at the moment.' I wished we didn't have to have these conversations but if we didn't talk about these things, what could we talk about? I suppose I could have told her about my lunchtime visit to the tower and about meeting up with Maggie, but somehow I didn't think she would be that interested. It just wouldn't press the right buttons for her. So I kept quiet and listened to the latest gossip that she had heard down the pub at lunchtime while we both walked briskly through Lime Street into Whittington Avenue.

Ten minutes later, we arrived in the warmth of the Metal Exchange, laughing at each other's wild-eyed look, fuelled by a bitter cold wind on the way down. As usual the traders stared as we approached but Debbie, being far more gorgeous, received most of the attention, for which I was eternally grateful!

'OK,' I told her, 'you go up into the gallery now and watch the session. After zinc I'll come up and explain a few things, OK?'

'Yea, great, Wow, I'm really looking forward to this! I'm so excited!'

I watched her walk slowly and rather deliberately up the stairs, before I entered the trading floor. I considered the contrast in our appearances, mine quite sober compared to hers. Still, skills come in many forms and I rather naively believed then that women would be valued for much more than simply their looks! But if vanity was the prerogative of women, then some showing off was allowed.

Entering the Exchange was still something of an experience for me, filled with a hushed sense of expectation that always made me nervous. The feeling was accentuated by numerous glances that told me I was still uninvited into this male sanctum. Often you could cut the atmosphere with a knife, but most of the time I tended to ignore this feeling. Today I was more aware of it because Debbie was watching and I wondered whether she was able to sense the atmosphere from where she was. I waved at her discreetly. I had a couple of lead and zinc orders to do but decided to trade a couple of hundred tons instead. This was so Debbie could see what it took and what it looked like for a woman to shout across the Ring, across all of those male voices, and be heard. I hoped to show her that we could do the biz just as well as any of them! But it was a quiet Ring and after I had done my bit, all I could do was lean back and wait for the closing bell. Hardly inspiring really, not like when I first saw James in action. I was so impressed with his performance, but I doubt whether Debbie has seen anything to impress her today!

'Who's that then?' I turned around and a dealer from another company was leaning over me, pointing at Debbie in the gallery. 'A new client? A very pretty new client!'

'No, that's Debbie, our trainee clerk and soon she'll be working down here for us. This is her first visit to the market so be nice, will you?'

'Is that why you traded two hundred tons of zinc, then, to impress her? Ha ha ha!' I rolled my eyes, hoping to discontinue the conversation, but to no avail. 'Blimey, they'll be loads of you down here soon.'

'Yup, with any luck,' I smiled and stepped out of the Ring.

Ignoring the dealer, I waved to Simon, who had just walked into the Exchange, but the man carried on talking. 'I mean you lot will have two lady clerks down ere, RCW will have one soon and I hear ATM are thinking of putting a female clerk down as well, and then there's OCO as well!'

I sighed. 'And your point is?'

'Well there will be bloody loads of you soon,' he repeated.

'Hmm, hopefully, now if you don't mind I've got some work to do. Now where is James?'

A minute later I caught up with Simon, who was on the phone checking his orders for the Silver Ring. I tapped him on the shoulder 'Where's James?' Simon shook his head. 'Do you know what copper orders need to be done?' He shook his head again, shrugging his shoulders.

The Copper Ring was filling up fast, and one of us would have to fill in for James, we couldn't possibly allow our seat to remain empty! But James not being here in time for the Copper Ring was not a good impression to give Debbie on her first visit. If we were not careful, all of this would go back to David in the office. I decided to go and sit in the Ring but Simon pulled me back. 'Wait, Gerry, not you, not in the Copper Ring. Here, take this phone, I'll sit in for James.'

'OK, but you don't know what the orders are for copper.'

'Ask David to check the order book again.' And he thrust the phone into my hand. I looked up at Debbie and smiled. I should have gone up to see her, I hoped she was OK on her own.

The bell sounds and the Ring begins. 'OK, David,' I say into the phone, 'we're about to start copper, are there any orders?'

'Yes, tell James all the ones from this morning that weren't done are still valid.'

'Can you repeat those to me please, just so we avoid any duplication?'

'No I can't, I'm far too busy. You've still got Debbie down there and I've got no help in the bloody office. So no, no I can't!'

Simon was looking at me expectantly, shaking his hand as if to say: give me the orders. There were just a couple of minutes to go. Where on earth was James? And then, as though he had heard me, I watched him jauntily swagger onto the Exchange without, it appeared, a care in the world. Suddenly I realised he was as drunk as a lord! I beckoned him over. 'Quick, James, quick, you've only got a few minutes.'

He winked and pulled a stupid face, a face he always pulled when he was tipsy. But give him his dues, he took on board his mission and approached the bench. I watched as he tapped an obviously annoyed Simon on the shoulder. 'Get up will ya, get up.' James continued to shake Simon, but Simon was not moving, he carried on staring into the middle of the Ring.

'Come on, Simon,' I added, feeling I could make a difference. 'James has got orders to do. Hurry, he's got all of those orders to complete for New York.' They had put through a lot of orders overnight and would be expecting some executions.

Simon was nodding as if in agreement but staring at Debbie, who was watching from the gallery. Despite this apparent agreement, he failed to move. Simon wasn't normally a rebel but looking at Debbie seemed to give him courage to be just that. I realised then that the chances of us all working together as a team in the future would be quite remote. 'Tell ya what, why don't you do what you always do, mate?' drawled Simon. 'Book em out! Cause I ain't moving, not till the Ring has closed anyway.'

In his frustration, James hopped from one leg to the other and then he slammed his fist into the back of the bench, making Simon jolt from the vibration. To make his point further, he pointed a sharp finger into Simons shoulder, he did it so hard it must have hurt but Simon still didn't flinch maybe because he knew there was only a minute of trading left. James closed his eyes, gritted his teeth and held tightly onto the bench in a supreme effort to control his temper.

At last the bell rang and Simon, still very annoyed, stepped out of the Ring. James grabbed my arm, almost roughly. 'Do as he says, Gerry, book New York out and I'll sort this out in the morning.'

We all knew that James liked a little something before the market, perhaps a whisky on the rocks, a chaser after his pint or two. But it was beginning to get out of hand and all of us recognised that James being drunk was not good for any of us – not for our reputations and not for our business. But the show wasn't over yet. James was going down fighting. I watched as his face turned ashen white with fury as he pushed and shoved Simon into the foyer for one last showdown.

I followed them out, intending to speak with Debbie in the gallery. I could hear Simon shouting back at James. This was not a good idea, we were supposed to be setting a good example to Debbie. I would have to say something.

'Look, can't you see this is going to get us nowhere? Do we really want the whole market to know our business? Can't we sort this out later in the office?'

There was silence for a moment as they both looked at me and then it started again. 'Next time I fucking tap your shoulder, you get out of the fucking Ring, do you hear, mate?'

Simon pulled away from James's grip, rearranging his jacket as he walked away. 'Are you all right?' I asked James.

'Suppose so, but I'm bloody pissed off with this lot, as soon as my bloody back is turned they fucking well start!' And then, still waving his arms around wildly, he walked back into the Exchange.

'Phew!' I turned to see Debbie standing on the stairs.

'Blimey! What was all that about?' She asked.

I shook my head 'Nothing, something stupid, it's often like that, let's forget about it and go upstairs. I can show you what's going on.'

'I'd love to know what it's like sitting in that Ring,' she said smiling. 'God, it must be so wonderful being down there! I mean, you must love it, all those men looking at you, and always being the centre of attention?'

I laughed. 'What, like just now? I don't think so! Ha ha! Seriously, though, it's not like that all the time, I'm just here to do my job. Besides, I don't think anyone really fancies me anyway.'

She gave me a long look as if she wondered what on earth I meant before changing the subject. 'I suppose when you get to be like James or Simon then you'll know. I suppose you'll really feel like a dealer then, won't you?'

'Yes, when I take my exam and pass I can take my badge off and sit in the Ring as an authorised dealer.'

'If you do that, can you trade any metal?'

'Yes, any metal but usually beginners stay with lead and zinc.'

'But wouldn't you want to trade aluminium when it comes onto the Exchange? David thinks it will be as busy as copper, better than copper even.'

I thought for a moment. 'Does he? Well yes, then I would probably want to trade aluminium if I can but it does depend who the client is.'

She squeezed my arm. 'God, it's so exciting. We're going to be the only women down on the floor! We'll be rich, beautiful and young, with loads of blokes to choose from. It's too good to be fucking true!'

'Well speak for yourself, the only thing I am is young!' Debbie laughed out loudly. I held my finger to my lips. 'Ssshh!'

''Ere, Gerry, listen, when I get back to the office tonight I'm gonna get Henry to make an application for me to come down onto the Exchange as well. Then I can be your clerk and we can be an all-women team, that'll show em, eh?'

I smiled, not knowing whether to take her seriously but I agreed with her anyway. 'Yes, I think we need to get your application in if you want to be the second woman on the Exchange because I know other companies are also looking to get women to work down here now.'

'Are they? Well that doesn't surprise me at all. Of course they want the pretty girls down on the Exchange, they don't want to be left out, do they? Just think, soon I could be standing behind you, this place will never be the same. I mean, why the bloody hell should we have to work in the office all the time? It's about time we showed ourselves off and what we are capable of, don't you think, Gerry?'

'Absolutely, of course I think it's about time.'

Debbie was fun if not a little over-enthusiastic. It was great having another woman to laugh with and I began to think I really was going to enjoy working with her.

Back in the office later, James was speaking with Henry. I didn't want him to leave the company but he had backed himself into a difficult corner and Henry had never been his number one fan. There was a lot of shaking of heads. Trevor, Simon and, unusually, even David were all agreed that James should leave. I watched Henry leave the boys to it; both Debbie and I had moved closer to listen in on the conversation. I was shocked to see them all turn on James.

'Come on, you know you have lost us loads of money!' Simon was yelling at James, but he was having none of it.

'So? We all lose money from time to time, especially those of us that have to take a position. Sometimes it goes right, sometimes it goes wrong!'

'Yeah, but he doesn't have to take the position all the time, does he?' Simon asked the others, pointing at James as he started to leave the room.

'No, he just does it cause he's too lazy to trade the market.'

'Rubbish, that not true!'

'He drinks and he's too lazy to trade the market.' They were all pointing and shouting at each other.

'Enough!' I butted in. 'It's not getting us anywhere, why not check the position first before deciding that he's lost us a fortune?'

'Oh shut up, you silly old cow, what do you know?' Simon slammed his book on the desk.

'Right, I've had enough for one day,' I said. 'I'm going home.' I managed a smile for Debbie as I left.

Just as I was passing by the boardroom, Henry called me in. I had seen James leave a few minutes earlier and I was hoping to be able to catch up with him. But it wasn't going to be likely now. 'Come in, Gerry, and shut the door, take a seat.' He paused for a moment. 'Firstly, I would like to say well done for all your hard work and I know next week is on your mind, but if it's any consolation to you, I'm sure you'll do fine. Secondly, do you think Debbie is ready to go onto the Exchange?'

'Yes, I think she's ready so long as David feels he can cope.'

Henry tapped his pipe on the ashtray. 'Good. I'm pleased. And you both get on well?'

'Yes, I think we do.'

'Good, very good. Now listen. As you know we're doing a lot with the Czechoslovakians and I'm sure we can do even more business with them so I want you to send your metals report over to them and include a recommendation on aluminium will you please?'

'Yes, OK, that shouldn't be a problem.' I looked up at the clock. Damn, I'd just missed my train. I took advantage of the situation to ask about James. 'What's this about James? He's not going, I hope?'

Henry looked up and grabbed some blotting paper to dab his signature with. 'What do you mean, what about James?'

'What's happening with him?' I asked.

At times like this Henry did his best to make me feel awkward. As though I didn't really have a right to ask the question. But I felt I had as much right to know as any of the lads; besides, James had trained me, I should know if he was going. Henry cleared his throat, still pondering his response. 'James has decided to leave and I'm making Simon head trader. He'll continue to do silver but now he'll do copper as well. You'll do lead and zinc and possibly aluminium later, but for now Trevor will do tin and aluminium. By the way, how was Debbie today?'

'Yes, she was good, I think she enjoyed herself.'

'Right, well, I want her clerking and then trading too on the Exchange. OK, have I made myself clear?' He seemed stressed.

'Yes, of course.' I looked up at the clock, another train missed. Sod it, I thought, I'm going to ask for more money.

'Henry, I know we haven't spoken about this for a while but last time we did you promised to consider a rise for me.'

'Yes, I know I did and I'm going to give you a rise.' He puffed on his pipe hard. 'I'm going to give you a £5000 rise as soon as you become an authorised dealer.'

'That's next week.'

'Yes, and I believe that will take you to fifteen thousand.

Oh, and I'm also going to give you all a bonus at Christmas based on the profits you make during the year. Now I can't be fairer than that, can I?'

'No. Thank you!'

'Well, are you pleased?'

'Yes, of course I am,' I replied unconvincingly.

But at that moment I was wondering how much Debbie was getting paid. A little voice in my head seemed to tell me that she was already on this amount and that was why Henry had responded so promptly. But I fought off the temptation to ask; after all, it would seem very ungrateful of me, wouldn't it?

The following week was going to be an important time for me and I was upset that James had left without saying a proper goodbye. Still, I hoped I would see him again on the Exchange. Simon and Trevor had slipped into their new roles and Debbie had taken to clerking on the Exchange, just like a fish to water. Of course, I was very nervous about my interview with the Committee of the London Metal Exchange. Who wouldn't be?

I wondered what would happen if I failed the interview. Would I be able to try again, or would that be the end of my career as a Ring Dealer?

At 2.30 on the day of the interview, I made my way to the entrance doors of the committee room. It was in a very dark corner at the back of the Exchange and I immediately felt out of place. I stood as close to the doors as possible, without appearing as though I was listening to the debate going on inside. Those large, glass embossed Victorian swing doors would usher me in, then back out again, my fate decided by those within. I peered through the doors and could just make out a lad standing in a suit, his back towards me. I won't look like that when I'm in there, I thought. Everyone will know it is me because I'm not wearing trousers. Often I had seen a welcoming party waiting just outside to greet the successful candidate, but I was quite sure there would be no welcoming party for me. The committee usually met outside of Ring trading hours and I was relieved that my interview with these great metal men would be held before the afternoon market. I had swotted up on the rules, regulations and history, and felt ready to answer any question they might throw at me. I knew that part of the entrance procedure was about how they felt I had performed in the Ring over the last six months.

I thought back to that morning, when a number of dealers had come up to me, wishing me good luck, smiling knowingly and patting me on the back. 'Hey, Gerry, best of luck, mate. I bet you're nervous!'

'Yes, just a bit'

'Ah, don't worry, you'll be OK.'

'Yes, hope so.' Trouble was, the more support they gave me the more nervous I felt. I had to keep telling myself: what will be will be and if I don't get in this time, I'll learn from the lesson and keep trying. And then, just when I didn't think I could think about it any more, 2.30 had arrived and it was time to go in.

The door opened and out stepped a very happy and presumably just authorised trader. 'All right?' I asked.

'Yes, great, I think it's your turn next.'

'Oh, shall I just go in or wait to be called?'

'I'd wait a minute, if I were you.'

None the wiser, I waited and then the call came. I walked into a large stuffy room smelling of cigars and pipes. 'Good afternoon, gentlemen,' I said, shutting the door behind me. Despite the dim atmosphere, some light reflected off a highly polished oak table, making it look very large indeed. Around it sat twenty elderly men. It may have been more. I searched for a friendly face to focus on but they all looked the same to me. Now the whole place smelt of a mixture of polish, port and cigars. It wasn't an unpleasant smell but it was overpowering.

'Would you like some port, Geraldine? Ha ha ha!' Was he serious, I wondered, or were they testing me? So even though I felt like a drink, I said, 'No thank you sir, I don't drink.'

A chorus of laughter broke out in the room. I was pleased

they were happy with my response. 'I should think not, young lady. Not at this time of the day anyway!' They leaned back in their chairs and laughed, some patting their well-nourished bellies and others twiddling with their gold pocket-watch chains. It was all I could do not to laugh myself. During this light-hearted interlude, I had a chance to look around the room. Sporadically spaced but intentionally placed were awe-inspiring pictures of past chairmen and other dignitaries that I had become so used to seeing. There were black and white photographs and a couple of very large paintings in brown and white. Members of this club looked and dressed exactly the same. Normally top-hatted and tailed, some had obligatory bushy whiskers, while others, more sombre-looking, had long dark brown beards. A rather Darwinian look, I fancied, or did I mean Dickensian? Or perhaps draconian, even! Well, it would seem there hadn't been much change in the last hundred years. The images hanging on the wall were not very different from the men now sitting in front of me. Sitting there ready to say whether they were prepared to accept a change in their club, sitting there just like the men in the pictures above them, sitting there smoking their cigars, fiddling with their pocket watches and stroking their beards, polishing their glasses and stroking their whiskers. No, there was not much change to be expected here!

'Enough!' I jumped as a heavy hand slammed the other end of the table. 'Enough, I say, gentleman. Give the poor girl a chance now.'

I focused on the man who had taken charge, he had a very large booming voice and I recognised him as being supportive, but next to him sat the committee member whose face I had slapped! Now I was in trouble.

'Geraldine, we are each going to ask you a question in turn. You will answer loudly and clearly so that we can all hear. If we are satisfied with the answer you have given, we will nod so that another question can be asked. Do you understand?'

'Yes, Sir'

'Right, who would like to start?'

Several questions later, I was in the middle of a rather long answer when I realised that I had been in there for more than an hour. I turned slightly to the glass door behind me and I could hear the market was filling up with traders, ready for trading to begin. I could also see that there were two clerks waiting to be interviewed. I returned my gaze to my questioner. 'Well of course, I have been trading for nearly ten years, Sir, so it's not that new to me and I'm sure I will be able to cope. I'm just here to do my job, Sir.' I didn't like saying 'Sir' all the time but I knew they liked me to say it and that was the best way of showing them respect.

'Thank you, Geraldine, we have, as I am sure you know, been watching you for some time. You may now leave the room. And by the way, Madam, congratulations!' I couldn't believe my ears and I felt I had to confirm what had been said.

'I'm sorry, are you saying that I'm authorised?'

'Yes, yes, well done and send the next one in on your way out.'

'Thank you, gentlemen,' I said, stepping backwards and out of the door. I stood for a moment, breathing a sigh of relief and checking to see if I felt any different now that I was officially a fully authorised dealer. I didn't and I was surprised.

The market was filling up and I was at last beginning to feel some sense of achievement. Walking into the Ring, I noticed some photographers were standing at the back of the room. I sat down in the Ring without smiling and then all hell let loose. Flashbulbs went off all around me while I pretended I wasn't blinded by the lights! Committee members who had followed me out onto the trading floor were now standing opposite, pointing and smiling from the ringside.

They must have issued a press release because little trading activity was taking place. I looked to see who was standing behind me and was pleased to see James leaning over me. 'All right, love?' he beamed.

'Yes, I'm fine, where did you come from?'

'Ah, never mind, I wasn't going to miss this, was I?'

Thank God he was here with me because by now the market was beginning to resemble a film set. After the Lead Ring a photographer grabbed me. 'Please can you sit in the Ring again so we can take more photos of you trading?'

'Yes, of course.'

Later I was bombarded with questions – ironically, far more difficult to answer that those from the committee!

'What was it like to be the first woman to trade on the Exchange? Exciting?'

I could see huge expectancy in their eyes as they waited for my responses. But I didn't have a clue how to answer them. So I did what I usually do in such circumstances; I told them what I thought they wanted to hear. 'Yeah, very exciting!'

'It must be difficult, eh?'

'Yeah, very difficult!'

'How much money can you make?'

'Err… if I'm doing my job well, quite a lot, I suppose!'

'What's it like working down here as the only woman with all these rich, handsome men? Surely you must be tempted sometimes?'

'No not really! Err… well yes, I suppose so, but I fight it!'

'And lastly, can you tell us how you're feeling right now? You must be feeling on top of the world!'

'Oh yes, I feel wonderful, I don't have to wear this badge any more, I am the equal of any man sitting here and I'm very proud to be here! It's a really great day for me and I sincerely hope for the London Metal Exchange. I would like to say thank you to everyone who has helped me. That includes the Committee of the London Metal Exchange, my bosses Henry and Mark for supporting my application for authorisation and, of course, my fellow dealers who have helped me during the last six months.'

The Lead and Zinc Ring had come and gone and so had most of the questions. I could relax now even enjoy the moment.

'Halo, Allo, Ello, can I take a picture miss, OK? Can I take a picture please, outside, outside on the pavement if you like.' A young Italian-sounding photographer was gesticulating at me.

'Yes, it will have to be quick though as I have some dealing to do in the Copper Ring. Who are you anyway? What paper are you writing for?'

'No, not paper, magazine, Italian magazine 'Oggi'. Ha, you can be famous in Italy now, yes famous in Italy.'

I followed him into Whittington Avenue. There was no dramatic Metal Exchange building to show off so I posed beside the wrought-iron façade of Leadenhall Market. 'OK how's this? Can we be quick please, I don't have too much time.' I felt a bit of a fool, having my photo taken in the street and I didn't want the other traders to come out and find me posing. It was embarrassing because each time he tried to take a picture of me, pedestrians would get in the way or stop and stare. As a result, we constantly had to change our position and what should have been a five-minute shoot ended up being far longer. By now I was freezing and tired and could barely be polite. 'Please send me a copy of the photo and the article you write to go with it.'

'Yes, of course, but just one thing, so that I know I have it right. You are the first in London, first woman to trade on Exchange floor and first in the world yes, is that right?'

'Yes, I believe so.'

'So first in the world on an Exchange floor as recognised dealer yes?'

'Yes.'

'OK, just so I am straight, can I come to watch you trade now?'

'Yes, of course, if you wish, but from the public gallery, up those stairs there.'

'I'm not able to go with you through this door now?'

'No, I'm sorry you're not allowed to, you have to have special permission.'

'But I had special permission didn't I already?'

'Yes, well that was then, this is now. I'm sorry, I really must get back'

'Will you come out for drink later with me we can talk again for magazine?'

'No, I can't I'm afraid, but thank you for asking.'

I walked onto the Exchange floor just as the Silver Ring had closed. 'Sorry, Simon, were you busy?'

'No, we managed OK, didn't we, Trevor. Anyway what was James doing behind you in the Ring? He doesn't work for us any more.'

'Well, he always said he would be there on my first day in the Ring as an authorised trader and he was as good as his word. I'm glad he was here, it was very thoughtful of him to remember his promise to me.'

Someone tapped me on the shoulder. I turned to see who it was. 'About time we had that lunch, don't you think, Madam?'

'Oh yes, of course.'

'Well, you keep saying yes so when's it going to be, Monday, Tuesday?'

I thought for a second or two, I would have to accept since I didn't feel I could put him off again and still appear polite. 'How about next Thursday?'

'Good, I'll book a table at my club and we can celebrate.'

This was Mr Stevens, a committee member who had, for quite some time, been inviting me to lunch. Up until now I had managed to decline every invite. I felt he was far too familiar and didn't show enough respect. He just couldn't help himself. He had to touch me whenever he could. Usually he would pinch or slap my bottom as he passed and then wink and smile at the lads opposite. Eventually I had slapped his face and been quite rude to him. We didn't talk for a bit but then he forgot all about it and asked me out for a drink, which of course I declined. He soon became keener and a drink turned into dinner before I finally agreed to lunch. He must have been at least thirty years older than me but I felt that, so long as I could control him, he would be a good friend. After all, being an authorised dealer did not mean my troubles would now all go away. On the contrary, I expected a great deal more grief as a result of being qualified! My enemies had not disappeared, they had simply gone into hiding for the moment. Mr Stevens would be a great source of strength for me. Mr Stevens, or Thomas, as I later called him, made me laugh and I needed a friend like him, especially as James was not about any more. Thomas was a jolly aristocrat who was without doubt clever and powerful. He had many friends and, as we all found out later, just as many enemies as me. 'No one gets one over on me, my dear, ha, just let them try,' he once told me. 'I didn't get where I am today by being stupid.'

As I left the Exchange floor I was surprised to receive an enormous bouquet of flowers.. 'From all the dealers, welcome to the London Metal Exchange,' the Chairman said. I couldn't help but blush. 'Thank you.' I took a bow and they all clapped. This was a wonderful end to a wonderful day.

Afterwards, I went back to the office in a dream. David was standing there. 'What a bloody fuss about nothing! Honestly, haven't they got better things to do?' I smiled at his irritation. 'You'd better not get ideas above your station, that's all I can say.' He wagged his finger in pronouncement at me.

Henry walked slowly into the trading room, reading a report. Lifting his head, he smiled. 'Well, you did it, my dear, congratulations.' He bent down and kissed me on the cheek. 'You deserve it, Gerry.'

Mark was behind him. 'Yes, well done, we'll show em, eh?' He shook his fist in the air 'I just hope it's all worth it, that's all.'

'Of course it is, mate,' Debbie joined in 'It's brill! Can't wait to get down there and deal myself.'

I smiled. 'Thanks, and just another six months and you'll be in the Ring too. Not long to wait, is it?'

'Suppose not, but I'd be in there tomorrow if I could.'

'I know, but patience is a virtue, believe me!' I felt suddenly tired. Time to go home.

That weekend I relaxed and caught up with all those little jobs

I didn't have time to do during the week, like washing the car – a car I was still very proud of, despite it being dented on both sides from various accidents. No reason for it to be dirty, it was such a striking looking car and I was especially proud of the interior with its wooden and chrome dashboard and blue fitted carpets. But then, as I bent down to sweep the carpet, I felt a bump underneath. I wondered what it could be and removed a couple of the side studs of the carpet. The floor was grey, but something made me pass my hand underneath and it was then that I realised the car had a big hole in the floor. In fact there was hardly any flooring between the front and back seats. I was horrified to think of all my friends who had relaxed on the back seat as I took them home after a night out clubbing. All those feet resting on that back carpet and nothing underneath them accept the road!

I shuddered at the thought, How dangerous! At any time this car could have broken into two pieces. How it had managed to stay together at speeds in excess of a hundred miles an hour, I'd never know. Tanya and I could have easily been killed. Christ, all the troubles we'd had in the past with this car and now on top of it all, this. It really was the last straw, the car would have to go. What a fool to have bought it in the first place. It just goes to show, you can't judge a book by its cover! All that money spent and now we would have no car at all. Well, serve me right for being so stupid. I mean, who on earth would be so naive as to buy a car on the spur of the moment, the way I had!

I went inside and made a cup of tea. Later, when I told my mother, she gave me a knowing look. No good crying over spilt milk, I had to do something about it and selling was not an option. This car would have to go to the dump probably. I rang up a local garage and they agreed to take it away for nothing. 'If you can repair it you can have it, just come and take it away please.' The garage agreed to come the following week, so in the meantime I considered how I could buy another car. Perhaps work could help, maybe even give me a loan?

Determined to forget all about the car, I met my sister Patricia in the Ladbroke Arms for a lunchtime drink. Tanya said she would pop up too because she had arranged to meet Mike, her colleague from work, whom she promised to introduce us all to. Big deal! My sister was always able to pick up on stuff and, sensing my mood, she asked me, 'What's up then?'

'I dunno really. I mean, work is going fine but... well... the bloody car packed up on me yesterday and I feel I'm going nowhere fast. Do you know what I mean?'

'Yes of course I do, it's the same for me too. I'd just love to meet someone who could change my life. Someone you could really trust, someone who was good yet exciting, someone who was sensible but generous too, and oh yes, don't forget he would have to be very good-looking too!'

'Oh right, Mr Perfect. I don't think so!' I nudged her like I always did and like she always hated.

'Oh, shut up, I can dream, can't I?'

'Yes, of course you can because there is absolutely no chance of them ever coming true. Not these days, anyway. Look,' I continued, 'you've got just as much chance of that perfect person walking through that door now as I have and we both know it isn't going to happen.' We lit up a cigarette together. 'Ah, my life is just as boring as yours, all work and no play. Still, at least we have each other.'

'Yea,' I said, taking another sip of lager. We both watched as the door opened but we couldn't see who came in because of the sun shining though a haze of cigarette smoke. Subconsciously we carried on staring, waiting for the person to emerge. 'That person look very familiar, don't you think?' said Patricia finally. 'That person over there, the one who has just come in the door?'

I strained to see better. 'You know, if I didn't know better, I would have definitely said that it was Emily! It certainly looks like her.'

We watched as she sat down. 'She even moves like Emily,' I whispered, 'I'm sure it's her.' I got up and nodded to Patricia 'I'm sure it is!' The smell of musk was very convincing as I approached her. 'Emily, Emily, what are you doing here?'

She looked up and laughed out loud 'Gerry! Can you believe it? How long has it been? I didn't know that you came to this pub!'

'Yes, I always do on a Sunday, my sister's over there as well. But anyway, I thought you were in Austria?'

'Yes, I am, I'm over just visiting for a while. Actually I'm waiting for my brother, he lives just round the corner and we said we would meet here for a drink.'

'God, this is amazing, it must be all of five years since I last saw you and I see you've put on a little weight, but it suits you.'

'Yea, and I suppose you're still as rich as ever? Ha ha ha!' I didn't bother to reply since I had never considered myself rich. Emily threw her head back and laughed again.

'Well, have you got long enough for a drink or do you have to rush off somewhere?' I asked.

'That's a stupid question, isn't it? I've just arrived, haven't I, and when haven't I had time for a drink? Besides, I told you I'm waiting for my brother?' I beckoned my sister over and Tanya and Mike joined us later.

Time flew as we reminisced, it was 3.30 already. I noticed that Mike and my sister were getting on very well but Tanya looked a bit out of it. I felt sorry for her for a moment but couldn't steal myself away from Emily, who was now brushing her hair, signalling an imminent departure. 'Let's meet up tonight, shall we?' I said to Emily.

'Yes, that's sounds like a good idea, I'm already meeting some friends for a drink, why don't you join us?'

'I'd love to, and I'll see if Tanya wants to come as well.'

The evening was wonderful and, as usual when Emily was around, quite eventful. Emily was great company but I knew she was thinking of Molly in Austria. Still, we were all having a great time and she introduced me to some of her friends, including a girl called Mary. Tanya was in a quiet mood and hardly said a word all night – she hadn't been keen on coming in the first place but I had persuaded her. I just couldn't be doing with her sulks tonight and she had a habit of bringing me down when she was like this. Besides, Mary and I were getting on very well, laughing, drinking and dancing nearly all night together. It was great. We shared the same sense of humour, and had the same amount of energy, and we were the only ones left dancing at 11.30. Wow, we were really having a ball! But then Tanya finally flipped her lid and threw a pint of lager over me as I sat down for a rest.

Emily found it all very funny. 'Serves you right, Gerry. Fancy upsetting Tanya like that! What do you think you're doing?'

I laughed outwardly but inside I was mad. 'Well, there's no need to chuck lager all over me,' I said, brushing down my suit. 'I don't know why she's getting so upset.' Tanya was now ignoring me completely. Mary shrugged her shoulders. 'Well it's about time we went anyway, isn't it?'

I had to agree. 'Yes, shall we share a taxi?'

'What all three of us?' said Tanya scowling.

'Well, why not?' Mary asked.

Shame the evening was ending. 'I'll see you again soon, won't I?' I said, kissing Emily a reluctant goodbye.

'Yes, perhaps we can get together sometime next week before I leave for Austria?'

'Yes, that would be great.' I gave her another hug and turned to see Tanya still staring at me. 'Are you ready to leave?' she asked impatiently.

'Yes, I suppose so. Come on, let's go then,' I said, walking towards the door.

There was an awkward silence in the cab after we dropped Mary in Holland Road. Tanya was upset, I could feel that, but there was no point in talking about it now. I didn't think there was anything to be done. I just hoped we could remain friends.

On my way to work the following morning, I resolved to speak to Henry about getting a company car. I knew the other traders had cars. Hopefully he would give me one too. Recently he had been very good to me and if push came to shove, well, I was happy to go without the Christmas bonus. As it happened, he agreed to my request. 'Yes you can have the spare brown Capri, you know the car James had before he left, it's got some mileage on it but it will be OK for a while. You can drive it for a year and then we can think about getting you a new car later.' I was gobsmacked; this was the second time Henry had promptly agreed to one of my requests; perhaps he was really beginning to value me! I was over the moon. A Capri! What a great car to have, and it wasn't going to cost me a penny. And I was still going to get my Christmas bonus too. Things were looking up, a new car and a new job!

As I was leaving the office, Henry asked me... 'Those Chinese, when are they coming to lunch?'

I thought for a moment. 'I think we said 8th of September and Mark was very happy with that day. Can you still make it, Henry?'

'Yes, I should think so, how many of them are coming?'

'Well, there are at least three. Let me see now, there's Mr Hao, Mr Yang, and Mr Hang. My Yang is about eighty-five years old, and Mr Hao I speak to on metals quite a lot. Mr Hao has been down the market and I know Mr Hang would like to visit the market.'

Henry shuffled some papers on his desk before replying. 'OK, and you are still sending your metals report to them?'

'Yes,' I replied.

'Good, and are you taking Debbie down onto the Exchange today?'

'Yes, if she'd like to come and clerk for me.'

Henry cleared his throat. 'I want her to clerk for you all the time and I want her to take her exam as well, when she's ready, of course.'

I wondered whether I should tell him about my lunch date with the committee member but I decided against it. He might get jealous or even think he was trying to poach me. Henry was still quite protective towards me, although I noticed he was becoming less so since Debbie had started working with us.

Debbie's first day on the market went well. I watched as she stood, pen in hand, ready to record my trades in her book. Right from the start she made an impact and she had no problem conversing with the other traders, especially newcomers. She was not shy at all and her voice, although female, added to the Essex dialect that was now emerging as the dominant force of trading, usurping the more traditional public school accent. Debbie, I'm pleased to say, got on well with everyone and she did a good job clerking for me. I came to rely on her completely.

My lunch with Thomas, the committee member, was enjoyable but had got off to an awkward start when he tried to take me to his club in Lime Street. As we walked in, the manager said to us, 'Good morning, Sir, we are serving lunch at the moment!'

'Yes, I know, I'd like a table for two, please.'

'I'm sorry, Sir, but women, are not allowed in this club.'

Thomas wanted to argue but I said, 'Leave it, don't spoil our lunch.' Besides, I had my own ideas about writing a letter to the owner of the club. 'Sexual discrimination is against the law,' I said to Thomas as we left. 'Surely I have as much right to use that club as any man?'

'Of course you do, my dear,' he said rather quietly.

Eventually we found an Italian restaurant called Mario and Franco's. We had plenty to drink, starting off with Bloody Marys, followed by a bottle of wine served with our pasta a la pesto and several brandies to round it all off. The conversation consisted mainly of how we had both got to where we had in life. His was a much longer story and included family details, which mine did not. Some of the questions he asked me were rather personal – questions such as did I have a boyfriend and what did he do, or was I married or going to get married. Trouble is, I played the game because I couldn't be honest! I was forced to lie to them and I knew that each lie I told moved me further from telling them the truth.

Some men that I had confided in assumed they could teach me a thing or two, given enough time. So whilst they outwardly accepted my preferences, inwardly they were all the while planning to win me over to their wicked way! By the time I was twenty-eight, I knew full well that what was in the heart was often the exact opposite to what was said. Oh yes, white man he speak with forked tongue!

Little did I know then that over the next few years, I would dine with all sorts of men, often from different nationalities and cultures, and all in the name of business. They were, of course, all my clients and they expected to be wined and dined as part of the service! Some of them would try to get me drunk but I would usually succeed in drinking them under the table. However, I managed to gain and maintain their respect and avoid those awkward questions about my personal life. Often they would try to find out what clients we had and who we were doing business with. I was constantly on guard. But it was important to network and to be able to exchange information with each other without giving the game away. Sharing food and drink provided an opportunity to network and build relations of trust. Bonding was an important part of being a successful trader and this was done over lunch or dinner. Lunch I could partake of, dinner I avoided like the plague!

Anyway, back to my story. After lunch I rushed back to the office to pick up some orders, when Harry stopped me in the corridor. I was in a hurry and didn't want to be late for the market but he wanted a quick word with me. I knew what his quick words were like! 'I wonder, Gerry, if you can do a small favour for me next week? It's an errand. Would you mind flying to Germany and delivering some metal warrants and at the same time getting this contract signed for me?'

I thought for a moment. I was surprised that he had asked me but on reflection, we were doing a lot of business with the Czechoslovakians and they had made it known that they wanted to do even more aluminium trading with us. In the past they had visited our office and signed contracts. I wondered why we now had to visit them and I also wondered why he hadn't asked Ben or Rick, the new desk trader. Why was it he needed me to go? After all, I wouldn't be able to trade on the floor that day, and if they could do one day without me then they could do every day without me! In the end I gave up trying to work it out and agreed to his request. The experience would, after all, be good for me.

But rushing down to the Exchange, I couldn't help but mull over Henry's unusual request. Obviously the metal warrants were too valuable to be sent by post, but why send me? I wondered then whether David had something to do with all of this. Perhaps it was his way of getting me off the Exchange. I didn't want Henry to think that I couldn't cope but at the same time I didn't want to meet these people on my own. I simply didn't feel safe travelling on my own in a strange country with men I didn't know. I decided to ask Henry if Rick could travel with me. I felt sure he would agree; after all, if it was important for me to have the experience, it was surely just as important for Rick. And I could do with the company!

Back on the afternoon market, Thomas greeted me, smiling and waving from across the other side of the Ring. I smiled and waved back.

'Come on, hurry up, you're late, where ave you been, mate? Look, you got this big zinc carry from New York to do.' Debbie handed me a piece of paper full of orders. 'They're from this morning and I've just got another one from New York, so take this down will yer?'

'Christ!' I said, looking at the clock 'I've only got four minutes, quick, what's the order then?'

Debbie read out from her book 'Yea, now let me see, New York changed it just now, so the one you got this morning is wrong. Now you got to lend eighty lots of cash to three months at market close first Ring this afternoon.'

The one I got this morning? I couldn't remember what order that was. 'Eighty lots, that's two thousand tonnes, that's a big order for New York, I hope the first afternoon Ring can take that!' I said to Debbie as I walked into the Ring and sat down. I could feel her behind me and for some unknown reason it made me feel quite nervous. Still, this was a big order and I didn't want to cock it up and certainly not in front of her. But I couldn't think how much the spread was.

'Cash to three months!' I shouted across the Ring.

There was still no response from any of the dealers. I looked at the clock again, just two and half minutes to go. It was no good, I'd have to suggest a rate, no one was making it easy for me today! 'I'll lend at fifteen.'

Still no reply, just a row of disinterested, motionless blank faces staring back at me. Two minutes to go. 'I'll lend at fifteen!' I shouted as loud as I could and a senior dealer turned from his conversation to look at me. 'OK!' I bellowed. 'I'll lend at sixteen contango then!'

Uproar ensued in the Ring and I wondered what was going on. Debbie was leaning over my shoulder, shouting in my ear, but I couldn't understand a word of what she was saying. I pushed her away and leaned forward in my seat. Traders were standing up and pointing at me and Debbie was frantically tapping me on the shoulder but I shoved her away. 'Not now,' I said but I doubt whether she heard me. Ten dealers were now jumping up and down in their seats pointing at me and shouting, 'Yes, yes, yes!' I *'how muched'* them and they took five hundred tonnes each and that was a good job too because just then the bell rang, indicating the Ring was closed. I leaned back against the bench, relieved that most of the order was done. Debbie was again leaning over me. 'What?' I asked.

'It's a backwardation!'

I stared into thin air, unable to fully absorb the ramifications of trading a backwardation instead of a contango. 'A backwardation! When did the market move into a backwardation?' I asked Debbie.

'This morning, Gerry, don't you remember?'

The uproar in the Ring continued, but I ignored it. I walked out of the Ring as calmly as possible, paying no heed to the pointing fingers, rude comments and accompanying laughter. Well, who could blame them? This was my first big dealing mistake. I wouldn't have minded quite so much if all the clerks hadn't been laughing out so loudly as well. 'Ha ha, yea what a dealer eh?' I was an idiot to have made such a stupid mistake. Granted, it was an easy mistake to have made because the market had just moved into a backwardation, but I knew that they would not let me forget it. Debbie was watching me in disbelief.

'Fucking ell! What av you done? You idiot, av you got any idea ow much you've just lost the company? Bloody ell, you must have lost us a fucking fortune.' I brushed past her, making my way over to the phone booth. Debbie followed me as though she wasn't sure whether I had heard what she was saying. 'It's not a contango, it's a backwardation and you fuckin wouldn't listen to me, you just kept on lending. It was mad, I can't believe you did it, and when Henry finds out, well, you're dead meat, ain't yer? You ain't no bloody dealer, Gerry, you're an asshole!'

'Oh shut the fuck up, will you, Debbie, and let me think! What have you told New York?'

Debbie turned a whiter shade of pale, she wasn't used to me shouting at her like that. 'Nuffing yet, why?'

'Right, OK, tell them their order is executed at £16 backwardation then!'

'What on all two thousand tonnes?'

'Yes, on the lot.'

'No! You're fucking mad. I'm not doing it.' I watched her stride off into the crowd. There was nothing for it but to take control.

'Right,' I said to myself as I grabbed the phone to the office. 'David, tell New York I lent two thousand tonnes at £16 backwardation and base it off the official prices, please.'

'Yes, thanks, Gerry, that's a great execution. What's all the noise down there anyway, what's going on? Has someone famous just visited?'

I laughed at the thought. 'No I don't think so, not that I can see anyway!'

I put the phone down, relieved to have given the execution but shaking from the fact that I could have made such a costly mistake. Debbie was clearly still shocked at what I had done. She was standing opposite me again, shaking her head from one side to another. 'What?' I snapped at her.

'You're fucking mad and I'm not clerking for you any more, it's terrible what you've done. You should not be able to deal, and I'm not checking those stupid deals at a fucking contango. It's too embarrassing.' She slammed her book into my hand and walked out of the Exchange.

I didn't have to look round to know that all eyes were upon me and I didn't have to be a mind reader to know what they were all thinking. Well, the deals would have to be checked and clearly it was now down to me to check them. Debbie was right – it was going to be embarrassing but the deal was done and that was that. So what! I had made a mistake, a very expensive mistake and I would have to live with the consequences. I ignored the smirking clerks and their obvious snide comments such as 'Don't you know the difference between a backwardation and a contango, Gerry? Ha ha ha!' I walked away, unable to defend myself because, well, what was the point?

Then another dealer came surprisingly to my defence. He obviously felt sorry for me. I watched incredulously as he actually stuck up for me. 'Oh shut up, Charlie, I suppose you've never made a mistake have you?' He smiled at me. What was I to say back to him? Thank you? Well, I wanted to, but I couldn't bring myself to be nice to anyone at that moment because I felt such a fool and him being so nice, well, that made me feel worse. In any case, I didn't really need him to come to my aid; I was perfectly capable of defending myself. Besides, the others would only sneer even more. So I walked away, shaking my head and muttering, 'Dear, oh dear, oh dear' in reply to the well orchestrated comments being muttered around the Exchange: 'How long has she been a dealer?', 'She can't last now, surely!' 'I bet she's finished now, silly cow!'

And where had Debbie stormed off to? Perhaps she had gone back to the office. Then I spotted her in the foyer talking to the other dealers. I would be annoyed if she was running me down to them and I would be annoyed if she was sticking up for me too! She should be in here clerking for me, not taking advantage of the situation. She should show some solidarity; after all, we were both women and I'd told her before how important it was for us to stick together. Divide, I'd said, and we will be conquered. Us women, we are bloody useless at sticking together when it really counts. Men, they have it all worked out. They are big on clubs, loyalty, memberships, their secret societies that make members feel so welcome, so wanted, so accepted. They are just so good at sticking together when it counts. But what can be said for us? That we stand by our man, oh, and the family, of course. Why, I ask myself, is it true that, when push comes to shove, we feel threatened by other women? It's as if we have no faith in ourselves, it's as if we have been indoctrinated with a false premise that we are born to fail or are only half as good as any man. If we don't believe ourselves to be equal, how can any man think of a woman as his equal and treat her with the respect they themselves demand?

Debbie's actions reflected my thoughts but I couldn't be bothered with her now. It was clear she would not support me and I knew I was in big trouble. Since I had just qualified, I anticipated that my days were numbered. Debbie was walking slowly towards me and her serious face told me that she was contemplating her next move. Two can play at that game, I thought, so, attack being the best method of defence, I asked her, 'Where have you been?'

She responded as indignantly as I would have done. 'What do you mean, where have I been?'

'You should have been with me, clerking, that's what you're paid to do, isn't it? You should not have left the Exchange floor. What kind of message do you think that sends?'

She acknowledged my outburst with the respect it deserved – by ignoring it. 'Do you know how much you av lost us, Gerry? Sixty-four thouzand paoundz, that's ow much. What do you fink Henry is going to say about that then, eh? Any fucking ideas, mate?'

'Thanks for your support, Debbie, but I'll face that one when I get to it, and it won't help, you having a laugh at my expense either.'

'I wasn't, and if only you but knew it I...' she said, pointing her finger in her chest rather severely '...I've been bloody sticking up for you out there, mate!'

I stared back at her, not believing a word. 'Yes, right, of course you were! Just like Trevor and Simon, both of whom were getting on with their work and, I might add, ignoring all the bloody awful comments!'

'Well, if you adna dun wat you ad, I wouldn't ave ad to, would I?'

'What?'

'Stuck up for yer, that's what!'

'Oh for God's sake, Debbie, just leave it, will you! Let's just get on with the rest of the day's trading shall we?'

Later, the walk back to the office was miserable. We were marching with hands in pockets and heads down through a drizzly cold rain. None of us wanted to speak to each other. After we crossed Fenchurch Street, the sound of our clicking shoes on the pavement reminded me horribly of the word 'sixty'! Yes, sixty-six, sixty-six, sixty-six! Sixty thousand bloody pounds had been lost that day, thanks to me. A whole month's jobbing profits straight down the drain! Why, oh why on earth, couldn't I have just made £60 000 instead of losing it? There was no point in crying over spilt milk but, my reputation as a dealer was right on the line. I imagined Henry sacking me as soon as I walked in. We turned into Mark Lane. It was bite the bullet time now! I'd better prepare myself for the worst. My end is nigh!

We walked into the office, our heads still bowed. It was quiet, so quiet you could have heard a pin drop. Debbie was the first to smile, heralding an aggressive response from David. 'Well? Hmmm? Well? What happened down there? We all want to know, Gerry. Come on, what happened? Hmm?' Before I could answer, he had tutted very loudly and slammed his book on the desk. 'Look, New York says you did the deal the wrong way round and everyone is talking about it. For Christ's sake, on both sides of the Atlantic! How much did you lose? Come on, how much did you lose?' I sat down and buried my head in my hands hoping he might feel sorry for me.

'Gerry, now you listen,' he continued. 'Listen to me, how much was it, for God's sake, why won't you tell me?' I wished he wouldn't swear like that, it really didn't suit him. He continued shouting loudly and I was getting angry. I mean the whole office could hear. What was he trying to do to me? I raised my head slowly from my hands, guessing that I had smudged my mascara all over my eyes. David handed me his handkerchief. 'Dry your eyes, my dear, I don't like to see you cry tears like this.'

'I'm not crying, it was the drizzle on the way back'

'Tsk, tsk, I knew it was too much for you today, and you see, now I'm proved right! It has been a disaster having you on the Exchange. Admit it, Gerry, I was right and you were wrong! Now how much have you lost us?'

I shook my head. 'Too much,' I replied.

'How much is too much?'

'Oh for evans sake, David, stop the bloody interrogation, will ya?

'Would ya like a coffee, Gerry?'

I pretended to think for a moment. 'Yes I would, Debbie, thanks and, David, I'll speak to Henry about this, not you! Where is he, do you know?'

David stood up, red in the face, and furious that I wouldn't speak with him. 'I told you, you should be up in the office from now on! Servicing your stupid Chinese clients. You wait till Henry sees what you've done. You'll be for the chop, mate!'

'Calm down, David, why are you getting so worked up? It isn't anything to do wiv you, is it?' Debbie was shaking her hand at him, annoyed at his continued outburst.

'Gerry, come in here please. Now!' The master's voice had spoken and it was time to face the music! Henry was seated in

216

his usual position at the boardroom table. 'Shut the door, will you? Now what happened this afternoon on the Exchange?'

I shuffled around, wondering whether I should sit down or continue standing. I resented feeling awkward but tried not to show it in my reply. 'I made a mistake, I lent at a contango when I should have lent at a backwardation. It was my mistake, and that's all I can say.'

Henry took a deep breath and put his pipe down on the table as though considering some appropriate sentence for me. 'Did you know that you had made a mistake?'

I rolled my eyes up towards the ceiling and immediately wished I hadn't. 'No, of course not, otherwise I wouldn't have done the deal!'

'Well how much do you think it has cost us, this dreadful mistake of yours?' I hated it when he was in this mood, because he was nice right up to the second that he was nasty, and because most of the time he was warm and understanding, it came as a shock when he suddenly turned ruthless and cold. I watched him closely to determine the exact moment of transition from Dr Jekyll to Mr Hyde. This was so that I could be prepared for the onslaught, as I intended to give as good as I got! He looked at me out of the corner of his eye while stretching his arm across the table, to pick up his pipe. He started to poke it, rather maliciously, I thought, to loosen the tobacco. 'Well?'

I shuffled again. 'I'm thinking,' I replied uneasily.

'I don't pay you to stand there and think. I pay you to make me money, Gerry!' I could tell he was getting angry as he impatiently dug and scratched the inside of his pipe sending my teeth on edge.

'Do you mind if I open the door it seems to be getting rather warm?'

'As you wish,' he replied.

I walked back to the table and pulled out a chair to sit on. Henry was now tapping his pipe as loudly as he could on the side of the ashtray. I watched the burnt offerings fall, releasing an obnoxious aromatic smell into the room. I knew that I would be punished no matter what I said in my defence but I thought he must have to consider any mitigating circumstances, surely? And what, I wondered, did £60 000 worth of punishment look like?

'Well, answer me, I haven't got all bloody day. How much did you lose?'

'Probably about £60 000, but I think we could appeal against the trading procedure because I didn't know that the market had moved from a contango to a backwardation! I mean, the price was right, wasn't it?' Henry lit his pipe up again and was sitting behind a thick cloud of smoke. 'No the price was not right,' he said. I peered through watery eyes as the smoke became thicker and swirled around the room, despite the door being open. Henry handed me his handkerchief. 'Here, don't upset yourself.'

'Well those dealers, they knew they were taking us to the cleaners and that I had made a simple mistake. They were taking advantage of me. I know a gentleman's word is their bond, Henry, but I don't think they are gentlemen to knowingly capitalise on a mistake that I made, do you?'

Henry puffed hard on his pipe, releasing yet more smoke into the room. Mr Hyde had not appeared yet and I was surprised. Perhaps he was lulling me into a false sense of security, or maybe he simply admired my honesty. So I continued to explain. 'Do you know what I am saying, Henry? After all, everyone should be lenient with a newly authorised dealer. I mean, only last week I remember Brian being let off a mistake he had made. Everyone deserves a chance, don't they?'

Henry cleared his throat, and slid back in his chair. 'Open that door wider, will you, it's getting very smoky in here.' I did as he requested and returned to him just in time for the next question. 'Hmmm. So when exactly did the market actually go into a backwardation, then?'

I shrugged. 'Apparently earlier this morning, but it's only just happened and quite unusual as you know.'

'I know something funny is going on in the zinc market. It is really hairy at the moment.' He sounded as if he understood but I knew better than to be led into such a false sense of security. I watched him fiddle around in his pocket, first with one hand, then the other. He was looking for something and I suspected it was his tobacco pouch that was lying on the table.

I waited until he had both hands in his pockets before leaning forward. 'Henry, it wasn't my fault,' I said handing him his pouch. He said nothing and drew deeply on his pipe. I watched as the bowl lit up bright red and I wondered how his hand didn't burn when he covered and then uncovered it like that.

'I suppose it take years of practice,' he muttered.

'What?'

'Nothing.'

Henry, so it appeared, was being very understanding. I started to draw circles on the boardroom table. Then I thought he might find this annoying so I stopped. He looked up at me, still silent, contemplating my future as he shuffled papers lying on the table.

I fixed my gaze on a beautiful wooden mural on the wall. It had been carved in the Ivory Coast and it was only now, as I sat here, that I realised it was the Garden of Eden. Spotting the tree in the middle, I looked for the serpent and found it. Henry spoke again. 'Are you happy on the trading floor, Gerry?'

'Yes, why?'

'I just get the feeling that maybe you would rather be in the office.'

'No, Henry, honestly, I want to carry on dealing in the Ring. I like it down there.'

'Are you sure? I mean life is going to be very difficult for you down there now!'

'Is it?'

'Well yes, of course! You've made a big idiot of yourself, haven't you?'

'Have I?'

Henry stood up, knocking his knee against the table as he made his way over to the drinks cabinet. I wondered why men never gave themselves enough room when getting up from a table. If I had a penny for all the times I had seen them knock themselves, I would be very rich indeed! Henry was right, I had made a fool of myself, and what a time to do it, right in the middle of the London Metal Exchange dinner week. This was a time when we were supposed to impress potential clients - many of whom would have seen this mistake of mine. I shivered at the thought - how embarrasing.

I watched as he poured himself a large whisky, I was hoping he would offer me one but he didn't, after all, if anyone needed it I did! I considered what he might say and what my response would be. Surely he wasn't going to make me come back into the office?

'Everyone makes mistakes, I'm only human, just give me one more chance.'

Henry tutted and, shaking his head, sat down slowly, reaching for his pipe again. 'One mistake,' I repeated.

'Yes, a very, very expensive one and we can't have too many of those, can we?'

'No, and I promise it won't happen again, Henry.'

'No, it won't. Now leave me. Get out. The sight of you makes me sick.' He waved his arms wildly at me and I left the room as quickly as I could.

Back in the trading room, David was concerned and wanted to know what had happened. 'Well?'

'Well what?'

'Well, what's happening?'

'I'm going home, that's what.' I grabbed my scarf and left for the day. Well, at least Henry hadn't sacked me but I wasn't out of the woods yet. Tomorrow was going to be awkward but I didn't want to ruin my evening so the less I thought about it now, the better. I didn't like to take my work home with me.

On the way home I passed the Norman tower and wondered why it had never opened again since my last visit. I found myself taking a mental trip around the place, recalling those special visions. This helped me to unwind and relax before reaching the crowded tube station. Who, I wondered, dusted and kept the place so clean?

Chapter Seven

Daughters Wine

The following morning I walked into the office and no one looked up as they usually did. I didn't want an atmosphere and I didn't want anyone feeling sorry for me. I was going to carry on as usual. 'Morning, everyone.'

'Morning,' a bored chorus responded.

I ignored the air of expectancy as Henry came towards me.

'About the Czechoslovakians,' he said. 'I believe Rick is flying out with you next Tuesday. But I want you, *you*, to make sure they sign these aluminium contracts, do you understand, Gerry? Once they are signed I expect us to get a lot of business from them, especially carries, and I expect you to do them. They want you to trade for them in the Ring. So, everyone, the less said about yesterday the better!'

Debbie, Simon and David, who were clearly surprised at Henry's decision, said nothing, while Rick nodded in agreement. 'All right everyone?'

I was relieved it was over and done with and we could get on with the business in hand.

Later, Debbie sat next to me. 'Lucky cow to get away with that, aren't ya, mate?' She smiled and asked me for a cigarette.

'Why don't you buy your own bloody fags, Debbie? What do you think I am, made of money?' She seemed shocked at my outburst but characteristically ignored it. I liked that about her. She had no time to waste on frivolous words. But from now on I was going to change. I was going to toughen up my act. I was going to treat people the way they treated me. I wasn't going to be nice any more!

We sipped our coffee and checked our trading cards. 'Are you all right now then?' she asked me a little while later, putting her hand across my arm. I put my pencil down on the desk.

'Will you be OK when we get down on the Ring? I mean, you won't be scared or nothing like that, will ya?'

'No of course not, I'm human, and all humans make mistakes, don't they?' I smiled and then looked away.

'Yeah, but you have to admit, that was a bloody big one, Gerry.' She threw her head back and laughed out loud.

'Look, Debbie, are you going to keep on about it? I expect you to stand by me, all traders make losses and that's an end of it, so today we just carry on as normal. I don't want you speaking to the other traders on the floor behind my back and taking the piss all the time.'

'Yea, all right, keep your air on, mate!'

David looked up from across the desk 'Yes, Gerry, I don't think you should be on the Exchange anyway, not now, not after that big mistake.' I ignored his comments.

Debbie leaned across. 'Look, Gerry, let's be mates again, tell me one of your funny stories, one you haven't told me before.'

I thought for a moment. 'Well I can't think of a funny one but how about this. Do you remember that time when I received that letter with the House of Commons seal on it?'

'Oh yeah, what was that all about then?'

'Well I never said anything to anyone about it because I didn't want to cause any jealousy, but it was from James Callaghan, the Prime Minister, inviting me to a party at Number 10 Downing Street, to celebrate fifty years of women's right to vote.'

'Bloody ell, you are joking, ain't ya?'

'No, seriously Debbie, I was delighted and of course a bit scared as well. But I couldn't miss out on the opportunity to meet all the first women in the land or visit the Prime Minister's residence!'

'Ere, wait a minute, I'll get us a coffee. White as usual, Gerry?'

'Yes thanks.' I watched her get up and couldn't help wondering whether the story I was about to tell her would bring us closer or make her even more distant from me. I hoped it might help her to understand me better. Well, I had started it now, and Debbie was eager to hear the rest. Two minutes later she was back. I waited for her to sit down and lit a cigarette. 'Want one?'

'Yes, why not? Now where was I? Ah yes. On the day, I was ushered into a surprisingly narrow hall. I don't know why but I had expected something much grander. The hall was painted a cherry red and as I climbed the stairs to the drawing room, I noticed photographs hanging on the wall, the residents of Number 10 were rising with every step, but there was not one woman amongst them.

'These great men of distinction would certainly be surprised to see a woman in their midst! But secretly we were all hoping that Margaret Thatcher, who had just become leader of the opposition, would join them shortly.'

'Wow, did you meet her then?'

'Yes but hang on let me tell you the story, because believe it or not, there was someone far more important in the room.'

'Yes, but do you like her Gerry?'

'Like who?'

'Margaret Thatcher.'

'How can you not like her? Yes, of course I would vote for her if I had the opportunity. After all, how could a woman not be good for the country? Fifty years was long enough to wait for a woman Prime Minister and she would help all women to achieve equality with men. It's great to see more women succeeding in what have previously been male-dominated professions. Anyway, Debbie, you might not know this but the Equal Opportunities Commission has really made a big impact under the guidance of Baroness Lockwood.'

'Baroness Lockwood, who's she?'

'I've just told you. Anyway, stop interrupting and let me finish the story! It was four o'clock on a warm sunny afternoon in July when I made my way into a large but cosy drawing room. Here I came face to face with a hundred women or more. We chatted over champagne, strawberries and cream. The constant chatter rose to an excited hum, indicating the arrival of someone very special. It was Margaret Thatcher, or Maggie, as some liked to call her. As she entered the room, everyone headed towards her. I felt quite embarrassed but she understood their enthusiasm for meeting her. I would have liked to have spoken too but knew I had little hope of getting anywhere near her as they all formed an orderly queue to greet her. The clearing of half the room gave me the opportunity to walk across to the french windows and look at the beautiful gardens.

'As I stood there, I had the distinct feeling someone was watching me. Looking down, I noticed a frail old woman sitting in her wheelchair. As we spoke, I was amazed to find out that she was the only surviving suffragette – probably the most important person in the room.'

'Wow, that's amazing but shouldn't she have been guest of honour?'

'Yes, I think she should have been. Anyway I told her, "But for your actions none of us would be here". We spoke for ages and I went to get her tea and strawberries. As I recall it, she was almost ninety-eight. She told me many stories of the Feminists' struggle and some of the protests she had been involved in. I was shocked to hear her best friend had been killed when she threw herself under the king's horse at the Derby, and she had chained herself to the railings in Downing Street.'

Debbie interrupted me again. 'What was her name?'

'Who?'

'The one who threw herself under the king's horse, of course!'

'Emily Wilding-Davison, I think, she was a martyr for the cause. Now look, we haven't got long so please stop butting in!'

Debbie laughed. 'Go on then.'

'Well, I loved talking with her but it was difficult to hear everything she was saying because there was such a noise in the room. Anyway, she told me she had been imprisoned several times and, after starving herself in protest at women not having the vote, she was forcibly fed. Listening to her, I was full of admiration. I thought it was a shame that no one else had spent any time with her. I knelt on the floor beside her wheelchair so she could hear me as I explained my job to her. Once or twice she nodded or smiled at what had been achieved, and at other times looked out into the gardens. I wondered whether she understood all that I was saying. She sometimes appeared very distant, lost in her own world. And then a funny thing happened as we fell quiet for a moment.'

'What?'

'Well, I know this sounds funny but I could hear music and I realised it was Jerusalem.'

'What do you mean, Jerusalem?'

'You know, the song.'

'No, I don't know it'

'Well it goes like this: *And did those feet in ancient times walk upon England's fine...* You know, William Blake. Oh, how does the rest go? *I will not cease from mental fight, nor shall my sword sleep in my hand, till we have built Jerusalem in England's green and pleasant land.*'

'Ha ha ha! Gerry, I didn't know you could sing so well!'

'OK, very funny, do you want to hear the rest then or not?'

'Yes go on.'

'So, having spent quite some time with the most important person in the room, I said a fond farewell. I could see she was getting tired.'

'Anyway, just as I was thinking about leaving the party, I caught sight of another pair of eyes watching me. Margaret was looking at me from across the room. Then she turned to leave as well. She was surrounded by just about everyone in the room and her progress towards the door was slow. I was sure I would be able to catch up, but I felt she was weary from all the attention, even though she was still smiling and listening. I watched from a distance as she made her way towards the exit, knowing that I would never get the chance to actually speak to her. With piercing blue eyes, she was clearly mistress of all she surveyed and I smiled at her, sorry to have missed the opportunity. But sensing my disappointment at not being able to get close, she winked at me from a distance and I felt on top of the world. No words passed between us – we were like ships that pass in the night.'

I stopped, having finished my story, and looked up at the clock.

'Yes, and then what?'

'Well, that's it, there's no more, that's my story!'

'Well how long ago did that happen?'

'I remember it well, it was the July 3rd, 1978.'

'What, and you never told anyone about it?'

'No, why should I? But I'll tell you what, I've never forgotten that wink, and sometimes I like to think that one day we'll meet.'

Debbie chortled and began to sing. '*We'll meet again, don't know where, don't know how, but I'll know we'll meet again some sunny day!* See Gerry I can sing better than you!'

'Yes, you can, but look at the time, we're going to be late for the market if we don't go now.'

As we left the trading room, Mark and Henry were talking seriously in the corner.

'I wonder what that's all about?' I asked.

'Dunno, I heard the Buffer Stock Manager mentioned and something about new tin business.' Debbie replied grabbing her bag.

'I must ask David about that later.' I thought.

As Debbie and I made our way down to the Exchange, we agreed from now that we would give each other a hundred per cent support. I was relieved, because despite what I had said to her, I was fearful of the likely reaction to me from the other dealers on the Exchange. I knew what they could be like when they ganged up and I felt stronger knowing she was on my side.

As we arrived, we were met by a few traders having a

cigarette out on the kerb. Thankfully, they said nothing. Debbie squeezed my arm. 'It'll be all right, you'll see.' I smiled bravely but felt nervous as more traders came into the Exchange. Feeling rather subdued I walked into the Ring and sat down. I managed to trade a few carries before the bell thankfully rang and I was able to step outside of it again. I clerked for Simon through the next Ring but still felt as though some dealers were talking about my awful mistake. I had it confirmed later when I went to check some deals for Simon. It was then that several of the dealers gathered in front of me.

'I'm surprised you're still here, Gerry, and you haven't been sacked for that loss you took yesterday. Or have you, and you're just serving out your notice? Ha ha ha!' This was Charlie, a notoriously cocky dealer, who was always surrounded by the same gang paying homage to his sarcastic but often amusing performance. Charlie ensured their patronage by, buying them copious amounts of beer. I considered walking away from them, but I knew by experience that it was better to face up to them. They were prone to tormenting and tormentors never left anyone alone for long.

'No, I haven't and as you can see, I'm still dealing!'

'Well, you bloody should have been!' another dealer shouted.

'Well, as you can see, I really haven't been sacked. On the contrary, next week I shall start trading aluminium.'

I pushed my way through the crowd towards the foyer.

Charlie shouted out again, 'You shouldn't be ere, you lost too much money, you're a crappy dealer. Why don't you let Debbie take your place and go back to the office where you belong?' I smiled.

'How many of you would still be allowed to trade on the Exchange, after losing sixty grand?' I asked. 'See what you've got to understand is this – if I can lose all that money and still have a job, then my company must think I'm worth it. They still want to keep me.' I shoved the swing door in front of me open and walked through. Once on the kerb, I lit up a cigarette, hoping that would be an end to it.

That lunchtime I decided not to have a drink and went back to the office for a quiet lunch and to read up on the new aluminium contract. David, as usual, was at the desk 'How was it?'

'Yes, just as you would expect!'

'Oh good,' he said, not noticing my sarcasm. 'Do you want a coffee?' he asked. He was pleased I was back from the Exchange and could relieve him for lunch. 'I'm going to Blooms later, do you want a salt beef sandwich?' he asked.

'Yes, I'd love one, thanks, and I'll have a white coffee while you're there, thanks.' As David was getting the coffee I picked up some tin contracts lying on the desk.

'What's this about the Buffer Stock Manager, have we a new tin client then?' I aked him when he came back.

'Yes – not that it's any of your business.'

'Oh, don't be silly, I think that's great news, well done. I know you've been working on him for a while, but you do know he trades with nearly everyone on the Ring and that he needs to borrow money from the brokers to do his business?'

David screwed his face up. 'Yes, so what! We lend him the money at a good interest rate, say about fifteen per cent, that's say five per cent above base, and then he buys cash metal and sells it forward for three months like anyone else does. All we're doing, Gerry, is financing his position and getting the commission too. Can't you see it's really good business for us!' David was shouting by now.

'Ssshh, David, don't get so excited!'

'Vell honestly, why are you always questioning me about my business? It is gud, believe me it is very gud!'

I watched him leave the trading room. I wanted to tell him that I had heard stories about the Buffer Stock Manager and his large positions and that I was concerned because they involved such large amounts of money. Anyway, David would say that I shouldn't listen to the gossip!

Aluminium was a new contract, a new start. Some said it would be as big as the copper contract but I wasn't sure. In any case, I was concentrating on my Chinese clients and they had only expressed an interest in copper, although I knew of course they traded other metals too.

They were coming for lunch and it was our opportunity to make a big impression on them. They were not impressed that easily and when I was in conversation with them they always left me with the feeling that they knew a lot more than they actually said. They were reticent, humble and quiet, yet they demanded respect.

Even though we didn't speak the same language I thought we understood each other well. Sometimes I thought that they could speak English better than they said. But I played the game, explaining everything very slowly, using a mixture of hand signals and smiles interspersed with a good deal of nodding of my head and yet another smile to end the sentence. They were especially responsive when I communicated in this way and it made me feel as though I was one of them. I was amazed that they got by on so little knowledge of English. I was in complete awe of them and even though they were communists, I believed them to be inherently good. So I wanted to do good by them. I instinctively understood what they needed and required from a broker. They treated me with the utmost respect and they trusted me as much as I trusted them. Since there were not too many people in that category, I was at complete ease with them, and if in the future I had to lend them money to trade, well, I would have absolute confidence that they would repay the money. They were a class A client, and besides, I always enjoyed myself in their company – which reminds me of the time when they invited me to a favourite restaurant of theirs in Queensway. I felt hungry on arrival as I smelt dishes of the day being prepared. Embarrassed by my stomach rumbling loudly, I sat down to await their imminent arrival. My watch had stopped so I had no idea of the time. I looked around the room and realised I was the only one seated. Surrounding me were dragons. They were both large and small, some almost six feet tall. From floor to ceiling and even across a doorframe, they dominated the room. One was a friendly blue and white, another a vibrant red and gold and there was a frightening one, his gold and black eyes only a few feet away, protruding from a highly lacquered gold, black and red striped head just a few inches off the ceiling. I was sure it had just moved! Perhaps he was a tiger, not a dragon? I finished looking around the room and decided that I was happy to be here, as well as a little intrigued. It was unusual for clients to pay for their brokers and I would be lying if I said I didn't feel just a little nervous. I lit a cigarette, hoping to calm my nerves. There were a couple of reasons why I felt nervous. Firstly, I would be lunching on my own with at least eight Chinese, who were a variety of ages. Secondly, I didn't speak Mandarin and was not particularly familiar with their customs. In addition, Chinese food was a bit of a mystery to me. I was not sure about the etiquette or what I would be given to eat but I was sure that I would make the effort and eat with chopsticks.

I stubbed my cigarette out just as they arrived, and stood up to greet them. I felt awkward being the only woman and the only westerner at the table. Nine men, not the expected eight, had arrived and after a lot of bowing and scraping and pleases, everyone was seated in their right places. There was no surprise in the hierarchy. My Hao was the most important man at the table and when he spoke, he spoke for everyone there. Cigarettes that had just been lit were now placed in the large ashtray at the centre of the table as hot flannels were passed to each of us by the waiter. I copied the ritual and picked up my cigarette only after they all had.

They spoke in Mandarin when discussing and ordering from the menu. I allowed Mr Hao to order for me as I hadn't a clue about Chinese food. The food arrived surprisingly quickly and was placed, steaming hot, in the centre of the table. Mr Hao then served us all. We waited patiently for him to finish and as he put the steaming food in his mouth, we picked up our chopsticks and started to eat. 'It is good, yes?' Mr Hao asked.

'Yes, very good!' I picked up a bowl of rice wine and raised it. 'Cheers,' I said as more dishes arrived.

They all laughed 'Cheers!'

The pungent smell of the wine was unusual and made me heady. I could tell it was strong as soon as the hot fumes rose into my nose. But I couldn't allow myself to go fully with it, given the company I was in. So long as I eat I'll be all right, I thought, as Mr Hao handed me yet another small cup. 'You like this wine?' He asked.

'Hmm, very good!'

He was pleased. 'You like Dragons?' He asked, waving his arm around the room.

'Yes, I like dragons! I'm surrounded by them, am I not?' he laughed. Then he pointed at himself. 'No, I am a tiger. Aaarrrggg! Ah, tiger very powerful in China.' I watched as he put his hand in the air, mimicking a claw. 'Ha ha ha! But you, Miss Gerry, do you know your sign in Chinese astrology? You know there is two of everything! In China the dragon is the most powerful sign.'

'What, more powerful than the Tiger?' I asked.

Mr Hao laughed and everyone around the table joined in. 'It depends, whether fire or water! Every sign can be fire or water.'

I thought for a moment. 'So let me see if I have this right then. Fire tiger might be stronger than water dragon?' I asked, thinking that I was now beginning to sound Chinese myself.

'Ha! Yes, vely good But there are two dragons, water dragon and fire dragon. Which you think is more powerful?'

'Fire sounds like it might be,' I said hesitantly 'but on second thoughts, water can put fire out.'

Mr Hao laughed out loud and they all laughed with him again. 'Aah ha, but some water has fire burning in it, does it not, Miss Gerry?' I kept quiet, thinking of a volcanic eruption underneath the sea. 'Do you know what sign you are, Miss Gerry?' Mr Hao was leaning across towards me and I could smell garlic on his breath. I moved back before replying, 'No I haven't any idea but in western astrology I am a Capricorn.' I suddenly pictured this pathetic goat standing next to a tiger. 'Ha, Chinese not same as western, we go on year, so what year you born in?'

'Nineteen fifty-two.'

'Aaahh!' they all said. 'Beginning or end of year?'

'End, December,' I replied.

'Aaahhh, ha!' they all said again.

Mr Hao patted my arm. 'Ha, so now we know. Your secret is out. It explains a lot, Miss Gerry! Cheers! Ha ha ha! Now listen to me.' I leaned closer, smiling at the others, while he related yet another mysterious Chinese story. I kept wondering when we would talk about business and commission rates. But the subject was never raised and I felt it would be rude for me to suggest it.

'This is Daughter wine.' Mr Hao raised the jug of wine into the centre of the table for all to acknowledge. 'Daughter wine very important in China. When baby girl is born, family bury new rice wine in ground. Many years later, time for daughter to get married, dig up this wine, and serve to new family. This wine very special, buried when daughter born, drunk at daughter wedding, very special. So today is special, beginning of good friendship, so you drink daughter wine with us now.' They raised their cups of wine and we all drank.

'Thank you,' I said, feeling the least I could do was to show how honoured I was to be drinking this special wine.

I was concerned that we had not spoken about business but there was hardly any opportunity for me to speak. Obviously eating and drinking were the order of the day because every other minute a fresh course of food would arrive. Getting tired but trying not to show it, I watched as multi-coloured portions of food arrived in the centre of the table before being divided up into equal portions. What a feast of prawn crackers, duck, pork, steak, and sharks' fin soup it was! I had never seen anything like it before. I didn't like the sharks' fin soup as I could still see blood hanging from the flesh, so I discreetly abandoned it and tried the hot and sour soup. I loved the taste of the vegetables, rice dishes, pancake rolls and fried seaweed. It didn't seem to matter if we ate them all at once because Mr Hao kept filling my bowl up before I had even finished.

Finally, desert arrived and I had to find room for banana

fritters and more daughter wine. I was sure it must be four o'clock by now, and obviously I would not be going back to the City. I just hoped they would give me a big enough order so that Henry would not be annoyed with me. And then just as I thought the moment had come to speak of business, they made it clear it was time to go and somehow it would have been very rude to raise the subject, so I didn't. They all stood up and smiled at me before offering their hands. I wondered if they sensed my disappointment at not getting any new business.

How many other brokers had they taken out to lunch. I wondered!

'Next time we come to you, yes?' Mr Hao had said, offering his hand.

'Yes, certainly, yes all of you would be most welcome,' I said, comforted that he wanted to repeat the occasion. I left the restaurant well impressed but wondering how I could possibly match such a meal.

The following morning Henry asked 'What happened to you yesterday? Did you have to go all the way to Bejing for lunch?'

They all laughed as Trevor stood up and sang 'Ning nong, ning nong, ning nong, ning nong, ning nong- tiddeleyeho!'

'Oh shut up, will you? Have some bloody respect! I had a lovely time, but more to the point, they want the invite returned, and that, I'm sure, means that we will get new business from them! So the sooner we invite them, the better. How about next Wednesday?'

David spoke first, probably confirming all their thoughts. 'You see, Gerry, you're so stupid! Why do you think they would give you an order, why, after all the mistakes you make? Honestly, you must be mad.' And he laughed. 'It would be much better for you if you concentrated on your other clients, clients who pay commission to us, however small they are.' They all laughed again.

'Change the record, David, it's getting boring,' I said, reaching for the lunch diary. 'Next Wednesday looks good, Henry, how about it?' I reached for the first cigarette of the day, waiting for his reply. He said nothing. 'Look, they just need to trust us. Mark my words, it will be better once they have been here for lunch and met everyone,' I pleaded with him.

Finally Henry was convinced and agreed. 'Next Wednesday it is then,' he said, puffing on his pipe as he left the room.
The following Wednesday Sasha, who was responsible along with the Commissioner for organising the lunch, kept asking me questions, questions I could not answer. 'How many exactly are coming?'

'I don't know, anywhere between six and twelve,' I said, hoping it was no more.

'Well, it better be no more than twelve, the table isn't big enough,' Sasha had responded. 'Anyway, it should only be Mark and Henry having lunch with them, you're not so important as to be having lunch upstairs in that boardroom.'

'Thank you, Sasha, but I think they expect me there!'

'Are there any specific rituals or routines to follow?' she asked. I didn't know. 'Did they mind kosher food?'

'Haven't got a clue,' all I knew was the very elderly Mr Yang ate mainly vegetarian food. 'Look, let's just put out plenty of fruit, salads and vegetables. Make sure there's plenty of fruit juice and water on the sideboard. Also some red and white wine, I'm sure everything will be OK, so don't worry, Sasha.'

Even Henry and Mark were nervous but I reassured them. 'What will we talk about?' Mark asked Henry. Henry shrugged his shoulders and looked at me for an answer.

'Well, last time I had lunch we didn't talk about anything in particular, and I don't think it will do to bully them into giving us their business! Anyway, Mark is always good at making speeches, aren't you, Mark?'

He laughed. 'Yes, Gerry and I suppose they'll want me to increase their credit line, like everyone else does these days!'

I thought for a moment before answering. 'Well, even if they do, I should think The Bank of China will be good for the money, don't you?'

Mark looked serious for a moment. 'Do you really think they will want a credit line, Gerry? How much?'

'Well, anything less than five million pounds would be an insult.'

'And you think that if we give them this big credit line we'll get their business, all their business, Gerry?'

'Well, I don't think we'll get their business unless we offer them a credit line and good rates of commission, the two go hand in hand.'

By 12.30 things had calmed down a bit as we waited for our guests to arrive. I knew that this was an important occasion. There could be no mistakes made. They must feel welcome at all costs. As they arrived, I counted out nine, eight of whom I knew well. Mark, Henry and David were waiting for them in the boardroom on the fourth floor. Everyone was nervous, including me, and we were all desperate to make the right impression. Down in the reception area I held the lift open, explaining that it only took six and that I would have to come back for the rest of them. But they were having none of it and all squashed in behind me. I just managed to close the lift doors. Mr Hao and all his colleagues stood behind, breathing very heavily as I pushed the button for the fourth floor. The lift reacted, slowly moving up with a jolt at first and then with another jolt until it came to a halt somewhere between the third and fourth floors. The Chinese burst out into laughter and I laughed with them, although I didn't find it at all funny. They were all smaller and for some unknown reason thought they should lean against me. I tried politely to move them away but they were having none of it. They seemed to be enjoying the whole experience!

By now the lift was full of laughter, grunting and garlic fumes filled the air and, I started to panic. What if the lift was here for a long time, stuck? How were we going to get out? The laughing was beginning to get on my nerves and I needed to take control of the situation. 'We seem to have become stuck,' I said as calmly as possible. 'Just a minute, now let me see if I can stretch across to raise the alarm. Excuse me, Mr Hao, can I just get behind you to ring that bell?' It was getting really hot now and there was no air.

'Do you want me to do it, Miss, I can do it if you like?'

'Yes please, if you can reach it.' He rang the bell and we waited for a response. I wiped the sweat off my face as a couple of the others loosened their shirts. We all smiled but the situation was not in the least bit funny. I thought the Chinese were incredibly good tempered and I continued to giggle and apologise until we were rescued. Well, I say 'rescued'. Actually what happened was the commissioner had to force the door open with an iron rod. We then had to climb out of a tiny gap that was only about a foot wide, somewhere between the third and fourth floors. The Chinese were helped up onto my shoulders so they could reach the rescuers' hands. Some stood on my shoulders while others asked for a leg up. I was exhausted by the time the lift was finally light enough to move up of its own accord. As we emerged, two very concerned faces greeted us. Mark and Henry were peering into the darkness. 'Are you all right? Is everyone OK?'

'Yes, we're fine now,' I said. And considering we'd been in there for at least fifteen minutes, everyone was remarkably jovial! I laughed to pretend how relaxed I was. But I don't think I convinced Henry.

Once we were all seated in the boardroom, early nervousness was overcome and the lunch went well, despite the lack of conversation. Munching and nodding was interspersed with a lot of smiling and occasional grunting as food was passed around the table. At first I tried to encourage communication but gave up when I realised that no one else wanted to make an effort. I fought off the temptation to serve, even though I could see some plates were empty, instead, I watched the clock and made sure the Chinese enjoyed their food. Old Mr Yang didn't have any teeth but he very much enjoyed the bunch of grapes I gave him.

Towards the end of the meal, Mark leaned forward with a

wide grin and, speaking very slowly indeed, said to him, 'So, let me see now, em, first of all I would like to say thank you. Thank you very much for coming to have lunch with us, and I hope you have enjoyed your meal. Gerry will show you around our trading room. It is very modern and has all the most up-to-date technology and even though I say it myself, I think you will be very impressed! Can I also say before I leave that I hope you will trust us enough, and trust Gerry enough, to give us a little of your business!' I watched as he patted Mr Hao's arm. But just as Mr Hao was about to give a reply he was rudely interrupted by Mr Yang spitting a grape pip across the table. I looked at David, who seemed shocked at the response, but I noticed Mr Yang had his eyes closed and was probably half asleep anyway. This was not rudeness. Mr Yang was quite at home here. I watched in astonishment at how high the pip rose before descending towards Henry's eye. But luckily it hit the wall before landing on the carpet.

Mark appeared not to have noticed and carried on smiling at Mr Hao, who finally felt able to respond. 'Yes, thank you, yes we can see it now if you like.' Mark smiled and leant to his right as if to whisper something in Mr Yang's ear but instead took hold of his arm, quite firmly I think, because Mr Yang opened his eyes. A moment later, Mark moved his arm away. It was then that I saw Mr Yang reach for another grape. I watched incredulously as he carefully put it in his mouth and then, looking at me without smiling, squashed it between his lips, freeing the contents all over the white tablecloth.

After lunch a grand tour of the trading room was arranged and they all seemed impressed. There was appreciation for our sophisticated telephone network and the numerous banks of phones built into the trading desks. A big 'Aaahhh!' went up when I explained how many different markets we traded. I was sure we had done a good job impressing them and now all that was needed was to sit back and wait for their business.

I was surprised when they said that they didn't want to visit the Metal Exchange in the afternoon because I was looking forward to having them as my guests. But this was not to be and so, after thanking us for lunch, they left. I was glad the occasion was over but disappointed that we were still no nearer to getting that big deal.

'What did you expect, an order or something?' David laughed. I couldn't be bothered to reply. Perhaps he was right after all.

They were already trading tin when I arrived at the Exchange. The market was hectic and prices were moving up sharply in thin trading conditions. Something serious was going on because cash tin prices were now trading at over £100 premium to the three-month price. Yet another market in a backwardation! There were many worried onlookers as both brokers and clients found themselves short of cash tin. No one knew for sure whether the buffer stock manager was net long or short of cash. Everyone hoped he was long and could lend to the market but the fear was that he would not lend until a much higher price had been achieved. Was he squeasing the market and if so he didn't appear to be doing his job very well. By now he should have entered the market to maintain the agreed buffer range. The fact that he hadn't was the reason for these crazy market conditions. So, where was he and what was going on? Had an even greater force entered the market and if so, who could it be – the Chinese or perhaps one of the big American Commission Houses?

Of course part of a trader's job was to try and second guess a client's position but no one really knew the Buffer Stock Manager's position because he was trading through so many brokers and dealers. This was what was so frightening about the situation. The reason why the brokers were so lenient I thought, was because they were beholden to the Buffer Stock Manager. They had already lent him millions of pounds and if he went down, so did they! So, at whatever cost the brokers would continue to raise more money and lend it to the Buffer Stock Manager and he would continue to trade tin regardless of the price and his overall exposure to the market.

Some brokers were happy with this situation because they

felt the loans they had made were safe and covered by the warrants of tin being held. But at the end of the day a warrant is only a piece of paper, a piece of paper that would have been honoured by gentleman. But this Buffer Stock Manager was different. I met him several times in the office or on the Exchange. He would laugh out loud with his arms open wide and head straight towards me 'Gerry, hullo, Gerry,' he would say and then, grabbing me by the shoulders and pulling me towards him, he would say, 'Be nice to me, Gerry, because you know I am everyone's friend! Ha ha ha!' He would lean quite far back and laugh even louder so that by now we would had an audience watching. 'Ah yes, Gerry, I had such a good day. You know I made so much money, you can't believe it! Not for me, you understand. No not for me, ha, but for the Tin Council. Ah yes, they are very happy and you know everyone, yes everyone wants to do business with me.' He squeezed me closer to him. 'And you know why, Gerry, you know why?' He held me against him. 'Because I make them so rich, like me! Ha ha ha! I mean, who wants to work, Gerry, when you can have all this, and for what? An order here and order there, ah yes, life is so good, and you can have a bit of it too! Ha ha ha!' Finally, I pull away from him. I had to smile because he was laughing so much. I had to be polite but he was practically frothing at the mouth, and I knew he was very excited, so I had to listen to him! I wondered whether his gold teeth were making his breath smell, or was it the oysters he had had for lunch? 'I have all these friends because Gerry, they get rich and they have all my business, ha ha ha. No one has so many friends in the world as I do! Now come here, closer, ha ha ha! When will you have lunch with me, tomorrow, the day after, when? We don't have to talk business. You know what I mean?' I can smell the garlic on his breath as he gets closer.

To look at him, you could not believe that such a friendly man could create so much anguish and havoc in the market. But instinctively I felt that he was dangerous, and no good for the market. He appealed to the greed in people's nature. Once they were hooked, they could never be free again. What was happening to the brokers on the Exchange was about to happen to my company too, but I was not going to get involved with this man. I didn't believe everything I heard about him. One day you would hear that he had made two million pounds and another that he had lost half a million! The problem was that he was doing business with so many dealers on the Ring that it was not at all clear what his position was and whether he was making money or losing it.

But today, he looked slightly more worried than usual. He wasn't laughing quite as much. Still, all would be well when the warrants were delivered against the cash short positions, albeit at a ridiculously high price. As the positions were squared off, I could feel the atmosphere lighten and see the visible relief on those previously contorted broker faces. They had survived yet another nerve-racking day but I wondered: how long this could go on for? Someone had to say no to the Buffer Stock Manager, perhaps I could convince Mark of the merits of not doing business with him! Trouble was, David and Henry would not be happy; they considered the Buffer Stock Manager a very good client indeed.

Back in the office, David, Mark, and Henry were mulling over the day's events and I was astonished to hear they were considering raising his three million pound credit line. I didn't want them to because it would reduce the amount that I would be able to offer the Chinese and of course I feared the company would suffer massive losses when and if the Buffer Stock Manager went bust. To me it was a very real possibility! Somehow I had to get my ideas across to Mark so that he could make an informed decision. I was sure he didn't understand or know the full extent of what was going on in the market, and Henry and David never came down onto the trading floor, so how could they know the full score?

I asked to speak to Mark in his office. David and Henry both raised an eyebrow, wondering what it was I could only speak to Mark about. Mark sat down. 'Have a seat, Gerry. Now, what can I do for you?'

I got straight to the point. 'I'm a bit worried about the tin market!'

'I see.' He clasped his hands together and protruded his bottom lip. 'And why would you be worried. Gerry, you don't trade tin, do you?'

'No, but I'm still worried for the company!'

'But it's none of your business, is it? So please, Gerry, don't worry. You had a good time with the Chinese? And they seem very nice.' He patted my hand, adding, 'Now look, I suggest you worry about the Chinese, tell me how much business we've had from them today.'

'Er, well, er, none yet, I expect to have an order tomorrow, I think they're short a hundred tons of copper.'

Mark laughed. 'Well ,Gerry, that's hardly going to keep the wolf from the door, is it? What about the aluminium business, how is that going with the Czechoslovakians?'

'Yes, I think that's coming along nicely, but they aren't trading with everyone on the Ring!'

Mark looked confused. 'What are you talking about? You've lost me, Gerry.'

I leaned forward in my seat. 'Well forgive me if I'm wrong, but aren't you considering lending the Buffer Stock Manager even more money? What if he goes bust?'

Mark laughed. 'Don't be silly, the Buffer Stock Manager can't go bust! In any case, we're holding the tin warrants as collateral against the money he owes us and we're earning on the interest he's paying us as well as getting the commission for all his carries. It's a win-win situation. Don't you worry.'

'No,' I insisted, 'I don't agree, not for us it's not a good situation, his allegiance is elsewhere.'

Mark cleared his throat, he was going to ask me to leave, I could tell. 'Look, all I can say is don't worry, we know what we're doing, we're not going to lose any money, OK? '

If I carried on he would get angry but I couldn't stop myself. 'If... if he goes bust, which I know you say won't happen, but if he does go bust, what will the tin be worth? And besides, we don't know what he's doing with other brokers do we?'

Just for a moment there was an uncomfortable silence. I had stepped across the threshold and there was no going back. Mark's usual florid face had gone much paler, he was white with rage and I braced myself for the onslaught. 'Looook!' he screamed 'If the bloody Buffer Stock Manager goes bust, Gerry, there will be no fucking Metal Exchange and no fucking us either! Do you understand? '

I had to back off and apologise. 'OK, I'm wrong, sorry to have disturbed you I should have known that you would have thought of every eventuality.' I stood up and left the room as quickly as possible. I had never seen Mark so angry, not so angry with me at any rate!

The last thing I wanted to do was to upset him and I certainly didn't want him to draw similar conclusions about our potential Chinese business. As I walked into the trading room, David sniggered. Henry gave me an enquiring look but I said nothing, They were bound to find out soon enough anyway. I grabbed my coat. 'How are we doing with the Czechs then?' Henry asked David just as I was about to leave.

'Yes, good, we've done some more deals and there are some more contracts for them to sign. They've promised us lots more business but first we have to raise their credit line, I think.'

I had to laugh to myself. I wished they'd let me have an increased credit line, honestly, money didn't seem to matter these days. Perhaps it was me; I just didn't get the money game. It was far too complex. More to the point, how could I understand the markets and provide recommendations if I didn't understand the money game? David was right after all! I was really stupid. Fancy working my trading system in the face of such adversity!

Walking to the tube station, I could see it all so much clearer now. My conversation with Mark had alerted me to a new possibility. No longer were markets simply moving according to the natural law of supply and demand. The supply and demand of physical metal to the marketplace was in the real world determined by environmental, economic or political news. It was real news that created or destroyed jobs, real news because it happened out there in the community before it impacted upon the marketplace. But now the market's very survival would be threatened because a new law from the moneylenders had made everything about the marketplace irrelevant. The cost of physical commodities such as sugar, cocoa, coffee would no longer reflect a true value. The dawning of the financial instruments such as derivatives and options was upon us. The circulation and availability of money was now the single most important factor in the market. It would enable a market to behave in completely the opposite way it would have done if it had being governed by the more natural factors of supply and demand.

Now I knew what all economists have always known: money is the route of all evil! Jobs were bound to be on the line when markets could be so easily manipulated. Powerful agents were at work, cornering markets and getting even richer. The principle of the free market was at stake. I realised too that the new game in town would mean little difference between buying and selling or borrowing and lending or trading options. Now it didn't matter if a loss on the metal was made, so long as financial deals made more money. In other words, so long as the rates of interest charged made the deal viable. And of course so long as the client was making money, the brokers' commission would be safe. But what would happen if interest rates rose sharply? Would the deals become untenable? I realised then that the bubble could burst at any time. What would happen when the client started to lose large amounts of money and couldn't afford to pay the broker's commission or the interest rate? The broker would then be forced to lend more and more money to him! Was this what was happening already? I wondered. So long as the banks would carry on lending, the brokers' business would be safe but if they stopped the broker would be caught in the middle.

What if this client was so big that he was trading through

half the Ring dealers? I shuddered at the thought. Surely anyone looking at the situation would have come to the same conclusion as me? I must have missed a trick. There must be something more to the deal because otherwise the risks would outweigh the rewards.

I wondered how my trading system would react to increased volatility in the market. I reckoned that if the market became too erratic the system would signal to liquidate the position. However, I could not afford for that to happen, as my clients would get fed up with the amount of commission they would be charged when we opened or closed a position. Now I wasn't at all sure that my trading system could survive in such a manipulated climate and all my hard work would go to waste.

Stepping into the crowded tube at Bank, I thought about the implications for British tin producers, companies I had recently visited in Cornwall. They would have been hedging, selling their forward production into the market, but if for any reason they were unable to deliver, then they would be short and face massive losses. There could be serious consequences for the whole industry if this all went wrong.

That year I had seen for myself Cornish tin mining at its most dangerous. I willingly undertook these mini-adventures, confident that what I learned would be invaluable in developing my understanding of the real hard business of mining for metals. It was absolutely imperative that I understood how and where a commodity was produced and the costs of doing so, and my visit to a traditional tin mine such as Saint Piran helped me understand the problems old mines had in competing against a more modern mine such as Wheel Jane.

A visit to a rocky outcrop of the Cornish headland near Redruth provided a welcome break from the office. I remember holding my breath as we dropped several hundred feet in an old rickety wooden crate. My helmet had a small torch on it that lit the way as we slowly made our way through damp, lightly flooded tunnels. The smell of wet, warm rock was musty, basic, and distinctly Neanderthal. We walked in single file as the rock face became steeper and the passages even narrower. I was so disorientated that I could not tell whether we were climbing down or up! It was pitch black and the temperature was continuing to rise. I felt claustrophobic and every now and again a jet of steam would appear in front of us. As we came to the bend I could just see the man ahead of me as he turned to look back. 'It's OK!' he shouted to me. The water was past my ankles, and I hoped it would not get any deeper.

Suddenly I heard a rattle to my right and then another. I thought it might have been rats but of course it wouldn't have been at that depth. Another light flashed in my face, this time from below. It was a miner eating his sandwiches! 'Sorry,' I said, 'I didn't mean to disturb you.'

'It's OK,' he replied. Perhaps he was used to visitors at lunchtime.

I passed through the tunnel that finally opened up into a huge cave. All six of us were for the first time in an hour or so able to stand fully upright. Our guide was explaining about the ore and how it was being mined from the seams. 'And now we are mining over here but the quality of the ore is not as good and so we must mine much more of it. Of course, with the price of tin moving higher we hope to be able to keep this mine profitable although we have had to lay many people off already. The mine is very old and as you can see in need of substantial repair.'

It was then that I heard a rustle above my head. 'What's that noise?' I asked the guide.

'Ah, that is…' He listened, cupping his hand over his ear. 'Yes, that is… can you all hear? Can any of you guess what we are all listening to?' he asked, raising his arm towards the ceiling.

'No, I have no idea – a miner eating his lunch? Ha ha ha!' one of the team laughed.

'No, it is the actual seabed! You are underneath the seabed and that is the debris, perhaps shells and the like, being moved around on the seabed by the tides.' Well, I stood there with my mouth open. This was awesome! I was actually under the sea!

Rather stupidly, I then imagined a hole appearing in the ceiling above my head and the ocean pouring in. But it brought home to me how dangerous mining could be, so now having seen it all I wanted to get out as quickly as possible. 'Can we leave now?' I asked.

'Yes certainly.' Our guide was very polite. 'And if you like we can have some lunch before visiting Wheel Jane this afternoon. That's a more modern mine, not such a frightening place,' he said, giving a reassuring smile.

As we walked back through the shafts, I observed the wooden supports holding back the now streaming rock face and tried not to think of mining accidents. I passed where the miner had sat eating his sandwiches in the tunnel and looked to see if he was still there. He was, but now he was standing up, drinking from his flask. I imagined him doing this day after day, year after a year. What a life! I saw the whites of his eyes as I passed and I wondered what he might be thinking. 'Have a good day' I said as we passed by on our way back to the wooden lift.

Four of us got into it and that felt like too many. Slowly the lights below us disappeared as we were hoisted higher in a lift that swung and then knocked us from one side of the shaft to the other. On one occasion we hit the side of the shaft so severely that the lift came to a sudden halt hanging at a precarious angle to the cliff face. Not wanting to think the worst I put on a brave face. There was a loud clunk and click as another pulley was attached and we started to move higher again. I was so relieved when we finally arrived safely at the summit.

Later after a Cornish pasty and a beer in the local inn we were taken to Wheel Janes the very antithesis of Saint Piran. Wheel Jane was an enormous mine, a cavern full of modern engineering. Underground lorries appeared as if by magic, ferrying their loads of copper, tin and silver from one end of the cave to the other. Although this was the largest mine I had seen, our guide told us there were much larger diamond and gold mines in South Africa. One day, I thought, I would visit them.

The tube jolted to a stop and the lights went out to a

prolonged and predictable sigh from the passengers. Why was it that British engineering, considered the best in the world, could so often let you down, especially when you relied on it the most? I suppose the answer must lie in its age. A lot of it had been built in Victorian times when demand for the service wasn't quite as high as it was now. The trouble was that we had all come to rely on it so much and there was hardly any time when it wasn't in use. When could it receive the attention it needed to ensure that it didn't break down? The train jolted forward and the lights came on again. I picked up the Financial Times and started to read about an impending oil price rise. Oh dear, I thought, all we need now is for the interest rates to move higher.

I was up at 5.30 the next morning, preparing for my flight to Dusseldorf. Rick and I had arranged to meet in the departure lounge at Heathrow at seven o'clock. By 7.15, he still hadn't arrived and I realised I would probably be taking the flight on my own. I was annoyed about this. I had never been to Germany before and although I was looking forward to the day trip, I was apprehensive about meeting the Czechoslovakians on my own. Sitting in Club Class, I half expected Rick to show but he didn't and by the time the plane took off I had accepted that I would have to journey alone – something I was not looking forward to.

During the trip, I read the paper and ate a full English breakfast. I was getting more nervous about the meeting ahead of me and checked several times that my briefcase was still beside me. Staring out of the window, my mind turned to the previous day's conversation with Mark. The more money you had, the more money you could make. It was all so simple. The more money you could lend to clients, the more business clients would give you, the more knowledge you would have about the market and the more commission you would make! I felt quite foolish now; how stupid I must have sounded, wittering on about a potential strike at Bunker Hill when the real news was what the Buffer Stock Manager was up too. Still what else could I put in my reports? It wouldn't be right to say that today there were more rumours in the market about the Buffer Stock Manager borrowing an extra five million!

What on earth had David been thinking of when he had said, 'Because we hold the warrants of tin we're safe!' How could we be if there was no money for trading it! Those who needed money would sell the warrants and without any buyers the price must surely fall! So where, I wondered, was our security? How do we get our money back from the market when all the other brokers are selling as well? I hated the build-up of events, leading to an impending disaster because there was nothing to be done but watch them unfold as systems broke down and chaos ensued. When the expected no longer happened and the unexpected lurked at the back door. When situations no longer felt good, no longer felt honest, no longer felt worthwhile. When the writing was on the wall, and every minute of every day brought you closer and closer to the moment when your fear would be realised. I hated it because negative energies began to feed off each other and grow. Because what was light was now dark and darkness seemed to absorb everything into it. Because like a sponge when it has absorbed enough, it would be wrung out and hung up to dry! And all of this was for what? Just so a few people could become immensely rich. What a waste! This wasn't the market I had grown up in and, worse, I was in a quandary about the Chinese. Say they wanted a massive credit line? What was I going to do if they asked me for one? Their business was legitimate. They had a country to modernise and electricity to put in. China had the highest population in the world and I would move heaven and earth to help them, profit or no profit!

My thoughts came to an abrupt halt as the plane turned to make its descent. I quickly opened a letter with an interesting postmark. It was an invite to the Woman of the Year Luncheon. This wasn't what I had been waiting for, but I would be very pleased to accept.

I thought it a shame that Rick could not be with me. He had been with me on my visit to a tin plant in Holland to watch tin ingots being manufactured. Afterwards, our host had taken us out for a drive to Arnhem to see the crossing. It was a cold damp and foggy day as we arrived at this rather depressing place. We discussed with our host what had happened here in the Second World War and as he spoke in broken English, I had no trouble imagining the scene. I suppose it was the knowledge that all our families had suffered this common experience of a war that now cemented our friendship in this sad place. Words came from out of the blue and I knew they would be with me all day long. *'Like a circle in a spiral, like a wheel within a wheel, never ending or beginning like an ever spinning wheel, like the circles that you find within the windmills of your mind.'*

On landing, I wasn't sure who would meet me. Eventually a board held up with my name guided me to a black Mercedes. We sped through Dusseldorf at high speed with my hand grasping my briefcase full of contracts that needed to be signed. The chauffeur was polite but did not speak, although his eyes watched me constantly in the mirror. I was pleased to get out of the car as we arrived at a modern office block. Once inside I was seated for a while before being ushered into a small room. In the middle was a round table and surrounding the round table were men in black suits. I walked in, held my hand out and smiled at them. I was relieved to see some smile back as one very serious man came up to me, grabbed my shoulders rather hard, drew me towards him and kissed me on both cheeks. I smiled but said nothing. I was sorry not to have been able to speak Czech to them. So I stood motionless until I think they asked me if I had a good journey. I was not sure whether to answer 'Ja' or 'Da', so I just nodded and smiled, keeping silent most of the time.

Once we were all standing around the table a drink was poured out, a very strong drink, and all glasses were raised. I drank it slowly at first but faster when a fat hand gestured to me from across the table. He was asking for me to put the briefcase on the table. I nodded and laid it on the table. I then decoded the lock and snapped it open. A large chair was pulled up and the most senior man in the room sat himself down. The atmosphere in the room lightened and another chair was brought to the table. 'Pleez seet down.' I didn't need to be asked a second time! There were a lot of contracts to sign and after checking the first few, I noticed that Mr Kiepjinsky, as I came to know him, didn't seem to check any more but carried on scribbling out his signature.

After half an hour or so, everything seemed in order and he leaned over to me. 'Ve have got somver gud for lunch today, I zink you vill enjoy eet!' He stood up and beckoned to a few people and myself to follow.

Outside there were three black Mercedes, and as we got in Mr Kiepjinsky beckoned for me to sit next to him. 'You vill like the Black Forest, I zink? You see ve go for not too long a ride and then ve have some lunch and then ve bring you back to ze office for tea and then ve take you to the airport for your flight to England, OK?'

'Yes, thank you!' I replied, trying not too sound frightened.

We sped through the forest at one hundred kilometres an hour and even though I kept looking I did not see any other cars on the roads. Eventually we pulled up outside a large chateau standing in its own grounds with pale stone walls and clay coloured turrets.

'This is a famous place for us to eat, I hope you enjoy,' a man called Sergei had said as he took my coat and guided me to the room where we would have lunch. 'Apparently it's an old hunting lodge and vos alvays in use until now ven it is a hotel and restaurant,' Mr Kiepjinsky explained. 'You like vild game? Some quails' eggs, or salmon perhaps?'

'Yes, thank you, salmon will do very nicely.'

As I looked around the room I was sure it had been used in a recent World War Two film that I had seen. It had a certain air about it, a sense of mystery that I wasn't particularly comfortable with. I decided to put the thought aside and concentrate on the party. Before long the wine was flowing and despite the language barrier, we were all laughing.

Suddenly Mr Kiepjinsky clapped his hands. 'Ve must go now.' I looked at my watch, goodness, it was nearly three o'clock! Reading my mind, Mr Kiepjinsky said. 'Don't vorry, ve vill have plenty of time, I know a short cut back to ze office and the airport is not far as you know, so don't vorry OK.'

'No, I won't then.'

He was as true as his word. No sooner had we arrived back at the office than the tea arrived, just as I was saying my thank you for a lovely lunch. 'Ve have a present for you and ve hope you like it' He handed me a very large cardboard box. 'But you must not open it until you get to England.'

'Is this for me or is it for the company or for a colleague?' I asked.

He screwed his face up. 'No, eet's for you, something from Czechoslovakia. Now you must go and ve vill see you again very soon, I'm sure.' Without further delay I was hurried out of the room and into the car. Shortly afterwards I was boarding my return British Airways flight.

When I got home to Holland Park at about 7.30, Mary, my new flatmate had cooked a superb meal – not that I was particularly hungry. We opened the present after dinner together. It was a beautiful crystal vase made of Czechoslovakian glass. Then she handed me the letter I had been waiting for. 'Is this it?' she said, passing me a large brown envelope.

'Yes, looks like it could be.' I opened it and out fell what I was looking for.

'Blimey what's all that about then?' Mary asked, genuinely interested.

'To tell the truth I'm not really sure, but it's to do with the Guildhall and becoming a Freeman of the City of London.'

'What, didn't Dick Whittington start that all off? Didn't you tell me once that he was Lord Mayor of London? Ere, Gerry, remember that party we went to a year or so ago? When I dressed up as a black cat and you kept calling me pussy all night? What a laugh, I kept purring and licking you! And you got so annoyed, I thought you were going to hit me!'

I thought back to the evening and she was right, it was quite funny, well it was funny up until the time it wasn't! 'Yes, well you didn't have to keep calling me Dick all night, did you? I mean I think everyone knew who we were without you giving subtle hints!'

'Oh God, I've just thought of something else! Ha ha ha! Remember when you said if I was a pussy I should start to drink milk and lay off the wine.'

'Yes, vaguely, I think I left after that. Look.' I took the papers out of the envelope. 'It explains what a Freeman of the City of London is.'

'Well, why do you want to know about that? I mean, what good will it do being a Freeman, shouldn't you be a Freewoman? Oh sorry, there's no such thing as a freewoman is there? Ha ha ha!'

'No, not at the moment! Anyway, as a Freeman, apparently I can walk my sheep across London Bridge in the rush hour.'

'But you haven't got any sheep – mind you, I suppose you could always get some.'

'Oh, and if I want to I can set up any business in the street and I don't need a licence.'

'Well what's the bloody use of all those perks to us? It won't help us get a house, will it?'

I thought for a moment. I felt as if I owed it to the City to become a female member of its governing council. It was something I should do. I had been convinced by a Dame, Alderman herself who believed that there were far too few women becoming Aldermen. She would nominate me but first we needed to solve the problem of me not being a member of a Guild. She was a very sophisticated elderly woman who lived in the Barbican. I had visited her on occasions but of course never told Mary. She had told me that once you were a Freeman, you could become an Alderman and then eventually Lord Mayor of London. Mary was right, of course – there were no benefits as such to becoming a Freeman of the City of London. But to me it was a way of paying homage to the past and, however tenuously, connecting it to my future. I had never forgotten the strength and empowerment I had received in the early days from the traditional culture of the City.

Those big buildings, those guarded hidden places, the guides without names, the names without faces, the Roman ruins, and the knights who held their secrets so well. All of them, in turn had spoken and although I hadn't always understood their message, it didn't mean I couldn't acknowledge their role. So becoming a Freeman was my way of saying thank you to all of them for making sure my path had been as straight as it had.

That Saturday we visited a local pet shop as it was Mary's birthday and she wanted a puppy. We already had four cats living with us: Bilbo, Tuesday, Charlie and Robin. Two we had chosen and two had chosen us! Charlie had belonged to my aunt but she didn't want him any more and had given him to my brother, who didn't want him either so we ended up looking after him. He was a big, grey, fluffy and very huggable cat. Then there was Robin, a black and white cat who had been born a stray in Pottery Lane. But despite his unfortunate beginning, he wanted warmth and cuddles and regularly spent time with us. Luckily Mary and I had moved into the basement flat in Clarendon Road. This had a large garden that was big enough to accommodate those who were able to make their entrance and exit through our bathroom window!

We parked the car and walked over to the pet shop. There in the window were two of the cutest puppies ever imaginable. They were both King Charles Cavaliers. One was brown and white with the famous Blenhiem spot on her forehead. We called her Shambles because she made such a mess and the other one, who we purchased a week later, was a rather plump male who was black and white with brown eyebrows. I called him Badger in memory of the awful badger cull that took place that year.

The following week we drove down to Exmoor. Mary had been born in a small village called Porlock and she had often told me how beautiful it was. She was right. In fact it was the perfect village, with all the amenities you could want. The scenery was out of this world, with green fields and forests sweeping down to cliff-hugging bays with deep blue seas. We had some wonderful walks and played with the puppies, making sure that Badger didn't eat all Shambles's food and that Shambles didn't get lost when we were out walking. It was a world away from the concrete jungle that we both worked in and we felt great being down there. Just getting the fresh air in our lungs, smelling the pine forests and sitting by a real fire in the evening helped to blow away the cobwebs.

We were lucky to have spent a good part of the summer in Porlock But now it was time Mary and I had somewhere more permanent to live. London was expensive but we couldn't keep renting from my mother as she had now decided to sell the house. We agonised over whether it was right to buy in London where we both worked, or in Porlock where we both would have liked to live! The green fields were a real pull and although I was driving us down almost every weekend, the time spent there was never enough. Having a house down there would be ideal and property was so much cheaper.

On our last visit we had looked at a building plot and had been told by the developers that we could have a new three-bedroom house with a large front and back garden for £18 000. This compared very favourably with a one-bedroom town flat for £36 000. The problem was, where would Mary and I live when we were working in London? I saw no reason why we couldn't continue to rent a flat in Holland Park. But to buy the house in Porlock, I would have to get a mortgage. Borrowing money wasn't something I liked to do, but all the traders I worked with had no problem with the concept. You see, I had been bought up with the idea that you should only have what you can afford to pay for. But nowadays everyone seemed to think very differently. Life was all about living for today and paying for it tomorrow, and there was no shame to being in debt.

It was Debbie who finally convinced me to take the plunge and take a loan out. 'Everyone has to get a mortgage, Gerry, the way the market is going you'll never buy a house if you have to save up for it.'

'Yes, but how can I afford a mortgage with interest rates at fifteen per cent, and who knows, they might go even higher? It's going to cost me at least £3 500 in mortgage repayments a year and I have to rent in London as well. I mean on this salary I don't know whether I can cope, and then if I lost my job I'll be in real trouble.'

Debbie laughed. 'Course you'll cope, Gerry, housing is going up so you can sell it at a profit, and even so your salary is bound to go up now you're doing all this aluminium business. Henry said we will get a good bonus this year, I reckon we'll definitely get a couple of grand, maybe more.'

'Do you?' I was astonished at how much more she knew about future bonuses and the like. It was then that I suspected that some of the dealers were getting paid out a lot more often than I was. I wondered whether she was too. Perhaps I ought to be a bit more forthright in asking for more money for myself from Henry.

'Ere, what happened to you the other night?' Debbie was referring to the annual Metal Exchange Dinner held at the Dorchester in Park Lane.

'I went home, why?'

'Well it was such a laugh. We all went gambling and won loads of money, you should have come, and guess what time it was before I got home?'

'No idea, about four?'

'Yeah at least then, but I think most of the lads were out partying all bloody night. What a night we had, you should have been there.'

'Yes, sounds fun,' I said rather unconvincingly. I took a cigarette out. 'Do you want one?' I asked.

'Na, just put one out, mate, ta anyway. Now look, Gerry, there's one thing you got to remember, it's not *what* you know, it's *who* you know, that's what counts in this life.'

'Yes, I know that, anyway I can tell you some funny stories about the London Metal Exchange Dinner too!'

'Look,' she added, 'I'm not saying you should suck up to everyone, just the ones that count, yeah?'

'Well how do you know who the ones are that count and in any case, why aren't we the ones that count?'

'As usual you've lost me. Let's just forget this conversation, Gerry, it isn't going anywhere!'

Of course I knew what she meant. She probably had my best interests at heart but I didn't want to play that way. I didn't want to trade for favours. I didn't want to be dishonest. Sure, I wanted to get on, sure, I wanted to lead the way, I wanted to show that it could be done and that a woman could do it. I just didn't want to become corrupted to earn the easy buck, even though I saw many benefits from doing just that. I knew that Debbie thought of me as simple, stupid, weird even. 'Gerry,' she had said during one of our rather deep conversations, 'if I don't do it, someone else will, no one will benefit by me being honest. Can't you see that? If I don't take the money, a million others will. So, I might as well, yeah?'

I had argued differently. 'How will things change if we don't change? What about your soul, aren't you worried about that?'

'Na, why should I be? Honestly. Gerry. what are you talking about, soul? What bloody soul? I think you've lost the plot, really, you're on another fucking planet!'

For once I was speechless and had to agree it certainly seemed that way! I didn't really understand people talking about making money when all I could see was them doing was taking it from Peter to pay Paul, with a nice cut for themselves. I couldn't actually see any more money being made. All I could see was the wealth being distributed to fewer and fewer people.

'Tin,' I said, 'look at tin. That's a good example of people being greedy.'

'What?'

'People being greedy, doing things for money, not caring about who it might be hurting, or who might be suffering. Just so long as they make enough money to do what they want.' I lit my cigarette.

Debbie took her brush from out of her handbag and pulled the hair from it. I could tell she was annoyed. 'Oh lighten up, Gerry, for Christ's sake, it's not the bleeding end of the world to make a fucking profit!'

I looked away, upset at her apparent selfishness. Was I the only one who felt like this? Did no one else feel guilty at making easy money? I looked around the desk and the answer was clear: no, they didn't. Perhaps I was having a nervous breakdown? After all, I had been working very hard lately and even I had to admit I sounded a bit confused!

Debbie tapped me on the arm. She felt sorry for me, I could tell, or perhaps she was just picking up my vibes. 'I'll tell you what, I'll go and get a coffee and you can tell me one of your stories about when you first went to the metal dinner.' She looked deep into my eyes. 'Come on, you remember you said you had something funny to tell me, what was it? It must have been such a laugh. I would love to have been a fly on the wall watching you. Ha ha ha!'

When she came back with the coffees, I began. 'Yes, well, dining at the Grosvenor House was quite a big deal,' I said, trying to remember the first year. I was in awe of all these important metal dealers from around the world, congregating every year for the annual dinner. Dinner? I say dinner, but as far as I was concerned it was a banquet. Every year around two thousand men – no, I tell a lie, there were a couple of women there too – are invited by the Committee of the London Metal Exchange. It's a hugely important affair where issues affecting the industry are discussed and important speeches are made. For example, the Chairman – or was it the Chief Executive? – of Fords spoke to us one year. He was considered to be the best after-dinner speaker on the circuit and I must say he was very good. Although I didn't think much of a couple of the jokes he made that night.'

'You must have felt quite proud to be the only female metal dealer there, though surely, Gerry?'

'Yes I suppose so but I've got something funny to tell you in a moment, which shows that you're not always perceived the same way as you feel!'

'Wasn't that just what I was saying?'

I waved a hand impatiently. 'Anyway, where was I? Oh yes, every company would invite their most favoured clients up to their suite for pre-dinner drinks. The Metal Exchange dealers used to circulate through all the suites saying an innocent hello but really checking to make sure that the client that should have been with them wasn't in someone else's suite!'

Debbie laughed. 'Oh yeah, a great opportunity to nick someone else's client, eh? And I bet you got a lot of attention, being the only young woman?'

'Yes, I suppose so, and some of it I was happy with. By that I mean the respect shown by one dealer to another. But some of it I found far too personal. You know me, Debbie, and how I find it difficult to deal with flirtatious clients but this will make you laugh. There were a lot of confused faces and I think many of these clients, who I didn't know particularly well, thought I was a hostess. One even waved me over, shaking his empty glass and later another came over and told me about some spillage that needed mopping up. I thought: any minute now someone is going to ask me to collect the empty glasses or unblock the toilet!'

Debbie laughed hilariously. 'Oh careful, I'm wetting myself, what a laugh! Let's get another coffee. Usual, Gerry?' Within a minute she was back and we lit up another cigarette.

'We'll have to watch the time, Debbie, have you got all the orders and your card up to date?'

'Yeah, more or less. I'm just waiting for confirmation of a couple of lead orders, that's all.'

'Are you a bit scared about sitting in the Ring, Debbie?'

'Na, I'm looking forward to it. How bad can it be the first time? Any tips?'

I took a deep drag and thought for a second. 'Yes, it's a good idea when you sit in the Ring to keep your legs closed and your ears and eyes open!' Her mouth dropped open, not knowing whether I was joking. 'Oh, and only open it at the right time, make sure you do it loudly and clearly, not as though you're afraid to speak.'

'Blimey, you don't mince your words, do you?'

'No, but that doesn't make me a good dealer!' This made her laugh, I'm not quite sure why, unless it was because she had thought of something funny to say. She laughed so long it made me laugh at her laughing. I stubbed my cigarette out and finished my coffee. I didn't like smoking without having something to sip.

Debbie was still smirking to herself. 'Yeah, I'd better not be like you, Gerry, who doesn't know the difference between a contango and a backwardation! Ha ha ha! Ere… I tell you, mate… it won't be difficult to beat your performance! Anyway go on… tell me what it was like at that first Metal Exchange Dinner, you said you had a funny story to tell me.'

I ignored the quick succession of insults from her, which she was prone to do on occasions. 'Oh yes, so I did, now where was I? To reach the banquet you had to negotiate a huge winding staircase made up of really shallow steps. The journey was treacherous because nearly two thousand men would descend on it at the same time. That's because a stupid bell would sound off in all the suites and leave us with only fifteen minutes to get to our tables. Crazy, I know, but that's the way it was. It was pandemonium, especially when all came to squeeze into the lifts. You see, all the party suites were on the top floor and the banqueting room, well… it was almost in the basement. Imagine all that and then imagine me in the middle with a long evening dress that was cut lower than I would have liked.' I looked at Debbie and smiled. 'Not as low cut as you wear, but low for me, you understand.

'Anyway, having made it down in a very crowded lift to the ground floor, all of us then had to negotiate this stunningly huge winding staircase that ended up in the centre of the banqueting hall. Several large crystal chandeliers dominated the room where forty large white round tables were laid out immaculately for the diners. You can get a feel of how important the occasion was. Picture the scene for a moment, imagine the Oscars – it was just like that.'

Debbie got up to get a coffee, and I wondered whether the other traders minded me speaking so long with her. They were all hard at work and here I was gossiping! Well, it was important to share these moments together, to bond and she clearly enjoyed listening to the story. 'You're not getting bored are you?' I asked her when she got back.

'Are my eyes still open? Have I gone into a trance? No, of course not, so just carry on with the story, will yer?'

'Right, now where was I? Oh yes. As we were all about to descend the staircase en masse, someone decided to dim the lights. Picture me surrounded by all shapes and sizes of men from different countries speaking different languages. There was lots of laughter and smoke as the crowd moved slowly towards the top of the stairs. But everyone was so much larger than me and from a distance you wouldn't have known I was right in the middle of the huge crowd. Pretty dangerous really, it was an absurd situation to be in, and once I was in there, there was no easy way out, as I later found to my cost.

As the crowd moved forward, my turn came to negotiate the staircase. I was being pushed and shoved and knocked as a crowd of fourteen or so wide tried to squeeze into a place that could only take half that number. I was getting distinctly nervous about walking down the stairs in my heels. So I tried to move to the inside rail to steady myself but was pushed out by a very large, cigar-smoking German, who shouted at me before pushing me back into the centre of the stairs. I felt my dress rip, slowly at first, but then all at once I felt it go. From the hem at the bottom to my you-know-whats!'

She laughed. 'Your you-know-whats? What on earth do you mean?' she asked.

'You know!'

'No, I don't know! Do you mean your tits, Gerry?'

'Sssshhh, Debbie!'

She laughed out loudly 'Well for evven's sake, Gerry, can't you say the word?'

'Yes, well, I don't want everyone to hear, do I?'

'OK, go on then, get on with the story.'

'Well, someone or several people had stood on my dress. I was so angry I grabbed the top part of the dress and hoisted it up as best I could while at the same time locating the culprits and asking them to move their bloody great clobbers off my dress!'

Debbie laughed again. 'I bet you caused a bloody stir.'

'Yes, I did but you should have seen the guy who did the damage, he was a big German fellow with a fat cigar in his gob. After I had spoken to him he waved his red hand in my face and pushed past me as if I was less than human. I was so upset, my beautiful dress was all but ruined and I was left standing with it in tatters while all of them just carried on down to dinner.'

'So what did you do then?'

'What could I do? I had to excuse myself from the crowd with great difficulty. Have you tried to walk in the opposite direction of two thousand people?'

'No, but I would have thought it's something you're used to doing, Gerry!'

'Anyway, I hurried as fast as I could to the loo where I pinned my dress together and made my way back to the banqueting hall.'

'God, you didn't go back with a torn dress, did you?'

'Well yes, by this time they were all seated and I stood on the staircase alone.'

Debbie burst out laughing again. 'Yes she stood on the stairs at midnight, her lips all a flutter, she gave a cough, her dress fell off and ended up in the butter!'

'Yes, thank you, Debbie, very funny! Anyway, as I descended very slowly, everyone was watching and I really hoped that I wouldn't trip up or make a fool of myself. But how on earth was I going to find my seat amongst all those tables? I told you, the room was a fantastic shape and the chandeliers were stunning. As I came slowly down the stairs I tried to see if I could pick out Henry's face or our table but it was impossible.'

'How long did it take?'

'Ages, I think, can you imagine me trying to be invisible in a half-torn dress, creeping around the tables while the starters were being served? Honestly, I felt such an idiot. Luckily for me, by the time I arrived at the right table most of the dealers were engaged in animated conversation with their guests and hadn't seen me searching for the seating plan.'

'Then what happened?'

'Some people at the neighbouring tables were quite shocked that I was actually going to sit down. But as the evening progressed they accepted my right to be there. After all, I hadn't shown disapproval at the after-dinner jokes, and I didn't mind too much when the waiter refused to serve me port.'

'You're joking?'

'No, I'm not. He said, "I'm, sorry that's normally reserved for the gentleman, Ma'am!" and he even bowed to me as he said it!'

'What a cheek!'

'Yes, I know. Anyway. "That's perfectly all right and I understand your position," I said. "Now please bring me an Armagnac and a slim cigar".'

'Brilliant, what did he say?'

'"As you wish, Ma'am!" So by the time I lit up my cigar and was on my third brandy, I was feeling quite at home. That is, until I left the table and it was then that I realised getting home would be a journey in itself!'

'What do you mean?' Debbie asked, looking at the clock. 'Shit, I think we have to leave for the market.'

'Yes, OK, I'll just tell you this one quickly then. After dinner and a lot of socialising and running between suites, I finally decided enough was enough and about 2.30 asked the doorman to get me a cab to take me home. Now you think I would be safe from trouble by now, wouldn't you? but no, towards me came this client we all know, but I'm not giving names, and just as I was getting in one side of the cab, he got in the other. Then, as we sped on down Park Lane, he grabbed hold of me and tried it on. It was terrible, he just wouldn't leave me alone and he was drunk as a Lord. Eventually I fought him off, stopped the cab and told him to get out. Thank God.'

'We'd better go now, Gerry.'

'Yes, come on then, I'll tell you this story as we walk down to the market.'

But the very worst thing had happened to me the following year when someone too important to mention, a very well-liked gentleman from the east, had offered me a lift home in his chauffeur-driven limousine. 'This was an invitation I should have declined,' I explained to Debbie, 'but his behaviour was a complete surprise to me since, before this, I'd had no reason not to trust him implicitly!'

'Well, who was he?'

'I can't tell you, not now, maybe later. Anyway, as I was saying, he had never given me any reason for concern. He was at least sixty- five years old and held a very senior position.'

'Do I know him?' she persisted.

'I'm not going to say, Debbie. Anyway, the company he works for is an international organisation and has huge global presence. I mean, you'd think he would have a reputation to maintain, wouldn't you? Surely I had a right to feel safe with such a man?'

'If it's who I think it is, he's married, isn't he?'

'Yes, he has at least one family, although his religion would allow for more if he could afford it, which of course he can.'

As we passed the tower, Debbie squinted up at it. 'So this is the Norman tower you're always saying I should visit?' We stopped for a moment and Debbie pointed at the locked wooden door, 'It is always shut? It's not very inviting is it?'

'No, that's why I find it so mysterious.'

'Yes, I think you would enjoy it. Anyway getting back to what I was saying. Haven't you had any similar experiences then?'

Debbie thought for a moment. 'No, not really. Oh, don't worry, I av a good time, don't get me wrong, but I don't get myself into the bloody mess you seem to get yourself into! I wouldn't be so bloody stupid!'

'I know. Anyway, let me finish the story, you'll never guess what's coming next. I was in a difficult position now, stuck in his car driving rather slowly through Soho. I knew I had to be very careful how I dealt with him, after all I didn't want to offend him, even though I didn't care if we lost his business.'

'Well, what did he say to you then?'

'"Here's the deal, Gerry," he said as he took one of my hands. "You know, I think you are a very pretty girl and I must say I like your attitude and the way you deal. But you don't earn too much money and I can help." Then he moved even closer, begging me not to be worried and saying that no one would have to know about it. "Please," he said, "don't get worried now, it's nothing too serious, in fact I think it's a really good idea. How would you like to have your own flat, a penthouse flat overlooking the whole of this part of London, and you don't have to pay a penny?" Naturally I was disgusted by the thought and told him as much. But he insisted. "No, listen, Gerry, you don't understand, I would pay for it all. The carpets and furniture and whatever else you need and you can take some time to think about it. You don't have to decide now".'

'Bloody hell!' Debbie said. 'Do you think he meant it?'

'Yes, of course. And he wasn't going to give up easily – he tried to convince me again and again. In fact he's never given up. He makes the offer every time I see him. Luckily enough, I only see him four or five times a year!'

'So what was it he didn't understand about the word no?'

'I don't know, some men just won't take no for an answer.'

'Still, you got home safely, didn't you?'

'Yes, eventually I got home. So you see, Debbie, I never really look forward to the London Metal Exchange dinner even if it *is* held at the Grosvenor House!'

Walking onto the Exchange floor, I noticed that, for the first time in a long while, the gallery was packed full of visitors.

'That's what you get at this time of the year and especially during London Metal Exchange week,' I said, pointing up at the gallery.

'Unless, of course, there's another reason?' Debbie smiled.

I wasn't sure what she meant by the remark and ignored it. Some of the visitors were Chinese, although I didn't recognise them. In any case, they were with another broker. Debbie got her book out to check some pre-market deals. She smiled and leaned towards me, whispering, 'Yes, but you always seem to attract eastern men. I mean, look at you with the Chinese – they love you and you spend so much time on them, yet you never really get any business from them, do you?'

'No, but one day I'm sure we will.'

'David says not.'

'I know, but he can talk. I'm not happy with that tin business. Everyone is in the same boat and if something goes wrong it will be awful. I don't think the business is safe. We're just lending money into a black hole.' She looked at me and I could tell that she didn't agree with me. Perhaps she thought I was jealous of David. 'Anyway, just think, it won't be very long before you're sitting in the Ring and then you'll see what it's like to be a woman dealer on the Exchange.'

I walked into the Zinc Ring as she shouted, 'Hey, Gerry, I'm not worried, it'll be great, I hope the other girls who are clerking try it too. Yes, as many as possible, that will do for me!'

After the Zinc Ring I phoned Mr Hao directly from the market. I knew some of his colleagues were up in the gallery but I still hoped he would give me a copper order. In any case, I didn't trust David to provide him with a decent commentary from the office. 'Good morning, Mr Hao, would you like to listen to copper today?' I was expecting him to put me on the speaker as he usually did. At the very best I could expect a market order for a hundred tons. But I was to be surprised.

'Yes, thank you, I will listen. Why aren't you in the Ring, Miss Gerry?'

'Well, because I don't trade copper in the Ring.'

'When you trade copper then?'

'Well, I can trade in the office any time but we have a new copper dealer who is very good. You can give me the orders and I will make sure you get a good execution.'

'Ha, no we want you trade copper for us.'

'Well if you want, I can ask.'

'Yes, we want. When this afternoon you phone me, when New York opens, you don't tell anyone.'

I was getting excited. All this secrecy! I could barely contain myself. 'Copper is very quiet today, Mr Hao.'

'Hmmm, what volume on Ring?'

'Thin, there is not much trading at all.'

'Hmm, OK, you phone later.'

Excited from my conversation with Mr Hao, I rushed back to the office, grabbed a sandwich and smoked far too many cigarettes. David sensed my excitement. 'What's up then?' he asked. A better person couldn't have asked, I was about to be vindicated and I couldn't help but smile. 'Come on, don't keep it to yourself. What's up?'

This was like the good old days. 'Nothing, I'm just thinking that's all.' I'd say anything to shut him up while I watched anxiously as Comex, the New York Market, opened. I wondered whether the Chinese were buying on the opening in New York.

David, who still couldn't get over his surprise that I was back in the office at lunchtime, was still trying to get information from me. 'OK, what's the occasion?'

I continued to ignore him, while I checked to make sure there were enough trading sheets and pencils were sharpened. 'Nothing, why?'

'Well, you're not normally back here, are you?' Are you expecting a call or something? If so I could have taken it for you.'

'Thanks, David, that's very sweet of you but I'm expecting a call from a journalist who wants to do an interview with me.' That should shut him up for a moment, I thought.

He sneered back. 'Oh, not that stupid old rubbish again! I don't understand what there is to talk to you about. Really, Gerry!'

'Want a coffee?' I asked, changing the subject

'Yeah, black no sugar.'

That was easy, I thought! It was important that David had absolutely no idea that I might have a big order from the Chinese. He would try and trade on the back of it and tell his clients, and that would ruin the market. 'Here, black no sugar, right?'

David looked up and gave a rare smile. 'Were you pleased with your bonus, Gerry?'

'Yes, it was OK, why?'

'Just wondered.'

Actually, I had been upset when I received it, not because it wasn't very generous but because of the conversation I had overheard from two other members of staff.

As I'd opened my envelope, two of the girls from upstairs were talking. One was moaning about not getting more money because the company couldn't afford it and the other had been warned of an impending redundancy. I felt guilty, imagine them knowing I had just received a £4000 bonus! I felt sorry for them and wished I could help. Still, if my big deal comes off they'll all be better off next year.

I sat down and waited for the phone to ring, and it soon did. It was Mr Hao. 'Hullo, Gerry, what's three months copper?'

'800 at 802 at the moment.'

'OK you make me five hundred-ton market please?'

I put my hand over the phone. 'David, do you know what our house position is on copper?'

'I think we're short about three hundred tons, why?'

'I need to make a market for five hundred tons.'

He looked at the screen. 'OK, make 801-802 if it's with commission.'

'Hello, Mr Hao, 801-802 is my market.'

'OK, I sell you five hundred tons.' And before I could answer, he had hung up.

'We've got five hundred tons at £801, so that makes us long two hundred tons if we take that in against our short of three hundred. Do you wanna cover them in or leave them?' I asked David.

'No, I'm not worried. New York might pick up later and anyway, it's a small profit. It won't do us any harm to be long a couple hundred tons.' David seemed relaxed. 'Who was that, anyway?'

I pretended not to hear him. 'So did you enjoy yourself last night, David?'

'Not really, you know I hate those false get-togethers.'

I had to agree with him. 'Yes, I expect everyone's still got a hangover from all the partying. This afternoon should be quiet, none of the clients will be back in their offices until tomorrow or the day after.'

David looked up, astonished at what I had said. 'Well, they can still trade when they're in London.'

'Yes, of course they can, of course they can,' I repeated, grabbing my jacket. God, he was always so serious, I was only making idle conversation with him anyway.

'Well, tata, I'm off to the market, see you later.'

I wasn't really, I just had to get away from him. Anyway, I was hungry. I hadn't eaten anything for ages so I headed over to the café for a sandwich. Warming up my hands on a hot cup of tomato soup, I wondered how big an order we would get. If Mr Hao was selling, the market must be going down. I mean, the Chinese, they were clever. They would not sell into a rising market, would they? I mean that would just be plain foolish.

It was just as I was finishing my soup that for some unknown reason, I recalled the old Jewish trader who had given me the paperweight all those years ago. 'Keep this by your bed and you'll never be poor.' I had believed in what he had said and I had never been poor again. Perhaps I was about to be rewarded for all my years of loyalty now. Then it dawned on me why I hadn't yet had the big order. It was because they wanted me to actually trade the copper, not to give it to another dealer to trade. It wasn't the company I worked for that mattered to them, it was me. I rushed back to the office to speak to Henry.

He was in his usual place for that time of day. 'Henry,' I blurted out, 'I must speak with you now. You know I'm trading zinc at the moment and Debbie will be coming into the Ring next week and she ought to trade lead and zinc so I was wondering, if I could get some experience in trading copper, perhaps on a quiet Ring this afternoon?'

He looked at me and puffed on his pipe slowly. 'This is unlike you, Gerry, thinking of Debbie's needs!'

'Not at all, Henry, Debbie and I get on very well indeed and it makes sense for everyone to have experience of trading all the metals in the Ring. don't you think?'

'Well, you have aluminium, so why do you need copper? I mean the markets are quite similar and I hardly think we need to take the copper card away from Simon just yet!'

My plan wasn't going to work. I had to think fast. 'OK, I'll tell you what I think. Simon has really got to concentrate on the tin market. I mean, have you seen how volatile it is? And we have so much of the buffer stock business. I think, that Simon needs to have the time and space to be able to concentrate on it.' Henry sat down slowly 'Are you all right?' I asked.

He looked up at me and I could see he didn't look very well at all. 'Just the usual aches and pains,' he said, rubbing his chest.

'You want to watch that, Henry. Don't forget last week what happened when I was in the Ring. Geoffrey had a heart attack right next to me!'

'Oh yes, I meant to ask you how is he? Is he recovering?'

'As far as I know but he's still in hospital and I don't think they'll allow him to trade in the Ring when he gets back.'

'Hmm...' He was silent for a moment 'I noticed that Simon was spending a long time on the tin position this morning, trying to offload some of those carries he had to take on yesterday. Do you think he's under stress then, Gerry?'

'No, I don't think so.'

Henry puffed on his pipe again. 'Perhaps it is a good idea to take some pressure off him at the moment and as you say, Debbie also needs the Ring trading experience. I'll speak to him tonight. Now you get off to the market, otherwise you'll be late.'

Great. I was well pleased. I rushed down to the Exchange, walking straight into the Ring as the bell sounded for zinc. Debbie leaned over me. 'Where have you been, you're a bit late?'

'Yes, sorry, I was speaking to Henry.'

'What about?'

'You, as it happens. Now ssshhh, I'll tell you later.'

Afterwards I phoned Mr Hao for the Copper Ring and got nothing. I was so disappointed. Perhaps they just wanted us to make them markets, perhaps they didn't trust us enough to work an order for them.

Later, on the way back to the office, I explained to Debbie. 'Don't say anything until Henry has had a chance to speak to Simon because I don't want him getting upset.'

'Why would he get upset?'

'Well, he might, copper is such a macho metal to trade and this will be the first time a woman has sat in a Copper Ring.'

She shook her head 'Oh don't be so stupid, it's no fucking big deal, we've hardly got any copper business anyway, just a few carries for New York and a couple of David's German clients. Honestly, the way you carry on! Trading copper is no big deal, believe me!'

I wondered what she was getting so hot under the collar for. 'I know, I'm only joking, I don't know why you take me so seriously all the time!'

The following morning I felt the butterflies in my stomach for the first time in a long while. Hopefully Henry would already have spoken to Simon by the time I got in. It was quiet as I grabbed a coffee and looked around the trading desk.

'Yes?' Debbie raised her head. 'What's up?'

'Nothing, is everyone happy today?'

'Yes, why shouldn't we be?' David looked at me across the desk and I noticed that he had very dark rings under his eyes.

'The tin position is really taking its toll on you lot, I can see that,' I said, trying to kick-start a conversation.

'Yes, well we can't all have super duper clients like you, Gerry!' David snapped back sarcastically. 'And don't get above yourself just because you're going to trade copper this morning either.' I glanced at Simon who just finished rubbing out a position on his card. Thankfully he smiled and was obviously OK about the whole situation. Well, why shouldn't he be? It wasn't a permanent thing it was just for a short while.

'It's only a temporary change just so Debbie can have a go at both the lead and zinc markets.'

'Yes,' she said pointing to herself. 'Then you'll see what a real trader in the Ring looks like and, you'll all see what a bunch of toss-pots you all really are! Ha ha ha!'

'Very funny,' I said. 'But watch it, pride comes before a fall!'

'Yes, you should know, Gerry!' she laughed.

Grabbing a coffee, I went across to the telex to write the metals report. What could I say different about the copper market that hadn't been said before? It certainly looked very cheap to me but then I had been talking bullish about it for quite sometime now. David had called it wishful thinking; others had called me out of touch. The market was in the doldrums and it wasn't surprising with what was going on with the tin market. Millions were being invested in supporting the tin price, which had moved from over £3000 to nearly £7000, more than a hundred per cent increase in the price over the last couple of years! What was there to say about tin, other than that the market was completely monopolised by the Buffer Stock Manager.

The tin producers must have been very pleased with him, but what about the consumers? Most of the time he was the only buyer in the market, bidding up the price without trading it. At other times, when he did trade, he was simply trading against himself through a variety of different brokers whom he paid large amounts of commission to square out forward positions for him. Surely it couldn't go on. One day the bubble would burst and create a tidal wave that would threaten the very existence of the London Metal Exchange. But for now I just had to think about what else I could say about tin that I hadn't already written. My recommendation was already to stay long. All there was left to do was watch the market go up rather tediously!

It was 11.30 when I lit up a cigarette and looked at the overnight orders from New York. There were a couple of copper carries and some possible selling if the market ran higher. The phone rang and I picked it up.

'Hullo, Miss '

I smiled. Good, it was them. 'Is that you, Mr Hao?'

'Yes, I have an order for you, sell one hundred tons of copper on the opening of the first Ring.'

'OK, Mr Hao. Would you like to listen to the Ring?'

'No, just phone me back with the execution.'

'Yes, OK, will do.' I put the phone down and rubbed my hands together, even though I was a little disappointed at the size of the order. Why, I wondered, were the Chinese selling when I was clearly recommending buying in my report? Surely with the market so low and their need for copper so great, they should be buying? I mean, just look at what had happened to the tin price. And aluminium and zinc – they had all gone substantially higher. Oh well, at least I would be actually trading this order.

I barely even noticed that it was time to leave for the market until Debbie came up to me. 'Come on, Gerry, what's the matter with you? We'll be late if you don't hurry. It's your big day, come on.' She could see I was despondent. Life, I told her, was becoming incredibly predictable, even boring. And in any case, what was the big deal in sitting in the Ring, even if it was the Copper Ring, if you didn't have a big order to execute?

But by the time we had arrived at the Exchange she had cheered me up. We both looked into the gallery as we always did. 'Seems quite crowded up there,' she said.

'Yes, it often is for the morning rings. Is that Mr Yang I can see standing there?'

'I dunno, I can't see.'

'Can you see who he's with, which broker is he standing with?'

'No, I can't see, honestly, Gerry!'

'Here,' I nudged her gently, 'next week you'll be trading zinc in the Ring, that'll be exciting.'

'Yes, I know, I can't wait.'

'Ah, that reminds me, I promised Michael a trip to the Exchange.'

'Michael?'

'Yes, Michael – the scrap dealer from Kent, you remember the one I told you about. He'll do a lot of business on lead so, Debbie, you should phone him.'

The bell rang, signalling the beginning of the Copper Ring. I smiled. 'Here goes then!'

'Yeah, good luck, mate'

Well there was nothing to be nervous about because nothing really happened. I traded the copper for the Chinese in very quiet market conditions and after a boring three minutes of staring at blank faces across the Ring, the market closed. After the Ring I phoned the Chinese to give them the execution. 'Hello, Mr Hao you have sold one hundred tons of copper at £799, would you like to listen to the next Ring?'

'No, no thank you, but I give you an order now. Buy ten thousand tons of copper at market. You can work it slowly throughout the day and don't tell anyone else. Do it slowly, quietly, and then phone me later with execution, OK?'

'Yes, Sir, will do and thank you.' I put the phone down in total shock. This was it! I had been right all along!

This was the big deal I had been waiting for. But then I pondered the current circumstances. I would have to trade this carefully. There was hardly any volume in the market. I would have to get Henry's agreement first. I had to make sure that we had all the right finance in place. There would be margins to pay on such a large open position. Why had they been selling when really they wanted to buy? Had Mark agreed to the five million pounds credit line? I just couldn't remember. This was probably the biggest order anyone had ever had. What was the copper price? £795 last traded.

I looked up at the gallery, there was no sign of Mr Yang, thank God – no one to spy on me. Act normal, I told myself, whatever you do, act normal. By now I was pacing around outside the telephone booth.

'What's the matter? What's wrong with you, are you not well?' Debbie was staring at me. 'You nuf gonner funny colour, mate, are you sure you're all right?'

'Yes, yes, I'm fine, Debbie, just fine.'

'Oh dear, that Copper Ring has got to you, hasn't it?'

'Yes, you could say that.'

'Well, what the bloody hell is it?'

'I've got a massive order to buy 10,000 tons!' Debbie's jaw dropped open, something it was prone to do when she was in shock.

'Just let's say we're going to be very busy on copper today. Get me Henry on the phone, quick, I need to talk to him.'

Debbie handed me the phone 'He's on there now.'

'Henry, I haven't got long,' I whispered so that the dealer next door couldn't hear. 'I've got a very big order on copper for you-know-who.' There was silence on the other end of the phone. I could almost hear him laughing at me 'Henry are you there? I've got ten thousand tons of copper to buy at market for you-know-who.'

I heard a sharp intake of breath and then Henry's hand went over the phone. I guessed he was speaking with David. Within a second he was back. 'OK, Gerry I heard you.' Henry at least was calm.

'Are they good for the volume?' I asked.

'Yes, the credit line is in place, don't worry. Are you going to trade this order or do you want Simon to do it?'

'No, I'm doing the trading today, Henry.'

'Well, don't let's have any fuck-ups then! OK?'

Back at the Exchange, there was just eight minutes to go until the Copper Ring opened. I thought Debbie looked nervous and I didn't blame her. I would have felt the same! She would have to catch all the deals and that wouldn't be easy, not in a busy Ring, and not the way I liked to deal! Both of us knew we had to do our best and for a successful outcome we must be able to rely on each other totally. 'Debbie!' I called her over. The butterflies were really beginning to take hold of me now. Debbie's face was white.

'What?' she said hesitantly.

'The deal is on ! Are you ready?'

She smiled. 'Yes of course, it's not such a big deal!' she laughed, but I knew her laughter covered up her true emotions.

I patted her arm discreetly. 'Look, try not to worry, you'll be fine, just make sure you catch all the trades, and remember to check each one directly after the Ring. Don't leave it until the kerb because I'll be busy again. Remember, Debbie, if you want help ask Simon to be ready. But try not to let the other dealers see that I have two clerks standing behind me in the beginning, otherwise they'll suspect we have a lot of business to do. I don't want them knowing that until it's upon them!'

Debbie laughed and nodded. 'Yes, don't worry it'll be a doddle, just you wait and see!'

Satisfied that everything was well prepared, I went out onto the pavement and lit up a cigarette. I looked up to the sky and took a deep breath. This was the day that I'd known was coming and I had to perform like never before. I knew this wasn't simply about making money. This was an important job that had to be done for the People's Republic of China. Bringing a second, some would say third world nation into the twenty-first century. Providing her with the power (literally, because the copper would send electricity to millions of homes across China) to become a first world nation state. It was a deal to be proud of and I hoped I could do it justice.

I pulled out the latest metals report and chart from my pocket. What had the system said? Copper prices were trading around £800 per tonne. What would happen to the market if I bought ten thousand tons? How high would I take the price? I wanted to buy the copper as cheaply as possible. I could see there was likely to be big buy stops around the £815 level that would force the market rapidly higher without me being able to purchase the volume of copper I needed. The market would run up very quickly in thin trading conditions to around £845. At that level further resistance might force the market back down again, but it wasn't a risk I could take. Everything depended on how much copper I could buy in at the lower prices. Trading conditions had been slow for some months now and a lot of the glamour had gone out of the copper market with all the big money going into tin.

If I completed my buying around £845 and then attracted a whole load of speculative selling, the market would close lower than the average price I had paid. The client would not be happy, especially as the order to execute had been given at my discretion. If I wanted more business from them I would have to get this right! No wonder I was feeling nervous. A couple of dealers joined me on the pavement. I smiled but I didn't have time to chat. One made a move to come over but I turned my back, making it clear I was busy. 'Boy trouble, I expect,' I heard him say.

I looked at my report to see what I had written earlier. 'If the market falls through the support at £780 on close of second Ring sell stops could be triggered and we would not advise buying until £750 where we would expect to see considerable support.' I returned to the floor of the Exchange in deep thought. If I could hit them hard the market would go into freefall and hopefully it would be much easier to buy back later. But if I got it wrong I would look a complete idiot when it came to buying it all back again. Mr Hao had said I could take all day but if New York opened higher the tide would be against us. I wondered then if the Chinese were already buying in New York. I would have to be careful. I didn't want to get stitched up!

The Copper Ring was about to start. I glanced across to Debbie, Simon and Trevor, who looked fully prepared as I walked into the Copper Ring. I sat down and thought of James. I could certainly do with his advice now. What was it he used to do? Oh yes, he would lean back as if he hadn't a care in the world.

I leaned my head slightly to the side and back so that it touched the base of the wooden bench. My neck was stiff and I hadn't even noticed. I thought it must be a little bit of tension. 'Debbie, are you ready?'

'Yes,' she whispered.

Opposite, the dealer called out to the Ring 'Three months?' There was no reply, just silence from the other dealers. You could hear a penny drop, or should I say a copper! Anyway, I noticed a couple of them move forward in their seats, apparently getting ready to trade. One of them shouted 'I'll give £795.' That was well down from the previous Ring, but it didn't mean the market was going down. On the contrary, dealers would often open the market where they would like it to be! An offer to sell at £797 was ignored as a dealer offered the market at £796, only a pound away from the bid. This was my chance. So I shouted as loud as I could, 'I'll sell at £795.' Because I had suddenly leaned forward in the Ring, it had unnerved a few of the dealers. Well, that was the intention. I edged forward again, this time sitting sideways. 'I'll sell at £795!' I shouted again, this time waving my hands and looking at the clock as if I didn't have very much time left. With that the Ring broke into a chorus of voices.

'I'll sell at 794!', 'I'll sell at 793!', 'I'll give 790!', 'Sell at 792!' another said. Before I knew it, the market had dropped to £788. I looked at the clock, it was imperative that I had enough time to trade before the Ring closed and the way this market was going, everything was happening far too slowly.

I edged forward in my seat again. I could no longer sit with my legs crossed but it didn't matter because I had a long skirt on. I was hoping to be able to make a multiple strike at breakneck speed. I needed the market much lower than this and I didn't want to sell too much copper getting it there. I wanted them to think that I was a crappy dealer so they would take full advantage of me and not suspect that I had a different agenda in mind! I got the attention of the Ring by some animated gesturing and by shaking my head, so that my hair flicked across my face once, twice, and a third time as I shouted out, 'Yes, yes, yes!' Then, just for a second the Ring went quiet, before bursting into absolute uproar again as once again I offered the market lower.

By now I was pointing at everyone who had bid but because they thought I was a heavy seller they backed off, only taking twenty-five tons at a time. This was exactly how I wanted it. I leaned back in the seat. 'Are you managing to get all this, Debbie?'

'Yes, I think so.' I wasn't too worried because I knew that Trevor and Simon were also discreetly noting the trades. I had less than a minute to get the market through that important support level of 780. If I succeeded the market would collapse.

'Yes, I'll sell at 786!' I shouted out again. 'I'll sell at 785!'

There were no takers and the market had gone deadly quiet. This was not what I wanted. I looked at the clock again – I had just thirty seconds to get that market down. I sat a little further back in the seat as though I was unsure of what I was doing. 'OK, I'll sell at 784.'

The dealer opposite grinned. 'I'll sell at 783.' Oh, he liked that, offering the market ahead of me! I pretended I was upset. 'I'll sell at 782!' I heard him saying. He watched as the second hand started to move, the bell was about to ring. This was it. 'I'll give 778, sell at 780!' I shouted at the very top of my voice. The room fell silent for a second and then the biggest uproar ever as the bell signalled the end of trading. Relieved, I sat back in the seat with my task completed.

'Gerry, Gerry weren't you supposed to be…?'

'Sshhh, Debbie sshhh, how much do you think I've sold?'

'I dunno, about three thousand tons? I'll have to check.' I could tell Debbie wasn't happy but I didn't have time for that now.

I smiled at her, trying to calm her down. 'Well what's my average price, about £784?'

'No, I think it's better than that, say about £786.' She frowned 'You must be mad, Gerry, I thought that you're supposed to be buying, not bloody selling?'

'Ssshhh, I'll explain later, I've got to speak to the office first.' I picked up the phone 'David, have we any orders from New York for the kerb on copper?'

'Yeah, but look, why the hell are you selling? I thought you were supposed to be buying? And yes, we got one thousand tons to sell at £780 on stop and another one thousand to sell on stop at £778.'

'OK, got to go now, the kerb has started.'

Of course copper dominated the kerb as the stop levels were hit. I decided I wouldn't sell any more if I could help it. Anyway I knew it wouldn't be long before the Chinese would ask me for an execution! I just hoped that they realised I was doing all of this for their benefit.

During the morning kerb all metals traded in a twenty-minute session. This was after the official prices had been agreed and published. Normally chaotic by nature, it was today dominated by the copper market. We took it all in turns to sit in the Ring but in the end it became obvious that I had to stay there, so Simon and Trevor along with Debbie stood behind me. I sat back watching the market drop sharply. I booked out the sell stops from New York against my own short position. I'm glad to say that at these lower levels I was no longer a main player in the Ring. Commission House selling was now in abundance, offloading their huge positions before the New York market opened.

I sat back, considering the right moment to start purchasing. I had to give the Chinese an execution at the end of the session. At the moment I had nothing to give them! Whatever I did I would have to be careful. Letting the cat out of the bag would be dangerous and I simply couldn't risk being suspected by the other dealers of manipulating the market. If that were to happen they would bid the market up against me. Everything, yes everything would be ruined if that happened. So now I traded very discreetly. There was no shouting from me. I left that to everyone else. Instead, it was a wink or a nod. I even remember leaning across and touching a dealer's arm to get his attention!

I would do anything but shout. Because when I shouted, the whole Ring noticed! If they couldn't hear me they would think I wasn't trading. Like a stealth bomber, they would know I had hit when it was too late. Well, that was the game plan anyway! Besides, I still had at least ten thousand tons of copper to buy and we were already halfway through the day! At first I took just five hundred tons, then I took a thousand tons and still the selling was taking the market lower.

'£775 trading and a seller, 773 trading and offered,' I heard the exasperated commentary from behind me.

'There's no buyer in sight and the market's dropping like a stone.'

'It's crapping out of sight, man,' I heard another clerk say on the phone to his office. If only they knew! I leaned forward in my seat to guage the mood. There was a slightly more relaxed atmosphere, some traders were laughing but others had fallen back in their seats exhausted. Some of the heavyweights had even left the Ring!

I looked at the clock. There were just over nine minutes to go. Now I really must start buying. I couldn't afford to leave it all to the afternoon market, New York was far too unpredictable for that. Besides, there was no guarantee that London would open lower this afternoon and say the Chinese gave the order to buy at market to another broker! Then I would be in real trouble. They could demand an execution from me. I just had to get something in right now for them.

I edged forward again in my seat again, preparing to shout louder than the rest of them. 'Yes!' I pointed at a dealer offering at £774. 'Five hundred tons?'

'Done!' came an immediate response.

'Make it one thousand tons then?'

'Done,' he replied.

'Make it two thousand tons?' I asked.

'Done,' he replied again.

This was easy, I hadn't expected to get all my tonnage from one dealer! 'Make it three thousand tons then?' I asked tentatively.

'Done!' he said, grinning. What did he know that I didn't?

'Make it four thou—' I stopped. The market had gone quiet. I hadn't noticed but the Ring had filled up again. Eyes were staring at me, and some jaws had dropped open. I sat as still as possible, feeling the vibes, pensive, waiting for a release of emotion from the rest of the dealers who had probably sussed me out. *Tic-toc tic-toc.* I could hear the clock as it dawned on them that I was buying. It took a second for them to add up my apparent profit and their loss! And it only took a second for uproar to engulf the Ring. I heard the clerk behind me say, 'We got five minutes left of the kerb, and they have started to buy now, yes they're still buying and the market is moving higher again.' So the market commentary was showing us as buyers. Hopefully they would think I was just covering my short position. Well, the game was up for now so the less attention I attracted, the better.

The best thing I could do now was to walk out of the Ring and show that I had no more dealing to do. I got up just as Debbie was rushing over. 'The office is going mad, they want to know what you've done.'

'OK, just hang on a minute while I work it out. Did you get that last deal I did?' Debbie panicked. 'Well surely you know what you've done don't you?' I would have to calm her down.

'Yes, of course, I'm just checking, that's all, Ssshhh. What's that?' A dealer opposite was bidding up the market and smiling across as us.

'Christ, wait a minute,' I said, rushing back into the Ring. The market was rising fast and I couldn't afford for it to go any higher. I needed to get the market down again and the only way to do that was to start selling again. The market must believe that I was still a seller otherwise I wouldn't be able to get the balance of my purchases in at a decent price.

Sitting down, I watched as dealers shouted out simultaneously, 'I'll give 780!', 'I'll give 781!', 'I'll give 783!' They were doing exactly what I knew they would do. They were acting in unison and there was not a seller in sight. Everything was at stake now. I pointed at the dealer to the side of me. 'Yes, how much?' Then, shouting again, I pointed to the dealer opposite who was bidding 783. 'Yes, how much?' I asked him. I was sure he was bluffing and would take all that I offered. 'How much?' I asked again. He knew now that I was prepared to sell at least five hundred tons.

'Five hundred tons?' he responded – rather nervously, I thought.

'Yes!' I shouted back aggressively, trying to frighten him into withdrawing any other bids he might have up his sleeve. Damn, now I would have to act as though I had thousands of tons to sell. If I could make the rest of the dealers think that I was still a huge seller they might all withdraw their bids. After all, they were only bidding the market up because they wanted to make even more money by selling at the highest price to me. Time to call their bluff. By now they should have known that I was prepared to go to any lengths to get the price I wanted.

'Did he want more?' I asked, sporting a daring smile. 'How about four thousand tons?'

Another dealer jumped forward in his seat. 'I'll sell at 780,' he said while I carried on shouting my offer in the background, 'I'll sell at 780!' I knew that he would have to undercut me because I was first buyer in.

'OK!' he shouted, 'I'll sell at 779.'

Now the previous buyer had made it clear he didn't want to buy any more. 'No, five hundred was enough!' he shouted across the Ring to me. Relieved but not showing it, I turned round immediately as though desperate to find another buyer.

Clerks were now rushing to the side of the Ring and whispering new orders into the dealers' ears. Hopefully this was the stop-loss selling that I had been anticipating! The dealer next to me leaned forward in his seat, shouting as loud as he could amidst absolute uproar in the Ring. 'I'll give 776, sell at 778!'

'Here we go again, the market's taking another dive,' I heard the commentary behind me. I relaxed now. They all knew I had four thousand tons to sell. Hopefully that'd keep a lid on the market. I watched the market drop like a stone, wondering when would be the right moment to enter.

How was I going to buy back the tonnage I needed without them noticing? In such situations some dealers would have given their orders to other brokers to fulfil but I didn't trust anyone to do a proper job for me. Besides, that wouldn't have been fair on the Chinese. They were paying me the commission and they expected me to do the deal. So whatever way I looked at it, it was time to start buying again.

'I'll sell at 775!' the dealer opposite shouted out.

'Fifty tons!' I responded, pointing back at him.

'Yes!' he shouted. 'One hundred?'

'Yes. Make it five hundred tons then' I replied.

'Yes!' he shouted again.

The market had gone quiet. I could just imagine what some of them were thinking. There she is, playing our game, jobbing the market and just look, the bird has made a tidy little profit! One particular dealer always called me a tasty or dishy bird. So it was easy for me to hear his thoughts. I didn't mind them thinking I was jobbing, just as long as they had absolutely no idea how much copper I still had to buy!

'One thousand tons?' I asked gingerly.

'Yes,' he replied.

I had to go slowly I didn't want to give the game away. 'OK, make it fifteen hundred tons?'

'Yes, and that's it,' he replied. 'Now I'll sell at 777!'

But then the dealer next to me leaned over and said, 'I can sell you five hundred tons at 777.'

'Yes,' I replied. And then, just as I was about to buy more, the bell rang out loudly, signalling the end of the session. But where was the copper price?

'Last I heard it was 778 offered,' Trevor said.

Debbie was busy checking the deals, as I made my way over to the office phone. 'Hi, David, look, I'm not quite ready to give an execution back to the Chinese. I'm just waiting for

Debbie to check some extra deals and then I'll know exactly how much I've bought. If *you know who* phones, can you tell him that I'll phone him shortly?' For once he didn't argue. He knew I wanted to give a decent price to them.

Back in the office we checked and double-checked the position. In total I had purchased seven thousand tons for the Chinese. David had been very busy in the office as well and, surprise, surprise, he had also bought a thousand tons. We both agreed that it was important the house position was manageable because the market could move very quickly either way. We had to have something extra to play with.

Just after New York opened, I phoned the Chinese. They had expected a good execution and were pleased with their prices. Earlier David had said we could take a bit on the execution and still give them a good average but I had insisted on not taking anything from them. 'Isn't the commission enough, David?'

'It's never enough, Gerry, it just covers our overheads.'

'Well, if we give them a good execution, David, they might give us more business, It's about building trust, you know!'

'Don't you fucking lecture me, Gerry, Don't you think I know all about trust? Just you remember, I know more about this bloody business than you'll ever know!'

David was so stressed lately that I regretted upsetting him. 'OK, keep your hair on!' I said, trying to appease him.

During the afternoon, prices steadied but there was so much business from New York that it was easy for me to purchase the balance of the copper I needed for the Chinese.

Speaking later with Henry, I told him I was thrilled with the way trading had gone but I didn't want to have to trade that way every day! All that bluffing and counter-bluffing had taken it out of me and I felt exhausted. It wasn't so much the trading but the emotional turmoil you went through, concentrating on what everyone else in the Ring was doing. Trading in an open outcry market was extremely demanding.

'Yes it must really take it out of you, test your metal even, ha ha ha!' he joked. But no office trader could really know what it was like to trade in the Ring, especially if he had never sat in the Ring or been onto the Exchange floor during the busy periods. Still, I knew Henry appreciated me. He patted me on the back. 'You did very well, my dear. I'm sure this was the biggest order yet. You keep them satisfied and we'll get a lot more out of them yet! Why are they buying so much copper anyway?' It was unlike Henry to ask questions. I watched him withdraw his pipe from his jacket pocket.

'Well, I asked the same question and Mr Hao told me that it was for the modernisation of China. The copper-wire would be used to supply electricity to millions of homes throughout China, homes that had none at the moment.'

'Oh, trade business then?'

'Yes, of course, I never thought of it as speculative! They need, this copper.'

He lit his pipe, dragging deeply several times before a puff of blue smoke rose into the air. 'I wonder how much they still have left to buy. I've heard rumours they're in the market for at least one million tons, is it true?' he asked.

'I don't know and I don't much care, just so long as they keep giving us the orders! That's why I'm determined to give them the best execution. After all, everyone wants their business and we will do very well if we can keep it!'

'I'll say so!' Henry laughed a little before moving away from me. He was standing opposite David, who was on the phone, arranging yet another extension to the Buffer Stock Manager's credit line. 'Done?' Henry asked, raising his thumb optimistically.

'Yup, almost, nearly there now,' David replied, raising his thumb in return. I wondered what 'nearly there' meant? Did it mean we were coming to the end of our credit limit with the banks and if so how would that affect my future business with the Chinese? Mark had said to me many years before: 'Gerry, always remember we are the tail that wags the dog.' It was, at the time, a statement that could be interpreted in many ways.

Personally, I was never that comfortable with being the tail because of its proximity to another part of the anatomy. But now, as I watched the two of them, I wondered if the ability to access limitless amounts of cash and the obvious impact it was having on the tin market was, in effect, the same as the tail wagging the dog? And if so, what would happen to the tail if the dog sat down and refused to play the game?

These were happier days and I was determined to mind my own business and not worry so much about everyone else. The Chinese were still in the market and we continued to benefit from their large copper orders. Usually they were given as market orders to be executed at my discretion. I knew I wasn't the only one doing their business. Indeed I suspected there were many occasions when they gave orders to buy and sell at the same time through different brokers. Clearly they had a strategy and I believed they were sophisticated in their approach to trading such large amounts of copper. In any case, I was over the moon to be considered as one their principle brokers. Every day we got large orders to buy copper. We took our time executing the orders, buying slowly, sometimes absorbing sales from producers hedging their forward production, or from the speculators.

I often wondered why the Chinese didn't buy direct from the metal producers and chose instead to purchase their copper from a Ring dealer on the London Metal Exchange. I liked to think that it was something to do with trust and not just because we offered them a handsome credit line.

Shortly after that momentous day in the Copper Ring, I took over trading lead and aluminium, while Debbie traded zinc and nickel. The boys shared copper, tin and silver between them. Since I looked after the Chinese, I was rewarded with several increases in salary, regular bonuses and a new company car every three years. But soon I was to leave the Ring and spend my time trading from the office, doing what I liked best – analysing markets and providing clients with a commentary on the rings. But because the Chinese account was mine, I kept control of the copper business, controlling the rate at which the orders were executed. I found it much easier to be objective by trading from the relative calmness of the office. You could say I had the best of both worlds and I believe the experience of trading in the Ring made me a shrewd operator.

Life was good except for one black cloud that overhung every trading hour. The tin market was getting out of control and the Buffer Stock Manager was making larger and larger demands for credit. I tried not to think about it but it was always at the back of my mind. I detested the idea that we made our money this way and I couldn't get comfortable with how easy it appeared to be.

One day, as I strolled into the office around 9.30, I discovered David and Henry fully engrossed working out the level of collateral we required against the Buffer Stock Manager's tin position, along with the amount of money we would need to lend him. Both of them seemed concerned about the position. David was shaking his head in disbelief at what had just been said. Of course I couldn't hear what they were saying, but a sixth sense told me I needed to be worried. It was unusual for David to be having doubts. He was the eternal optimist. He was always saying, 'Don't worry, it'll be OK.' And so it usually was. But if he was now worried, we all had something to be worried about! It's true that sometimes the Chinese would require their credit limit to be extended and on occasions all of us would join in the debate on how to meet the growing demand for credit from new clients as well as old.

Of course we understood that the objective of the International Tin Agreement was to keep the price of tin within the range agreed by the International Tin Council. This was of paramount importance to both producer and consumer, so naturally the Buffer Stock Manager needed to trade when the price threatened to move either side. But no one had bargained for him to run out of money. He was in the habit of trading quite ferociously once an extension to his credit had been agreed. It's as if he wanted to spend the whole lot in one day. Needless to say, this was playing havoc with my trading system. When the cash price of tin went to a premium over three months, brokers started to lend even more money against the warrants of tin they held.

Henry and David's argument for continuing the business remained as it always had been. If we didn't get our money back we could claim on the warrants of tin that we held in reserve. But I worried about the availability of the warrants and whether there would be enough to go around if they were all called in. We had no idea what his position was with other Ring-dealing members. The situation in the tin market was beginning to affect other markets.

Because of this I decided to close down all my positions on the system and stand aside. Clients were surprised but as I explained, I still had a view on the market but it was a jobbing view; I didn't want to recommend holding a position for any length of time. I was nervous, there were too many uncertainties, such as the high interest rates and volatility of exchange rates. There was an unprecedented amount of volume trading from the trade and speculators and there was no doubt, the bubble was going to burst. It was simply a matter of time. When it did, it would deal a devastating blow and trading on the markets, especially the London Metal Exchange, would never be the same again.

That particular weekend I continued to think about the predicament in the market. I was happy with the Chinese business and I was pleased that we had managed to keep their credit line of five million pounds open. But I was increasingly nervous about the twenty-seven million pounds we had lent to the International Tin Council. So the following Monday I went to see Mark about my concerns. I didn't want him to continue lending money and if he wouldn't listen to me then the very least I could do was to convince him that he needed to increase the leverage on the tin warrants that we held as collateral. Although I was comfortable about talking about these concerns I wondered whether his take on the conversation would mean that he viewed it as a criticism of Henry and David. I knew he was close to them and in comparison, I didn't think he rated me at all. So I entered his office not knowing what to expect but hoping that he would agree with me.

Mark was sitting behind a large desk in the centre of the room as I entered. He smiled motioning for me to take a seat opposite him. 'What can I do you for, Gerry?'

I smiled because I appreciated his attempt to humour me, but I wanted to stay focused. 'Well…' I hesitated for a moment. I needed to choose my words carefully because Mark became intimidating when he got angry. His defensive reaction was to overcompensate by becoming aggressive. 'Well, it's about the tin market.' I paused,

'Yes,' he said leaning forward a little. 'What about the tin market, it's a good market, isn't it? and haven't we had this conversation before?' He looked sideways at me.

'Well, yes it has been up until now, but for how much longer?'

'Forever, I hope!' He sounded surprised at what I was trying to say. 'Well, yes, but realistically I don't think it will last!'

'And why is that, Gerry? What do you know that no one else knows, hmm?' He sounded menacing, it was a tone I didn't like, but I persevered.

'Well, let's face it everyone's in the same boat, lending money to the same client! What happens if… if one day a broker refuses to lend him more money?'

'And why would they do that, Gerry? Don't you think you're being a little stupid now? In any case, we'll lend him the money if he comes to us, so don't you worry, we have things under control.' He seemed very confident but I was sure he didn't know the full facts.

'Mark, everyone is trading for him, not just us!'
'So?'
'Everyone is lending him money against the warrants.'
'So?'
'So if the bubble bursts we'll all go down, won't we?'
Mark stood up, shaking his head, and then he rubbed his

chin, making a slow scratching sound, indicating he needed a shave. 'We have the warrants though, Gerry!' I stood still for a moment and then I realised he was holding the door open for me. At the risk of stating the blindingly obvious I blurted out, 'The problem is that when the market finds out the Buffer Stock Manager has gone bust, the price of tin will go into freefall as everyone tries to sell.'

He looked incredulous. 'But he hasn't gone bust and he isn't going to go bust! Now look, I'll tell you what I want you to do, Gerry, I want you to go away and forget all this nonsense about the tin market. You go away and concentrate on your Chinese customers and leave the tin trading to us, OK?'

I had no alternative but to agree. 'OK, thank you for your time, Mark.'

I was anything but happy and I felt it deserved one more go. 'Look, Mark, I just don't want us to lose money. I think we should stop lending now, otherwise it will be a close shave!'

He adjusted his red braces before twisting the waistband of his trousers round for a better fit. 'And what about your Chinese clients, eh? Shall we continue lending them money?'

'Yes of course.' I didn't want to say any more than that. Surely he could figure it out for himself! It was obvious that the two could not be compared. Besides, we had already lent seven times as much to the International Tin Council as we had to the Chinese. We were in danger of losing millions of pounds. The whole company would collapse. There could be no comparison and he knew it. I shuffled my feet, indicating that I was ready to leave the room, but he continued to stand in the way.

'Well, Gerry,' he sneered back at me. 'My answer to you is quite simple. If the International Tin Council goes bust then it won't just be our problem, it will be the whole of the London Metal Exchange's problem and then you can kiss goodbye to it all.' He blew a kiss to accentuate his point. Never a truer word was spoken and yet he was still prepared to risk trading with the International Tin Council. Perhaps they had reached the point of no return and they knew it!

I looked at him long and hard, trying to understand what he was saying to me. I pursed my lips together knowing that I had failed. He was right, we had had this conversation before and it hadn't made an ounce of difference.

Back in the trading room, Henry was agreeing to lend a further three million pounds to the International Tin Council. This was so that we could buy more cash tin for him the following day. I asked David at what interest rate we had lent the money but he wouldn't tell me the exact rate. I assumed that it was a couple of points above the base rate. But the problem was, the base rate kept moving higher and what appeared to be a good deal now might not in fact end up being so! I hoped we were trading the loan back to back and not taking a position, because we could then find ourselves liable for massive losses on both the metal and the money!

Over the next few weeks the situation was exasperated. Every day the Buffer Stock Manager would be on the phone requesting a further extension on his credit line Henry would agree finally at even higher rates of interest. Higher interest rates don't mean anything to a desperate insolvent! But Henry and David couldn't see what I was so worried about. 'Sour grapes if you ask me!' David had said before rubbing his hands with glee. 'That's another ten thousand we made, Henry.'

'Made my arse!' I said, feeling very angry one day. 'Where you see a profit, I see a loss. Where you see a profit, I see no future at all! There you are counting profits when you should be counting the loss! Here today gone tomorrow, easy come easy go. Robbing Peter to pay Paul is not the answer.'

'Money,' he had replied. 'Money-lending is the key to making a profit and that is what business is all about.'

I had to agree. 'Yes, you are very good at it except, as I keep saying, it's more important to generate wealth than to make money. Lending money at a higher price than what you borrowed it at simply incurs costs for the future! It adds to inflation. Surely you can see that? Look, capitalism relies on labour to generate a profit but it is the labourer who should benefit too. The benefit to the labourer should not be sacrificed at the expense of paying the profit to the moneylender. It is possible to be both a social capitalist and a capital socialist, you know!'

'You're just a bloody fascist who knows nothing, Gerry.'

'Well, I know not to make a profit regardless of the cost! Look, David, don't let's argue any more. It's silly, what's done is done, it can't be undone. More's the pity!'

It was a few months later that the news came that we had all been dreading. All we could do was sit back and watch events unfold, dumbstruck as everything we had worked so hard to achieve disintegrated in front of our eyes. First it started with a little rumour that a broker had refused to lend the Buffer Stock Manager any more money. But as it reverberated around the market, panic set in and like a tidal wave it inundated all the brokers who had lent the International Tin Council money. The banks had refused to lend the Metal Brokers more money and now positions worth hundreds of millions of pounds were at stake. The Buffer Stock Manager would have to sell his holding of tin and anticipating this, the market took an initial dive. Fearful of a total collapse in the market, the Committee suspended trading. The debts were now mounting up rapidly and the tin warrants became practically valueless.

The International Tin Council prevaricated for nearly a year and at first the refinancing package and rescue talks failed. Eventually the Committee decided on a ring-out formula where positions could be set off against each other at an agreed price between buyer and seller. As the deals where struck, so it became obvious just how large the losses were. Ours was twenty-seven million pounds and it would, in time force us to relinquish our seat on the Exchange. Many other dealers also found themselves in the same position. Of course the Committee had called on the International Tin Council to honour its debt but it didn't, and members had no alternative but to bear the losses themselves. It was a dreadful thing to have happened. We wrote to the Prime Minister's office requesting government intervention, but it was all to no avail.

The City was changing fast and new products were being introduced. There were fresh ideas such as merging the London Metal Exchange with the London Commodity Exchange and the introduction of a Clearing House – something that had been talked about for years!

The Financial Services Act decreed 'insider trading' as illegal and newly employed Regulators monitored Brokers to ensure they were *'Fit and Proper'* to carry out business.

The rules were changing the game. New markets with funny-sounding names such as 'Derivatives' and 'Financial Futures' were developing and currencies were no longer tied to the gold standard.

As for me, well, I didn't make a fortune, but that doesn't matter because wealth comes in many forms. Slowly but surely, trading in the City had changed me and I didn't much like what it had changed me into. It was time to leave and get a life. But deciding about when to finish was difficult. It was tempting to keep putting it off. I was at the top of my career and would be giving up a very lucrative salary package.

For many years I had gazed outside the office, hankering after natural woodland, green pastures and the sea. I used to think, there must be more to life than sitting here drinking coffee and smoking cigarettes all day. Now was definately the time to leave and start a new life in Porlock, away from the hustle and bustle of city life and the pressures of dealing.

I decided to pay a last visit to the Metal Exchange and standing on the balcony overlooking the Ring I watch as those around me get on with their everyday business. I think back to all those trying times I experienced in the Ring, and I want to commit to memory as much of those experiences as possible. So, taking one last look at those portraits of Victorian gentleman hanging on the walls, I recall my first days on the Exchange and they don't seem so frightening now as I say goodbye to each one in turn.

Debbie is smiling up at me as she sits in the Ring waiting to trade. Perhaps she guesses my thoughts. I waive, trying not to let her see my watery eyes.

I know she is feeling just as proud to be sitting in the Ring as I had on my first day and around her are quite a few women dealers and clerks. Part of me was sorry to leave and I knew Debbie would never understand my motivation for wanting to go, but the job was over.

'So you're leaving us to grow daffodils are you, Gerry? You must be mad!'

'Yes, that's about it,' I said, smiling. Knowing that there was a ring of truth to my reply...

But that's another story altogether!

CPSIA information can be obtained at www.ICGtesting.com
Printed in the USA
LVOW11s0604210416

484639LV00003B/114/P